Four Contemporary
American Plays

Four Contemporary American Plays

Selected and with Biographical Notes

by

Bennett Cerf

VINTAGE BOOKS

A Division of Random House

New York

Manufactured in the United States of America

Contents

Four Contemporary
American Plays

Paddy Chayefsky

The Tenth Man

TO TYRONE GUTHRIE

The Tenth Man was first presented by Saint Subber and Arthur Cantor at The Booth Theatre, New York City, November 5, 1959, with the following cast:

(*In order of appearance*)

THE CABALIST	Arnold Marlé
THE SEXTON	David Vardi
SCHLISSEL	Lou Jacobi
ZITORSKY	Jack Gilford
ALPER	George Voskovec
FOREMAN	Jacob Ben-Ami
THE GIRL (EVELYN FOREMAN)	Risa Schwartz
ARTHUR LANDAU	Donald Harron
HARRIS	Martin Garner
THE RABBI	Gene Saks
KESSLER BOYS	{ Alan Manson { Paul Marin
THE POLICEMAN	Tim Callaghan

DIRECTED BY Tyrone Guthrie
SETTINGS AND LIGHTING BY David Hays
COSTUMES BY Frank Thompson
ASSOCIATE: Caroline Swann

3

An Orthodox Synagogue

ACT ONE

Interior of the synagogue of the Congregation Atereth-Tifereth Yisroel.

It is a poor congregation, and the synagogue is actually a converted shop. A raised platform surrounded by a railing contains the lectern and the Holy Ark. This altar is surrounded by rows of plain wooden folding chairs which constitute the seating accommodations for the congregation. On the far side of the altar is an old desk at which THE RABBI *presides when teaching Hebrew school.*

A partitioned area downstage right is THE RABBI'S *study, a crowded little cubicle containing a battered mahogany desk and chair, an old leather armchair, a worn leather couch, and piles of black prayer books. On the walls are old framed pictures of bearded patriarchs in desolate obsession over their Talmuds and perhaps a few familiar scenes from the Old Testament.*

Downstage is a metal heating unit. There is a second heating unit upstage, and a door leading apparently to a bathroom. The front door is stage left.

It is 6:30 A.M. on a cold winter day.

At rise, THE CABALIST *stands in the middle of the synagogue, entirely wrapped in a thick white linen prayer shawl with broad black stripes, praying silently from a heavy prayer book that rests on the railing of the altar. Suddenly*

5

he pauses in his intense devotions, clutches at the railing as if to keep himself from falling. We have the impression that he is faint, near to swooning. He is a small, bearded man, in his seventies; his face is lean and lined, his eyes sunken and hollow. He wears a small black skullcap from beneath which stick out gray forelocks and sidecurls—a testament to his orthodoxy. After a moment, he regains his strength and returns to his prayers.

Three men hurry into the synagogue out of the oppressive cold of the street. They are THE SEXTON, SCHLISSEL *and* ZITORSKY. *They all wear heavy overcoats and gray fedoras.* SCHLISSEL *and* ZITORSKY *are in their early seventies.* THE SEXTON *is a small, nervous, bespectacled man of forty-eight. We know he is a sexton because he carries a huge ring of keys. The men rub their hands for warmth and huff and puff and dart quick looks at* THE CABALIST, *who is oblivious to their entrance.*

SCHLISSEL (*Muttering*) Close the door. (*Light pours down on the synagogue as* THE SEXTON *flicks on the wall switch.* THE SEXTON *scurries upstage to fuss with the heater in the rear of the synagogue.* SCHLISSEL *and* ZITORSKY *shuffle downstage to a small uncovered heater and stand silently—indeed a little wearily—for a moment.* SCHLISSEL *sighs*) So how goes it with a Jew today?

ZITORSKY How should it go?

SCHLISSEL Have a pinch of snuff.

ZITORSKY No, thank you.

SCHLISSEL Davis won't be here this morning. I stopped by his house. He has a cold. His daughter-in-law told me he's still in bed.

ZITORSKY My daughter-in-law, may she grow rich and buy a hotel with a thousand rooms and be found dead in every one of them.

6

SCHLISSEL   My daughter-in-law, may she invest heavily in General Motors, and the whole thing should go bankrupt.

ZITORSKY   Sure, go have children.

SCHLISSEL   The devil take them all.

THE SEXTON   (*Scurrying downstage; to* THE CABALIST *as he passes*)   Hirschman, are you all right?

(*He flutters, a small round ball of a man, to the door of* THE RABBI'S *office, which he now opens with one of the many keys on his chain*)

SCHLISSEL   Foreman won't be here today.

ZITORSKY   What's the matter with Foreman?

SCHLISSEL   His granddaughter today. This is the morning.

ZITORSKY   Oh, that's right. Today is the morning.

SCHLISSEL   Listen, it's better for everybody.

ZITORSKY   Sure.

SCHLISSEL   I told Foreman, I said: "Foreman, it's better for everybody." The girl is becoming violent. I spoke to her father. He said to me they live in terror what she'll do to the other children. They came home one night, they found her punching one of the little children.

ZITORSKY   Well, what can you do?

SCHLISSEL   What can you do? You do what they're doing. They're putting her back in the institution.

ZITORSKY   Of course. There she will have the benefit of trained psychiatric personnel.

SCHLISSEL   The girl is incurable. She's been in and out of mental institutions since she was eleven years old. I met the psychiatrist there, you know, when I was up there to visit Foreman last week. I discussed the whole business with him. A fine young fellow. The girl is a schizophrenic with violent tendencies.

(ZITORSKY *considers this diagnosis for a moment, then sighs*)

ZITORSKY   Ah, may my daughter-in-law eat acorns and may branches spout from her ears.

7

SCHLISSEL   May my daughter-in-law live to be a hundred and twenty,and may she live all her years in *her* daughter-in-law's house.

(THE SEXTON *has been tugging a large opened brown cardboard carton out of* THE RABBI'S *office, from which he now extracts two velvet bags which he hands to* SCHLISSEL *and* ZITORSKY. *A fifth old Jew now enters from the street, a patrician little man with a Vandyke beard and a black homburg. His name is* ALPER. *He bursts into shrill prayer as he enters*)

ALPER (*Chanting*)   "As for me in the abundance of thy loving kindness will I come into thy house; I will worship toward thy holy temple in the fear of thee. How goodly are thy tents, O Jacob . . ." (*As precipitously as the prayer had begun, it now drops into nothing more than a rapid movement of lips.* THE SEXTON *acknowledges* ALPER'S *arrival with a nod and darts back into* THE RABBI'S *office, where he plunks himself behind the desk and begins hurriedly to dial the phone.* ALPER'S *voice zooms abruptly up into a shrill incantation again*) ". . . in the truth of thy salvation. Amen!"

SCHLISSEL   Amen.

ZITORSKY   Amen.

(ALPER *joins the other two old men and they stand in silent, rueful speculation*)

THE SEXTON (*On phone*)   Hello, Harris? This is Bleyer the Sexton. Come on down today, we need you. Foreman won't be here. Davis is sick. We won't have ten men for the morning prayers if you don't come down . . . Services start in twenty minutes. Hurry up . . . Wear a sweater under your coat . . . All right . . .

(*He hangs up, takes a large ledger from the desk, and begins nervously to examine its pages*)

SCHLISSEL   Hirschman slept over in the synagogue again last night. Have you ever seen such pietistic humbug?

ALPER   Well, he is a very devout man. A student of the

8

cabala. The Rabbi speaks of him with the greatest reverence.

SCHLISSEL Devout indeed. I assure you this lavish display of orthodoxy is a very profitable business. I was told confidentially just yesterday that his board and food are paid for by two foolish old women who consider him a saint.

ALPER It can't cost them very much. He's been fasting the last three days.

SCHLISSEL And the reason he sleeps in the synagogue so frequently is because his landlady does not give him heat for his own room in the mornings.

ZITORSKY Ah, go be an old man in the winter.

ALPER I must say, I really don't know what to do with myself on these cold days.

SCHLISSEL I'm an atheist. If I had something better to do, would I be here?

ZITORSKY You know what would be a nice way to kill a day? I think it would be nice to take a trip up to Mount Hope Cemetery and have a look at my burial plot. A lovely cemetery. Like a golf course, actually. By the time one gets there and comes back, the whole day has been used up. Would you like to come? I'll pay both your fares.

ALPER Why not? I have never been to Mount Hope. I have my burial plot on Mount Zion Cemetery.

ZITORSKY Oh, that's a beautiful cemetery.

ALPER Yes, it is. My wife wanted to buy plots in Cedar Lawn because her whole family is buried there, but I wouldn't hear of it.

ZITORSKY Oh, Cedar Lawn. I wouldn't be buried in Cedar Lawn.

ALPER It's in such a bad state. The headstones tumble one on top of the other, and everybody walks on the graves.

ZITORSKY They don't take care in Cedar Lawn. My wife once said, she should rest in peace, that Cedar Lawn was the tenement of cemeteries.

ALPER A well-turned phrase.

ZITORSKY She had a way with words, God grant her eternal rest.

ALPER I'd like you to come to Mount Zion sometimes, see my plot.

ZITORSKY Maybe we could make the trip tomorrow.

SCHLISSEL Listen to these two idiots, discussing their graves as if they were country estates.

ZITORSKY Where are you buried, Schlissel?

SCHLISSEL Cedar Lawn.

ALPER Well, listen, there are many lovely areas in Cedar Lawn. All my wife's family are buried there.

ZITORSKY Come with us, Schlissel, and have a look at my grave.

SCHLISSEL Why not? What else have I got to do?

(ALPER *now slowly goes about the business of donning his prayer shawl and phylacteries, which he takes out of a velvet prayer bag. Among Jews, prayer is a highly individual matter, and peripatetic to the bargain. The actual ritual of laying on the phylacteries is a colorful one.* ALPER *extracts his left arm from his jacket and rebuttons his jacket so that his shirt-sleeved left arm hangs loose. Then, the shirt sleeve is rolled up almost to the shoulder, and the arm phylactery, a long thin black leather thong, is put on by wrapping it around the left arm seven times, three times around the palm, and three times around the middle finger. All this is accompanied by rapidly recited prayers, as is the laying on of the head phylactery. All the while* ALPER *walks, bending and twisting at the knees, raising his voice occasionally in the truly lovely words of incantation. In a far upstage corner,* THE CABALIST *huddles under his enveloping white tallith—prayer shawl—his back to everyone else, deeply involved in his personal meditations. The synagogue itself is a shabby little place, the walls yellowed and cracked, illumined by a fitful overhead bulb. There is indeed at this moment a*

10

sense of agelessness, even of primitive barbarism. During this, THE SEXTON *has dialed a second number*)

THE SEXTON Hello? Mr. Arnold Kessler, please . . . How do you do? This is Mr. Bleyer the Sexton at the synagogue. Perhaps you recall me . . . Did I wake you up? I'm terribly sorry. As long as you're up, according to my books, your father died one year ago yesterday, on the eleventh day in the month of Shvat, may his soul fly straight to the Heavenly Gates, and how about coming down with your brother and saying a memorial prayer in your father's name? . . . Let me put it this way, Mr. Kessler. You know we can't have morning prayers without a quorum of ten men. If you and your brother don't come down we won't have a quorum . . . As a favor to me . . . Kessler, may your children be such devoted sons, and bring your brother. You are doing a good deed. Peace be with you. Hurry up.

(*He hangs up, sits frowning, totaling, up on his fingers the number of men he has, scowls. In the synagogue,* ALPHER'S *voice rises for a brief moment*)

ALPER ". . . and it shall be to thee for a sign upon thy hand, and for a memorial between thy eyes . . ."

(THE SEXTON *rises abruptly from his chair and bustles out of the office to the front door of the synagogue*)

THE SEXTON (*To nobody in particular*) Listen, I'm going to have to get a tenth Jew off the street somewheres. I'll be right back. Schlissel, will you please fix that bench already, you promised me.

(*He exits.* SCHLISSEL *nods and picks up a hammer. For a moment, only the singsong murmur of the rapid prayers and the upstage tapping of* SCHLISSEL'S *hammer fill the stage. The front door to the synagogue now opens, and a sixth old Jew peers in. He is a frightened little wisp of a man, named* FOREMAN. *He is obviously in a state. He darts terrified looks all about the synagogue, and then abruptly disappears back into the street, leaving the syna-*

*gogue door open. Nobody noticed his brief appearance.
A moment later, he is back, this time leading a slim young
girl of eighteen wearing a topcoat, who is also distracted.
The old man herds her quickly across the synagogue to*
THE RABBI'S *office, pushes her in, and closes the door
behind her. She stands in* THE RABBI'S *office, almost rigid
with terror.* FOREMAN *scuttles back to close the front
door.* SCHLISSEL *looks up and notices* FOREMAN *and nods
to him; he nods back. Like his friends,* FOREMAN *wears a
heavy winter coat and a worn fedora some sizes too small
for him. He stands and watches the others apprehensively. At last* ALPER *reaches the end of his laying on of
the phylacteries, his voice climbing to a shrill incantation*)

ALPER (*To* FOREMAN, *moving slowly as he prays*) ". . .
and it shall be for a sign upon thy hand, and for frontlets
between thy eyes; for by strength of hand the Lord
brought us out from Egypt. Amen!"

FOREMAN (*Muttering, his head bobbing nervously*)
Amen!

ALPER I thought you weren't coming down today, Foreman.

FOREMAN (*His mouth working without saying anything.
Finally, he says*) Alper . . .

ALPER You seem agitated. Is something wrong?

FOREMAN (*Staring at his friend*) Alper, I have her here.

ALPER You have who here?

FOREMAN I have my granddaughter Evelyn here. I have
her here in the Rabbi's office.

ALPER What are you talking about?

FOREMAN I took her out of the house while nobody was
looking, and I brought her here. I am faint. Let me sit
down.

(*He sinks onto a chair. His friend regards him with concern*)

ALPER Here, David, let me take your coat.

12

FOREMAN Alper, I have seen such a thing and heard words as will place me in my grave before the singing of the evening service. "Blessed art Thou, O Lord, King of the Universe, who hath wrought the wonders of the world." (*Suddenly half-starting from his seat*) I must speak to Hirschman! This is an affair for Hirschman who has delved into the cabala and the forbidden mysteries of numbers.

ALPER Sit down, Foreman, and compose yourself. (FOREMAN *sinks slowly back onto his chair*) Why did you bring her here? Foreman, you are my oldest friend from our days in the seminary together in Rumni in the Province of Poltava, and I speak to you harshly as only a friend may speak. You are making too much out of this whole matter of the girl. I know how dear she is to you, but the girl is insane, for heaven's sake! What sort of foolishness is this then to smuggle her out of your son's home? To what purpose? Really, Foreman, a gentle and pious man like you! Your son must be running through the streets at this moment shouting his daughter's name. Cal him on the phone and tell him you are bringing her back to him.

(FOREMAN *stares at his friend, his pale eyes filled with tears*)

FOREMAN Alper . . .

ALPER David, my dear friend, make peace with this situation.

FOREMAN (*Whispering*) She is possessed, Alper. She has a dybbuk in her. A demon! It spoke to me. (*He stares down at the floor at his feet, a numb terror settling over his face*) It spoke to me. I went in to my granddaughter this morning to comfort her, and I said: "How are you?" And she seemed quite normal. She has these moments of absolute lucidity. (*He looks desperately at his friend again*) She seemed to know she was being taken to the institution again. Then suddenly she fell to the floor in

13

a swoon. I said: "Evelyn, what's the matter?" And she looked up at me, and it was no longer her face, but a face so twisted with rage that my blood froze in my body. And a voice came out of her that was not her own. "Do you know my voice?" And I knew it. I knew the voice. God have mercy on my soul. I stood there like a statue, and my granddaughter lay on the floor with her eyes closed, and the voice came out of her, but her lips never moved. "David Foreman, son of Abram, this is the soul of Hannah Luchinsky, whom you dishonored and weakened in your youth, and the Gates of Heaven are closed to me." And my granddaughter began to writhe on the floor as if in the most horrible agony, and she began to laugh so loudly that I was sure my son and daughter-in-law in the living room could hear. I flung the door open in panic, and my son and daughter-in-law were sitting there talking, and they heard nothing. And I tell you shrieks of laughter were coming from this girl on the floor. And I closed the door and besought God, and finally the dybbuk was silent. May God strike me down on this spot, Alper, if every word I tell you is not true.

(ALPER *has slowly sat down on an adjacent chair, absolutely enthralled by the story. He stares at* FOREMAN)

ALPER   A dybbuk?

FOREMAN   (*Nodding*)   A dybbuk. Could you believe such a thing?

ALPER   Who did the dybbuk say she was?

FOREMAN   You should remember her. Hannah Luchinsky.

ALPER   The name is vaguely familiar.

FOREMAN   You remember Luchinsky, the sexton of the Rumni seminary, with his three daughters? Hannah was the handsome one who became pregnant, and they threw stones at her, called her harlot, and drove her out of the city.

ALPER   (*Recognition slowly coming over him*)   Ooohhh.

14

FOREMAN   I was the one who debased her.

ALPER   You? You were such a nose-in-the-books, a gentle and modest fellow. Dear me. A dybbuk. Really! What an extraordinary thing. Schlissel, do you want to hear a story?

SCHLISSEL   (*Coming over*)   What?

ALPER   (*To* ZITORSKY, *who ambles over*)   Listen to this. Foreman is telling a story here that will turn your blood into water.

SCHLISSEL   What happened?

FOREMAN   What happened, Schlissel, was that I went in to see my granddaughter this morning and discovered that she was possessed by a dybbuk. Now, please, Schlissel, before you go into one of your interminable disputations on the role of superstition in the capitalist economy, let me remind you that I am a follower of Maimonides and . . .

SCHLISSEL   What are you talking about?

FOREMAN   A dybbuk! A dybbuk! I tell you my granddaughter is possessed by a dybbuk! Oh, my head is just pounding! I do not know which way to turn.

SCHLISSEL   What are you prattling about dybbuks?

ALPER   (*To* SCHLISSEL)   The voice of Hannah Luchinsky spoke to him through the lips of his granddaughter.

ZITORSKY   Oh, a dybbuk.

SCHLISSEL   What nonsense is this?

ALPER   (*To* FOREMAN)   Are you sure?

FOREMAN   (*Angrily*)   Am I sure? Am I a peasant who leaps at every black cat? Have I ever shown a susceptibility to mysticism? Have you not seen me engaging Hirschman over there in violent disputation over the fanatic numerology of the cabala? Have I not mocked to his very face the murky fantasy of the Gilgul with wispy souls floating in space? Really! Am I sure! Do you take me for a fool, a prattler of old wives' tales? Really! I tell you I heard that woman's voice as I hear the cold wind outside our doors now, and saw my granddaughter writhing in the toils of possession as I see the phylactery on your brow this moment. I was a teacher of biology for thirty-nine years at the Yeshiva High School. A dedicated follower of the great Rambam who scoffed at augurs and sorcerers! For heaven's sake! Really! I report to you only what I see! (*He strides angrily away, and then his brief flurry of temper subsides as abruptly as it flared*) My dear Alper, please forgive this burst of temper. I am so distressed by this whole business that I cannot control my wits. I assure you that it is as hard for me to believe my own senses as it is for you.

ZITORSKY   When I was a boy in Lithuania, there was a young boy who worked for the butcher who was possessed by the dybbuk.

SCHLISSEL   (*Scornfully*) A dybbuk. Sure. Sure. When I was a boy in Poland, I also heard stories about a man who lived in the next town who was possessed by a dybbuk. I was eight years old, and, one day after school, my friends and I walked barefoot the six miles to the next town, and we asked everybody, "Where is the man with the dybbuk?" And nobody knew what we were talking about. So I came home and told my mother: "Mama, there is no man with a dybbuk in the next town." And she gave me such a slap across the face that I turned around three times. And she said to me: "Aha! Only eight years old and already an atheist." Foreman, my friend, you talk like my mother, who was an ignorant fish-wife. I am shocked at you.

FOREMAN   Oh, leave me be, Schlissel. I have no patience with your pontificating this morning.

ALPER   Don't let him upset you, Foreman. The man is a Communist.

FOREMAN   He is not a Communist. He is just disagreeable.

SCHLISSEL   My dear fellow, I have never believed in God.

16

Should I now believe in demons? A dybbuk. This I would like to see.

FOREMAN (*Furiously*) Then see! (*He strides to the door of* THE RABBI'S *office and wrenches the door open. The others gingerly follow him to the opened doorway and peer in.* THE GIRL—EVELYN—*stares at them, terrified. In a thunderous voice,* FOREMAN *cries out*—) Dybbuk! I direct you to reveal yourself!

(THE GIRL *stares at the four patently startled old men, and then suddenly bursts into a bloodcurdling shriek of laughter. The four old men involuntarily take one step back and regard this exhibition wide-eyed.*)

FOREMAN What is your name?

THE GIRL I am Hannah Luchinsky.

FOREMAN Who are you?

THE GIRL I am the Whore of Kiev, the companion of sailors.

FOREMAN How come you to be in my granddaughter's body?

THE GIRL I was on a yacht in the sea of Odessa, the pleasure of five wealthy merchants. And a storm arose, and all were lost. And my soul rose from the water and flew to the city of Belgorod where my soul appealed to the sages of that city. But since I was debauched they turned their backs on me.

FOREMAN And then?

THE GIRL Then my soul entered the body of a cow who became insane and was brought to slaughter and I flew into the body of this girl as if divinely directed.

FOREMAN What do you want?

THE GIRL I want the strength of a pure soul so that I may acquire that experience to ascend to heaven.

FOREMAN I plead with you to leave the body of this girl.

THE GIRL I have wandered through Gilgul many years, and I want peace. Why do you plague me? There are those among you who have done the same as I and will

17

suffer a similar fate. There is one among you who has lain with whores many times, and his wife died of the knowledge.

ZITORSKY (*Aghast*) Oh, my God!

THE GIRL (*Laughing*) Am I to answer questions of old men who have nothing to do but visit each other's cemeteries?

ZITORSKY (*Terrified*) A dybbuk . . . a dybbuk . . .

FOREMAN Evelyn . . . Evelyn . . . She is again in a catatonic state.

(THE GIRL *now sits in the* RABBI'S *chair, sprawling wantonly, apparently finished with the interview. The four old men regard her a little numbly. They are all quite pale as a result of the experience. After a moment,* FOREMAN *closes the door of* THE RABBI'S *office, and the four old men shuffle in a silent group downstage, where they stand, each reviewing in his own mind the bizarre implications of what they have seen.* FOREMAN *sinks into a chair and covers his face with his hands. After a long, long moment,* ZITORSKY *speaks*)

ZITORSKY Well, that's some dybbuk, all right.

SCHLISSEL The girl is as mad as a hatter and fancies herself a Ukrainian trollop. This is a dybbuk?

ALPER I found it quite and unnerving experience.

ZITORSKY She caught me dead to rights. I'll tell you that. I was the one she was talking about there, who trumpeted around with women. Listen, when I was in the garment business, if you didn't have women for the out-of-town buyers, you couldn't sell a dozen dresses. Oh, I was quite a gamy fellow when I was in business, a madcap really. One day, my wife caught me in the shop with a model—who knew she would be downtown that day?—and from that moment on, my wife was a sick woman and died three years later, cursing my name with her last breath. That was some dybbuk, all right. How she picked me out! It gave me the shivers.

ALPER   Did you notice her use of archaic language and her Russian accent? The whole business had an authentic ring to me.

SCHLISSEL   What nonsense! The last time I was up to Foreman's the girl confided to me in a whisper that she was Susan Hayward. A dybbuk! Ever since she was a child Foreman has been pumping her head full of the wretched superstitions of the Russian Pale, so she thinks she is a dybbuk. The girl is a lunatic and should be packed off to an asylum immediately.

(ALPER *regards* SCHLISSEL *with a disapproving eye; he then takes* SCHLISSEL'S *arm and leads him a few steps away for a private chat*)

ALPER   Really, Schlissel, must you always be so argumentative? We are all here agreed that we have a dybbuk in our company, but you always seem intent on being at odds with everyone around you. Really, look at poor Foreman, how distraught he is. Out of simple courtesy, really, for an old friend, can you not affect at least a silence on the matter? And, after all, what else have you got to do today? Ride two and a half hours to look at Zitorsky's tombstone? When you stop and think of it, this dybbuk is quite an exciting affair. Really, nothing like this has happened since Kornblum and Milsky had that fist fight over who would have the seat by the East Wall during the High Holidays.

ZITORSKY (*Ambling over*)   That's some dybbuk, all right.

SCHLISSEL (*Frowning*)   All right, so what'll we do with this dybbuk now that we got it?

ALPER   It seems to me, there is some kind of ritual, an exorcism of sorts.

ZITORSKY   Maybe we should tell the Rabbi.

SCHLISSEL   A young fellow like that. What does he know of dybbuks? A dybbuk must be exorcised from the body by a rabbi of some standing. You can't just call in some smooth-shaven young fellow fresh from the seminary for

19

such a formidable matter as a dybbuk. This Rabbi has only been here two months. He hardly knows our names.

ALPER   He's right. You have to get a big rabbi for such a business.

SCHLISSEL   What has to be done is we must get in touch with the Korpotchniker Rabbi of Williamsburg, who has inherited the mantle of the Great Korpotchniker of Lwów, whose fame extends to all the corners of the world.

ZITORSKY   Oh, a sage among sages.

ALPER   I was about to suggest the Bobolovitcher Rabbi of Crown Heights.

SCHLISSEL   Where do you come to compare the Bobolovitcher Rabbi with the Korpotchniker?

ALPER   I once attended an afternoon service conducted by the Bobolovitcher, and it was an exalting experience. A man truly in the great tradition of Chassidic rabbis.

ZITORSKY   A sage among sages, may his name be blessed for ever and ever.

SCHLISSEL   It shows how much you know. The Bobolovitcher Rabbi is a disciple of the Korpotchniker and sat at the Korpotchniker's feet until a matter of only a few years ago.

ALPER   Listen, I'm not going to argue with you. Either one is fine for me.

SCHLISSEL   The Korpotchniker is the number one Chassidic rabbi in the world. If you're going to involve yourself at all, why not go straight to the top?

ALPER   All right, so let it be the Korpotchniker.

ZITORSKY   For that matter, the Lubanower Rabbi of Brownsville is a man of great repute.

SCHLISSEL   The Lubanower! Really! He's a young man, for heaven's sakes!

ALPER   Zitorsky, let it be decided then that it will be the Korpotchniker.

ZITORSKY   I only made a suggestion.

SCHLISSEL The question is how does one get to the Korpotchniker? One does not drop into his home as if it were a public library. One has to solicit his secretary and petition for an audience. It may take weeks.

ALPER I do think, Schlissel, we shall have to get a more accessible rabbi than that. Ah, here is Hirschman, who I am sure can give us excellent counsel in this matter. (THE CABALIST *has indeed finished his prayers, and is shuffling downstage, a small, frightened man.* FOREMAN *leaps from his chair.*)

FOREMAN Hirschman!

(*Everyone crowds around* THE CABALIST)

ZITORSKY Oh, boy, Hirschman, have we got something to tell you!

ALPER Zitorsky, please. Hirschman, you are a man versed in the cabala, a man who prays with all the seventy-two names of the Most Ancient of the Ancient Ones.

FOREMAN (*Blurting out*) Hirschman, my granddaughter is possessed by a dybbuk!

THE CABALIST (*Starting back in terror*) A dybbuk!

ALPER Foreman, please, one does not announce such a thing as baldly as that.

THE CABALIST Are you sure?

FOREMAN Hirschman, as a rule, I am given to whimsy.

THE CABALIST Was it the soul of a woman wronged in her youth?

FOREMAN Yes.

THE CABALIST I heard her cry out last night. I awoke for my midnight devotions, and as I prayed I heard the whimpering of a woman's soul. (*A strange expression of wonder settles over his face*) I have fasted three days and three nights, and I dismissed the sound of this dybbuk as a fantasy of my weakened state. For only those to whom the Ancient One has raised his veil can hear the traffic of dybbuks. Is this a sign from God that my penitence is over? I have prayed for such a sign. I

21

have felt strange things these past days. Sudden, bursting illuminations have bleached mine eyes, and I have heard the sounds of dead and supernatural things.

(*He lifts his worn little face, his eyes wide with wonder. The others are put a little ill-at-ease by this effusive outburst.* FOREMAN, *indeed, is quite overwhelmed*)

ALPER   Actually, Hirschman, all we want to know is if you knew the telephone number of the Korpotchniker Rabbi.

(THE CABALIST *with some effort brings himself back to the moment at hand*)

THE CABALIST   He is my cousin. I will call him for you.

(*He moves slowly off, still obsessed with some private wonder of his own, to the phone on the outside wall of* THE RABBI'S *office*)

ALPER (*Quite awed*)   Your cousin? You are the Korpotchniker's cousin, Hirschman?

ZITORSKY (*Hurrying after* THE CABALIST)   You'll need a dime, Hirschman.

(*He gives* THE CABALIST *the ten-cent piece*)

ALPER   Schlissel, the Korpotchniker's cousin, did you hear? Apparently, he's not such a humbug.

SCHLISSEL   I tell you, he gives me the creeps, that Hirschman.

(THE CABALIST *has dialed a number on the wall phone.* FOREMAN *stands at his elbow, hunched with anxiety*)

THE CABALIST (*To* FOREMAN, *gently*)   Where is she, the dybbuk?

FOREMAN   In the Rabbi's office.

THE CABALIST   You are wise to go to the Korpotchniker. He is a Righteous One among the Righteous Ones. We were quite close as children until I abandoned the rabbinate. (*On the phone, in soft, gentle tones*)   Hello? Is this Chaim son of Yosif . . . This is Israel son of Isaac . . . And peace be unto you . . . There is a man here of my congregation who feels his granddaughter is

22

possessed by a dybbuk and would seek counsel from my cousin . . . He will bless you for your courtesy. Peace be unto you, Chaim son of Yosif. (*He hangs the receiver back in its cradle and turns to* FOREMAN) Give me a paper and pencil. (*The others, who have crowded around to hear the phone call, all seek in their pockets for a paper and pencil and manage to produce an old envelope and a stub of a pencil between them*) That was the Korpotchniker's secretary, and you are to go to his home as quickly as you can. I will write the address down for you. It is Williamsburg in Brooklyn. And you will be received directly after the morning services.

(*He gives* FOREMAN *the address, sweeps his prayer shawl on and retires upstage again for continued devotions*)

FOREMAN Thank you, Hirschman. The eye of the Lord will be open to you in the time of your need.

ZITORSKY Oh, Williamsburg. That's quite a ride from here.

SCHLISSEL What are you talking about? Foreman, you take the Long Island Railroad to Atlantic Avenue Station, where you go down stairs, and you catch the Brooklyn subway.

ALPER Maybe, I should go along with you, David, because a simple fellow like you will certainly get lost in the Atlantic Avenue Station, which is an immense or conflux of subways

SCHLISSEL What you do, Foreman, is you take the Long Island Railroad to the Atlantic Avenue Station, where you take the Double G train on the lower level . . .

ALPER Not the Double G train.

SCHLISSEL What's wrong with the Double G?

ALPER One takes the Brighton train. The Double G train will take him to Smith Street, which is a good eight blocks' walk.

SCHLISSEL The Brighton train will take him to Coney Island.

ALPER Foreman, listen to what I tell you. I will write down the instructions for you because an innocent fellow like you, if they didn't point you in the right direction, you couldn't even find the synagogue in the morning. Where's my pencil?

(*He has taken the paper and pencil from* FOREMAN'S *numb fingers and is writing down the traveling instructions*)

FOREMAN (*Staring off at the wall of* THE RABBI'S *office*) What shall I do with the girl? I can't leave her here.

ALPER Don't worry about the girl. She knows me. I'm like a second grandfather to her.

FOREMAN I don't like to leave her. Did I do right, Alper? Did I do right, kidnaping her this morning and bringing her here? Because the psychiatrist said we must prepare ourselves that she would probably spend the rest of her life in mental institutions. The irrevocability of it! The rest of her life! I was in tears almost the whole night thinking about it. Perhaps this produced a desperate susceptibility in me so that I clutch even at dybbuks rather than believe she is irretrievably insane. Now, in the sober chill of afterthought, it all seems so unreal and impetuous. And here I am bucketing off to some forbidding rabbi to listen to mystical incantations.

ALPER The Korpotchniker is not a rogue, Foreman. He is not going to sell you patent medicine. He will advise you quite sensibly, I am sure.

FOREMAN (*Buttoning his coat*) Yes, yes, I shall go to see him. You shall have to hide her till I come back. My son has probably called the police by now, and sooner or later they will come here looking for her.

ALPER Don't worry about it. I won't leave her side for a moment.

FOREMAN I better tell her I'm going. She'll be frightened if she looks for me, and I'm not here.

(*He hurries quickly to the* RABBI'S *office, where he stands*

24

a moment, regarding THE GIRL *with mingled fear and tenderness.* THE GIRL *has sunk into the blank detachment of schizophrenia and stares unseeingly at the floor*)

SCHLISSEL So the girl is a fugitive from the police. The situation is beginning to take on charm.

ALPER Look at Schlissel. The retired revolutionary. As long as it's against the law, he believes in dybbuks.

SCHLISSEL I believe in anything that involves a conspiracy.

(*At this point, the front door bursts open, and* THE SEXTON *returns with the announcement—*)

THE SEXTON I've got a tenth Jew!

ZITORSKY Sexton, have we got something to tell you!

SCHLISSEL (*Shushing him abruptly*) Sha! Idiot! Must you tell everyone?

THE SEXTON (*He leans back through the open door to the street and says to someone out there*) Come in, come in . . . (*A fine-looking, if troubled, young fellow in his middle thirties enters; he is dressed in expensive clothes, albeit a little shabby at the moment, as if he had been on a bender for the last couple of days. His name is* ARTHUR LANDAU. *He stands ill-at-ease and scowling, disturbed in aspect. His burberry topcoat hangs limply on him.* THE SEXTON *has scooted to an open carton, from which he takes out a black paper skullcap, nervously talking as he does*) Harris didn't come in yet?

SCHLISSEL No.

THE SEXTON The two Kessler boys, I called them on the phone, they didn't show up yet? (*He thrusts the skullcap into* ARTHUR'S *hand*) Here's a skullcap, put it on. (ARTHUR *takes the skullcap absently, but makes no move to put it on. He is preoccupied with deep and dark thoughts.* THE SEXTON *heads for the front door*) The Rabbi's not here yet?

SCHLISSEL He'll be here in a couple of minutes.

THE SEXTON It's only seven minutes to the services. Listen, I'm going to the Kesslers'. I'll have to pull them out of their beds, I can see that. I'll be right back. (*To* ARTHUR) You'll find some phylacteries in the carton there. Alper, give the man a prayer book. Sure, go find ten Jews on a winter morning.

(*He exits, closing the front door*)

FOREMAN (*As he comes out of the office*) All right, I'm going. She didn't eat anything this morning, so see she gets some coffee at least. Let's see. I take the Long Island Railroad to Atlantic Avenue Station. Listen, it has been a number of years since I have been on the subways. Well, wish me luck. Have I got money for carfare? Yes, yes. Well . . . well . . . my dear friends, peace be with you.

ALPER And with you, Foreman.

ZITORSKY Amen.

FOREMAN (*Opening the door*) Oh, it's cold out there.
(*He exits, closing the door*)

ALPER He'll get lost. I'm sure of it.

ZITORSKY Oh, have you ever seen such excitement? My heart is fairly pounding.

ALPER Oh, it's just starting. Now comes the exorcism. That should be something to see.

ZITORSKY Oh, boy.

SCHLISSEL Oh, I don't know. You've seen one exorcism, you've seen them all.

ZITORSKY You saw one, Schlissel?

SCHLISSEL Sure. When I was a boy in Poland, we had more dybbuks than we had pennies. We had a fellow there in my village, a mule driver, a burly chap who reeked from dung and was drunk from morning till night. One day, he lost his wits completely, and it was immediately attributed to a dybbuk. I was a boy of ten, perhaps eleven, and I watched the whole proceedings through a hole in the roof of the synagogue. A miracle-working rabbi who was passing through our district was

26

invited to exorcise the dybbuk. He drew several circles
on the ground and stood in the center surrounded by
four elders of the community, all dressed in white linen
and trembling with terror. The Miracle-Worker bellowed
out a series of incantations, and the poor mule driver,
who was beside himself with fear, screamed and . . .
hello, Harris . . . (*This last is addressed to a very, very
old man named* HARRIS, *who is making his halting way
into the synagogue at this moment. He barely nods to
the others, having all he can do to get into the synagogue
and close the door.* SCHLISSEL *continues his blithe story*)
. . . and fell to the floor. It was a marvelous vaudeville,
really. I was so petrified that I fell off the roof and almost
broke a leg. The Miracle-Worker wandered off to work
other miracles and the mule driver sold his mule and
went to America where I assume, because he was a
habitual drunkard and an insensitive boor, he achieved
considerable success. Our little village had a brief month
of notoriety, and we were all quite proud of ourselves.

ALPER   Oh, it sounds like a marvelous ceremony.

SCHLISSEL   Of course, they don't exorcise dybbuks like
they used to. Nowadays, the rabbi hangs a small amulet
around your neck, intones, "Blessed art Thou, O Lord,"
and that's an exorcism.

ALPER   Oh, I hope not.

SCHLISSEL   Really, religion has become so pallid recently,
it is hardly worth while being an atheist.

ZITORSKY   I don't even know if I'll come to see this exorcism. I'm already shivering just hearing about it.

ALPER   Well, you know, we are dealing with the occult
here, and it is quite frightening. Hello there, Harris, how
are you? (*By now, the octogenarian has removed his
overcoat, under which he wears several layers of sweaters, one of which turns out to be one of his grandson's
football jerseys, a striped red garment with the number
63 on it. For the rest of the act, he goes about the busi-*

ness of putting on his phylacteries. ALPER *claps his hands*) Well, let me find out if we can help this young Jew here. (*He moves toward* ARTHUR LANDAU, *smiling*) Can I give you a set of phylacteries?

ARTHUR (*Scowling—a man who has had a very bad night the night before*) I'm afraid I wouldn't have the first idea what to do with them.

ALPER You'll find a prayer shawl in one of these velvet bags here.

ARTHUR No, thank you.

ALPER (*Offering a small black prayer book*) Well, here's a prayer book anyway.

ARTHUR Look, the only reason I'm here is a little man stopped me on the street, asked me if I was Jewish, and gave me the impression he would kill himself if I didn't come in and complete your quorum. I was told all I had to do was stand around for a few minutes wearing a hat. I can't read Hebrew and I have nothing I want to pray about, so there's no sense giving me that book. All I want to know is how long is this going to take, because I don't feel very well, and I have a number of things to do.

ALPER My dear young fellow, you'll be out of here in fifteen or twenty minutes.

ARTHUR Thank you.

(*He absently puts the black paper skullcap on his head and sits down, scowling, on one of the wooden chairs.* ALPER *regards him for a moment; then turns and goes back to his two colleagues*)

ALPER (*To* SCHLISSEL *and* ZITORSKY) To such a state has modern Jewry fallen. He doesn't know what phylacteries are. He doesn't want a shawl. He can't read Hebrew.

ZITORSKY I wonder if he's still circumcised.

(ARTHUR *abruptly stands*)

ARTHUR I'd like to make a telephone call. (*Nobody hears*

him. He repeats louder)   I said, I'd like to make a telephone call.

ALPER (*Indicating the wall phone*)   Right on the wall there.

ARTHUR   This is a rather personal call.

ALPER   There's a phone in the Rabbi's office there.

(ARTHUR *crosses to* THE RABBI'S *office*)

SCHLISSEL   Well, look about you, really. Here you have the decline of Orthodox Judaism graphically before your eyes. This is a synagogue? A converted grocery store, flanked on one side by a dry cleaner and on the other by a shoemaker. Really, if it wasn't for the Holy Ark there, this place would look like the local headquarters of the American Labor Party. In Poland, where we were all one step from starvation, we had a synagogue whose shadow had more dignity than this place.

ALPER   It's a shame and a disgrace.

ZITORSKY   A shame and a disgrace.

(*In* THE RABBI'S *office* ARTHUR *is regarding* THE GIRL *with a sour eye*)

ARTHUR   Excuse me. I'd like to make a rather personal call.

(THE GIRL *stares down at the floor, unhearing, unmoving, off in a phantasmic world of her own distorted creation.* ARTHUR *sits down at* THE RABBI'S *desk, turns his shoulder to* THE GIRL, *and begins to dial a number*)

SCHLISSEL   Where are all the Orthodox Jews? They have apostated to the Reform Jewish temples, where they sit around like Episcopalians, listening to organ music.

ALPER   Your use of the word "apostasy" in referring to Reform Jews interests me, Schlissel. Is it not written in Sifre on Deuteronomy, "Even if they are foolish, even if they transgress, even if they are full of blemishes, they are still called sons"? So, after all, is it so terrible to be a Reform Jew? Is this not an interesting issue for disputation? Oh, my God!

(*He wheels and starts back for* THE RABBI'S *office. The same thought has been entering the other two old fellows' minds, as has been indicated by a growing frown of consternation on each of their faces. They follow* ALPER *to* THE RABBI'S *office, where he opens the door quickly and stares in at* ARTHUR LANDAU. *The latter is still seated at* THE RABBI'S *desk, waiting for an answer to his phone call; and* THE GIRL *is still in her immobilized state.* ARTHUR *casts such a baleful eye at this interruption that the three old men back out of the office and close the door. They remain nervously outside the door of the office. At last, someone responds to* ARTHUR'S *phone call*)

ARTHUR (*On the phone, shading his face, and keeping his voice down*) Hello, Doctor, did I wake you up? This is Arthur Landau . . . Yes, I know. Do you think you can find an hour for me this morning? . . . Oh, I could be in your office in about an hour or so. I'm out in Mineola. My ex-wife lives out here with her parents, you know. And I've been blind drunk for—I just figured it out—three days now. And I just found myself out here at two o'clock in the morning banging on their front door, screaming . . . (THE GIRL'S *presence bothers him. He leans across the desk to her and says*—) Look, this is a very personal call, and I would really appreciate your letting me have the use of this office for just a few minutes.

(THE GIRL *looks up at him blankly*)

THE GIRL (*Hollowly*) I am the Whore of Kiev, the companion of sailors.

(*The bizarreness of this stops* ARTHUR. *He considers it for a moment, and then goes back to the phone*)

ARTHUR (*On the phone*) No, I'm still here. I'm all right. At least, I'm still alive. (*He hides his face in the palm of one hand and rubs his brow nervously*) I've got to see you, Doc. Don't hang up on me, please. If my analyst hangs up on me, that'll be the end. Just let me talk a couple of minutes . . . I'm in some damned synagogue. I was on my way to the subway. Oh, my God, I've got to call my office. I was supposed to be in court twice yesterday. I hope somebody had the brains to apply for an adjournment. So it's funny, you know. I'm in this damned synagogue. I'll be down in about an hour, Doctor . . . Okay. Okay . . . I'm all right . . . No, I'm all right . . . I'll see you in about an hour. (*He hangs up, hides his face in the palms of both hands and slowly pulls himself together. After a moment, he looks up at* THE GIRL, *who is back to staring at the floor. He frowns, stands, goes to the door of the office, opens it, gives one last look at* THE GIRL, *and closes the door behind him. He finds himself staring at the inquiring faces of the three old men*) Listen, I hope you know there's a pretty strange girl in there.

(*The old men bob their heads nervously.* ARTHUR *crosses the synagogue to a chair and sits down, his face dark with his emotions. The three old men regard him anxiously. After a moment,* SCHLISSEL *approaches* ARTHUR)

SCHLISSEL   A strange girl, you say?

ARTHUR   Yes.

SCHLISSEL   Did she say anything?

ARTHUR   She said: "I am the Whore of Kiev, the companion of sailors."

SCHLISSEL   That was a very piquant statement, wouldn't you say?

ARTHUR   Yes, I think I would call it piquant.

SCHLISSEL   What do you make of it?

ARTHUR   (*Irritably*)   Look, I'm going. I have a hundred things to do. I . . .

SCHLISSEL   No, no, no. Sit down. For heaven's sakes, sit down.

ALPER   (*Hurrying over*)   Don't go. Oh, my, don't go. We

need you for a tenth man. We haven't had ten men in the morning in more than a week, I think.

ZITORSKY (*On* ALPER'S *tail*)   Two weeks, at least.

(*At this point,* HARRIS, *who has finally divested himself of his muffler and the heavy, ribbed sweaters which were over his jacket, and is now enwrapt in a prayer shawl, bursts into a high, quavering prayer*)

HARRIS   "Blessed art thou, O Lord, our God, King of the Universe, who hath sanctified us by his commandments and . . ."

(*The words dribble off into inaudibility.* ARTHUR LANDAU *darts a startled look at the old man, not being prepared for this method of prayer, and moves a few nervous steps away from the other old men, then stands rubbing his brow, quite agitated*)

ALPER (*Whispering to* SCHLISSEL)   So what happened in there? Did she say anything?

SCHLISSEL   Yes, she said she was the Whore of Kiev, and the companion of sailors.

ALPER   Oh, dear me.

SCHLISSEL   I'm afraid we shall have to get her out of the Rabbi's office because if she keeps telling everybody who walks in there that she is the Whore of Kiev, they will pack us all off to the insane asylum. And let us be quite sensible about this situation. If Foreman has kidnaped the girl, he has kidnaped her, however kindly his motives —not that I expect the police to regard a dybbuk as any kind of sensible explanation. Whatever the case, it would be a good idea to keep the girl a little less accessible. (*The wall phone rings*)   Ah! I'll tell you who that is. That's Foreman's son calling to find out if Foreman and the girl are here. (*The phone rings again*)   Well, if you won't answer it, I'll answer it.

(*He crosses to the wall phone*)

ALPER   We could take her to my house. Everybody is still sleeping. We'll put her in the cellar.

(*The phone rings again.* SCHLISSEL *picks up the phone*)

SCHLISSEL (*On the phone*)   Hello. (*He turns to the others and nods his head, indicating he was quite right in guessing the caller. The other two old men move closer to the phone*)   Mr. Foreman, your father isn't here . . . Listen, I tell you, he isn't here . . . I wouldn't have the slightest idea. I haven't seen her since I was up to your house last Tuesday. Isn't she home? . . . If he comes in, I'll tell him . . . Okay . . . (*He hangs up and turns to the other two*)   Well, we are in it up to our necks now.

ALPER (*Stripping off his phylacteries*)   So shall we take her to my house?

SCHLISSEL   All right. Zitorsky, go in and tell her we are going to take her some place else.

ZITORSKY (*Not exactly inspired by the idea*)   Yeah, sure.

SCHLISSEL (*To* ZITORSKY)   For heaven's sakes, Zitorsky, you don't really believe that's a dybbuk in there.

ZITORSKY   If that's no dybbuk, then you go in and take her. (SCHLISSEL *shuffles slowly to the door of* THE RABBI'S *office*)

SCHLISSEL (*Pausing at the closed office door*)   It's getting kind of complicated. Maybe we ought to call Foreman's son and tell him she's here and not get involved.

ZITORSKY   Oh, no!

SCHLISSEL   Ah, well, come on. What can they do to us? They'll call us foolish old men, but then foolishness is the only privilege of old age. So, Alper, you'll deal with her. You know how to talk to her, and we'll hide her in your cellar. So we'll have a little excitement. (*He opens the door, and the three old men regard* THE GIRL *as she sits in sodden, detached immobility*)   Listen. Alper, let's get along, you know. Before the Sexton comes back and starts asking us where we're all going.

(ALPER *nods apprehensively and takes a few steps into the office*)

33

ALPER (*To* THE GIRL, *who doesn't actually hear him or know of his presence*) How do you do, my dear Evelyn. This is Alper here. (*She makes no answer.* ALPER *turns to the other two*) She's in one of her apathetic states.

ZITORSKY (*Darting back into the synagogue proper*) I'll get your coat, Alper.

SCHLISSEL (*Looking around to see if* ARTHUR *is paying any attention to what's going on; he is not*) Well, take her by the arm.

ALPER Evelyn, your grandfather suggested we take you to my house. You always liked to play with the children's toys in my cellar there, you remember? Come along, and we'll have a good time.

ZITORSKY (*Giving* SCHLISSEL *an overcoat*) Here. Give this to Alper.

(*He hurries off to the front door of the synagogue*)

HARRIS (*In the process of laying on his phylacteries*) "And from thy wisdom, O Most High God, Thou shalt reserve for me . . ."

(*He dribbles off into inaudibility*)

ALPER (*Placing a tentative hand on* THE GIRL'S *shoulder*) Evelyn, dear . . .

(*She looks up, startled*)

ZITORSKY (*Leaning out the front door, searching up and down the street*) Oh, it's cold out here.

ALPER (*To* SCHLISSEL, *who is hurriedly putting on his own overcoat*) I have a feeling we're going to have trouble here.

SCHLISSEL I've got your coat here.

ALPER Evelyn . . . (*A strange animal-like grunt escapes* THE GIRL, *and she begins to moan softly*) Evelyn dear, please don't be alarmed. This is Mr. Alper here who has known you since you were born. (*He is getting a little panicky at the strange sounds coming out of* THE GIRL, *and he tries to grab her arm to help her to her feet. She bursts into a shrill scream, electrifying everybody in the*

34

synagogue with the exception of THE CABALIST, *who is oblivious to everything.* ZITORSKY, *who has just closed the front door, stands frozen with horror.* ARTHUR, *sunk in despondency, looks up, startled. The old man,* HARRIS, *pauses briefly, as if the sound has been some distant buzzing, and then goes back to his mumbled prayers*) Evelyn, my dear girl, for heaven's sakes . . .

THE GIRL (*Screaming out*) Leave me alone! Leave me alone!

ARTHUR (*Coming to* SCHLISSEL, *who shuts the office door quickly*) What's going on in there?

SCHLISSEL It's nothing, it's nothing.

THE GIRL (*Screaming*) They are my seven sons! My seven sons!

ALPER (*Who is trying earnestly to get out of the office*) Who closed this door?

ZITORSKY (*Reaching for the front door*) I'm getting out of here.

SCHLISSEL (*To* ZITORSKY) Where are you going?
   (*But* ZITORSKY *has already fled into the street*)

ARTHUR (*To* SCHLISSEL) What's all this screaming?
   (ALPER, *at last out of the office, comes scurrying to* SCHLISSEL)

ALPER I put my hand on her arm to help her up, and she burst into this fit of screaming.
   (ARTHUR *strides to the open doorway of the office.* THE GIRL *stares at him, hunched now in terror, frightened and at bay*)

ARTHUR (*To* SCHLISSEL) What have you been doing to this girl?

SCHLISSEL The girl is possessed by a dybbuk.

ARTHUR What?

SCHLISSEL (*To* ALPER) Zitorsky ran out in the street like a kangaroo.

ALPER Listen, maybe we should call somebody.

ARTHUR Listen, what is this?

35

ALPER My dear young man, there is no reason to alarm yourself. There is an insane girl in the Rabbi's office, but she appears to have quieted down.

ARTHUR What do you mean, there's an insane girl in the Rabbi's office?

ALPER Yes, she is a catatonic schizophrenic, occasionally violent, but really, go back to your seat. There is no cause for alarm.

ARTHUR Am I to understand, sir, that it is a practice of yours to keep insane girls in your Rabbi's office?

ALPER No, no. Oh, dear, I suppose we shall have to tell him. But you must promise, my dear fellow, to keep this whole matter between us. (*To* SCHLISSEL) Zitorsky, you say, took to his heels?

SCHLISSEL Absolutely flew out of the door.

ALPER Well, I really can't blame him. It was quite an apprehensive moment. I was a little shaken myself. (*He peeks into the office*) Yes, she seems to be quite apathetic again. I think we just better leave her alone for the time being.

ARTHUR Look, what is going on here?

ALPER My dear fellow, you are, of course, understandably confused. The girl, you see, is possessed by a dybbuk.

ARTHUR Yes, of course. Well, that explains everything.

ALPER Well, of course, how would he know what a dybbuk is? A dybbuk is a migratory soul that possesses the body of another human being in order to return to heaven. It is a Lurian doctrine, actually tracing back to the Essenes, I suppose, but popularized during the thirteenth century by the Spanish cabalists. I wrote several articles on the matter for Yiddish periodicals. My name is Moyshe Alper, and at one time I was a journalist of some repute. (ZITORSKY *appears in the doorway again, peering nervously in*) Come in, Zitorsky, come in. The girl is quiet again.

(ZITORSKY *approaches them warily*)

ARTHUR Look, are you trying to tell me you have a girl in there you think is possessed by some demon? Where is her mother or father or somebody who should be responsible for her?

ALPER If there were someone responsible for her, would she be insane in the first place?

ARTHUR Of course, this is none of my business . . .

ALPER You are a good fellow and let me put you at ease. The girl is in good hands. Nobody is going to hurt her. Her grandfather, who adores her more than his own life, has gone off for a short while.

ZITORSKY To Williamsburg on the Brighton train.

SCHLISSEL The Brighton train takes you to Coney Island.

ZITORSKY You said the Double G.

ALPER All right, all right.

ARTHUR Of course, this is none of my business.

ALPER (*To* ARTHUR) I can understand your concern; it shows you are a good fellow, but really the matter is well in hand.

(*The front door opens and there now enter* THE SEXTON *and two young men in their thirties, apparently the* KESSLER *boys, who are none too happy about being roused on this cold winter morning. They stand disconsolately around in the back of the synagogue*)

THE SEXTON Here are two more, the Kessler boys.

ALPER Now we'll have ten for a quorum.

ZITORSKY Kessler? Kessler? Oh, yes, the stationery store. I knew your father.

(*There is a general flurry of movement.* THE SEXTON *hurries about the ritual of baring his left arm, donning the prayer shawl and phylacteries, walking nervously about, mumbling his prayers rapidly.* ARTHUR, *quite disturbed again, looks into* THE RABBI'S *office at* THE GIRL, *then moves slowly into the office.* THE GIRL *is again in a world of her own. He closes the door and studies* THE GIRL. SCHLISSEL, ALPER *and* ZITORSKY *watch him warily, taking*

37

off their overcoats again and preparing to stay for the impending services. HARRIS' *shrill quavering voice suddenly leaps up into audibility again*)

HARRIS "Thou shalt set apart all that openeth the womb of the Lord, and the firstling that cometh of a beast which thou shalt have, it shall belong to the Lord . . ."

SCHLISSEL (*To* ALPER) What are we going to do when the Rabbi tries to get into his office? He'll see the girl, and that will be the end of our exorcism. What shall we tell the Rabbi?

(*The front door of the synagogue opens, and* THE RABBI *comes striding efficiently in, right on cue. He is a young man in his early thirties, neatly dressed if a little threadbare, and carrying a briefcase*)

ZITORSKY Peace be with you, Rabbi.

THE RABBI Peace be with you.

ALPER (*Intercepting* THE RABBI *as he heads for his office*) How do you do, Rabbi.

(THE RABBI *nods as he strides to the door of his office, where* SCHLISSEL *blocks the way*)

SCHLISSEL We have ten men today, Rabbi.

THE RABBI Good. (*He reaches for the door to his office*) I'll just get my phylacteries.

ALPER (*Seizing* ZITORSKY'S *phylacteries*) Oh, here, use these. It's late, Rabbi.

THE RABBI (*Taking the phylacteries*) Fine. Well, let's start the services.

(*He turns back to the synagogue proper. From all around, each man's voice rises into prayer*)

THE CURTAIN FALLS

ACT TWO

Scene 1

Fifteen minutes later.

ZITORSKY *is reading the prayers. He stands before the lectern on the raised platform, singing the primitive chants.*

ZITORSKY   "And we beseech thee according to thine abundant mercies, O Lord . . ."

THE SEXTON   Young Kessler, come here and open the Ark. (*The younger* KESSLER *ascends the platform and opens the Ark by drawing the curtains and sliding the doors apart*)

ZITORSKY   "And it came to pass, when the ark set forward, that Moses said, Rise up, O Lord, and Thine enemies shall be scattered, and they that hate Thee shall flee before Thee. For out of Zion shall go forth the Law, and the word of the Lord from Jerusalem." (*Immediately, the rest of the quorum plunges into a mumbled response: "Blessed be Thy name, O Sovereign of the World! Blessed be Thy crown, and Thy abiding place!" Jewish prayers are conducted in a reader-congregation pattern, although frequently the reader's vocalized statements and the congregation's mumbled responses merge and run along simultaneously. In this specific moment of prayer, when the Ark has been opened and the Torah is about to be taken out, the demarcation between reader and congregation is clear-cut. The sliding brown wooden doors of the Ark are now open.* THE SEXTON *is reaching in to take out the exquisitely ornamented Torah, which, when its lovely brocaded velvet cover is taken off, will show itself to be*

39

a large parchment scroll divided on two carved rollers. When THE SEXTON *gets the Torah out, he hands it carefully to* ZITORSKY, *who has been chosen this day for the honor of holding the Torah until it is to be read from.* ZITORSKY, *who, as today's reader, has been reading along with the congregation although more audibly, now allows his voice to ring out clearly, marking the end of this paragraph of prayers)* ". . . May it be Thy gracious will to open my heart in Thy Law, and to grant my heart's desires, and those of all Thy people Israel, for our benefit, throughout a peaceful life." *(Pause)* "Magnify the Lord with me, and let us exalt His name together." *(Again, the congregation leaps into mumbled response. "Thine, O Lord, is the greatness, and the power, and the glory, and the victory, and the majesty . . ."* ZITORSKY *marches solemnly to the front of the lectern, carrying the Torah before him. Each man kisses the Torah as it passes him. There is now the ritual of removing the velvet cover, and the Torah is laid upon the lectern.* ZITORSKY, HARRIS *and* THE SEXTON *form a hovering group of three old betallithed Jews over it.* THE RABBI *stands rocking slightly back and forth to the left of the lectern. Off the raised platform, but immediately by the railing, stands* THE CABALIST, *rocking back and forth and praying.* ALPER *and* SCHLISSEL *stand at various places, mumbling their responses. The two* KESSLER *boys have removed their coats and wear prayer shawls, but still stand as close to the front door as they can.* ARTHUR LANDAU *stands, leaning against the wall of* THE RABBI'S *office, quite intrigued by the solemn prayers and rituals.* THE GIRL *is still in* THE RABBI'S *office, but she is standing now, listening as well as she can to the prayers. Her face is peaceful now and quite lovely. Again* ZITORSKY'S *voice rises to indicate the end of a paragraph of prayer)* "Ascribe all of your greatness unto our God, and render honor to the Law." *(There is now a quick mumbled conference among the three old Jews at the lectern, then* THE SEXTON *suddenly leans out and calls to the two* KESSLER *boys in the rear*)

THE SEXTON   Kessler, you want to read from the Torah?

THE ELDER KESSLER   No, no, no. Get somebody else.

THE SEXTON   Alper? (ALPER *nods and makes his way to the lectern.* THE SEXTON'S *voice, a high, whining incantation, rises piercingly into the air, announcing the fact that Moyshe son of Abram will read from the Torah*) Rise up, Reb Moses Ha'Kohan, son of Abram, and speak the blessing on the Torah. "Blessed be He, who in His Holiness gave the Law unto his people Israel, the Law of the Lord is perfect."

CONGREGATION (*Scattered response*)   "And ye that cleave unto the Lord your God are alive every one of you this day."

ALPER (*Now at the lectern, raises his head and recites quickly*)   "Blessed is the lord who is to be blessed for ever and ever."

CONGREGATION   "Blessed is the Lord who is to be blessed for ever and ever."

ALPER   "Blessed art Thou, O Lord our God, King of the Universe, who hast chosen us from all peoples and hast given us Thy Law. Blessed art Thou, O Lord, who givest the Law."

CONGREGATION   Amen!

THE SEXTON   "And Moses said . . ."

(*There are now four mumbling old Jews huddled over the lectern. It all becomes very indistinguishable;* THE SEXTON'S *piercing tenor rises audibly now and then to indicate he is reading.* ALPER *moves into the reader's position and begins to read from the Torah, bending his knees and twisting his body and hunching over the Torah, peering at the meticulous Hebrew lettering inscribed therein.* SCHLISSEL *and the* KESSLER *boys find seats where they were standing, as does* THE CABALIST. THE RABBI *and* HARRIS *are seated on the raised platform. In* THE

41

RABBI'S *office,* THE GIRL *decides to go out into the synagogue proper. She opens the door and moves a few steps
out.* ARTHUR *hears her and turns to her warily*)

THE GIRL (*Quite lucidly and amiably*)   Excuse me, sir,
are they reading from the Torah now?
(*She peers over* ARTHUR'S *shoulder toward the old men
at the lectern*)

ARTHUR   Yes, I think so.
(*He watches her carefully. She seems all right now. Still,
there is something excessively ingenuous about her, a tentative, wide-eyed, gently smiling innocence*)

THE GIRL   Is my grandfather here?
(*She peers nervously around the synagogue*)

ARTHUR   Which one would be your grandfather?

THE GIRL (*Growing panic*)   No, he's not here. I see Mr.
Alper, but I don't see my grandfather.

ARTHUR   I'm sure he will be back soon.
(*His calmness reassures her*)

THE GIRL (*She studies this strange young man*)   I think
all synagogues should be shabby because I think of God
as being very poor as a child. What do you think of God
as?

ARTHUR   I'm afraid I think of God as the Director of
Internal Revenue.
(THE GIRL *laughs brightly and then immediately smothers
her laughter, aware she is in a solemn synagogue*)

THE GIRL   You're irreverent. (*Frowning, she goes into*
THE RABBI'S *office, plops down on his swivel chair, and
swivels back and forth, very much like a child.* ARTHUR
*follows her tentatively, studying her cautiously, yet taken
by her ingenuousness. She darts a quick frightened look
at him*)   Were you in here just before?

ARTHUR   Well, yes.

THE GIRL   Did I—did I say anything?

ARTHUR (*Amiably*)   Well, yes.

THE GIRL (*Sighing*)   I see. Well, I might as well tell you.

I've been to several mental institutions. (*She looks quickly at him. He smiles at her*) You don't seem very disconcerted by that.

ARTHUR Oh, I expect it might be hard to find somebody who couldn't do with occasional confinement in a mental institution.

(*In the synagogue,* THE SEXTON *now calls* HARRIS *to read from the Torah*)

THE GIRL (*She frowns*) Did my grandfather say when he would be back or where he was going?

(*She starts from her seat frightened again*)

ARTHUR I understand he'll be back soon.

THE GIRL Are you the doctor?

ARTHUR No. You don't have to be the least bit afraid of me.

THE GIRL (*She brightens*) My grandfather and I are very close. I'm much closer to him than I am to my own father. I'd rather not talk about my father, if you don't mind. It's a danger spot for me. You know, when I was nine years old, I shaved all the hair off my head because that is the practice of really Orthodox Jewish women. I mean, if you want to be a rabbi's wife, you must shear your hair and wear a wig. That's one of my compulsive dreams. I keep dreaming of myself as the wife of a handsome young rabbi with a fine beard down to his waist and a very stern face and prematurely gray forelocks on his brow. I have discovered through many unsuccessful years of psychiatric treatment that religion has a profound sexual connotation for me. Oh, dear, I'm afraid I'm being tiresome about my psychiatric history. Really, being insane is like being fat. You can talk about nothing else. Please forgive me. I am sure I am boring you to death.

ARTHUR No, not at all. It's nice to hear somebody talk with passion about anything, even their insanity.

THE GIRL (*Staring at him*) The word doesn't bother you?

ARTHUR   What word?

THE GIRL   Insanity.

ARTHUR   Good heavens, no. I'm a lawyer. Insanity in one form or another is what fills my anteroom. Besides, I'm being psychoanalyzed myself and I'm something of a bore about that too. You are a bright young thing. How old are you?

THE GIRL   Eighteen.

ARTHUR (*Staring at her*)   My God, you're a pretty kid! I can hardly believe you are psychopathic. Are you very advanced?

THE GIRL   Pretty bad. I'm being instituionalized again. Dr. Molineaux's Sanitarium in Long Island. I'm a little paranoid and hallucinate a great deal and have very little sense of reality, except for brief interludes like this, and I might slip off any minute in the middle of a sentence into some incoherency. If that should happen, you must be very realistic with me. Harsh reality is the most efficacious way to deal with schizophrenics.

ARTHUR   You seem well read on the matter.

THE GIRL   I'm a voracious reader. I have so little else to do with myself. Will you come and visit me at Dr. Molineaux's hospital? I am awfully fond of you.

ARTHUR   Yes, of course, I will.

THE GIRL   It won't be as depressing an experience as you might think. If I am not in the violent ward, I will probably be allowed to go to the commissary and have an ice-cream soda with you. The worst of an insane asylum is really how poorly dressed the inmates are. They all wear old cable-stitched sweaters. I do like to look pretty. (*A vacuous look is beginning to come across her face*) They ask me to be in a lot of movies, you know, when I have time. Did you see *David and Bathsheba* with Susan Hayward? That was really me. I don't tell anybody that. They don't want me to make movies. My mother, I mean. She doesn't even go to synagogue on Saturday. You're the new Rabbi, you know. Sometimes, I'm the Rabbi, but they're all afraid of me. The temple is sixty cubits long and made of cypress and overlaid with gold. The burnished Roman legions clank outside the gates, you know. Did you see *The Ten Commandments?* I saw that Tuesday, Wednesday. I was in that. I was the girl who danced. I was in that. Mr. Hirschman is here, too, you know, and my grandfather. Everybody's here. Do you see that boy over there? Go away. Leave us alone. He's insane. He's really Mr. Hirschman the Cabalist. He's making a golem. You ought to come here, Rabbi.

ARTHUR (*Who has been listening fascinated, now says firmly*)   I am not the Rabbi, Evelyn.

(*She regards him briefly*)

THE GIRL   Well, we're making a golem and . . .

ARTHUR   You are not making a golem, Evelyn.

(*She pauses, staring down at the floor. A grimace of pain moves quickly across her face and then leaves it. After a moment, she mumbles—*)

THE GIRL   Thank you. (*Suddenly she begins to cry and she throws herself on* ARTHUR'S *breast, clinging to him, and he holds her gently, caressing her as he would a child*)   Oh, I can't bear being insane.

ARTHUR (*Gently*)   I always thought that since the insane made their own world it was more pleasurable than this one that is made for us.

THE GIRL (*Moving away*)   Oh, no, it is unbearably painful. It is the most indescribable desolation. You are all alone in deserted streets. You cannot possibly imagine it.

ARTHUR   I'm afraid I can. I have tried to commit suicide so many times now it has become something of a family joke. Once, before I was divorced, my wife stopped in to tell a neighbor before she went out to shop: "Oh, by the way, if you smell gas, don't worry about it. It's only Arthur killing himself again." Suicides, you know, kill themselves a thousand times, but one day I'll slash my wrists and I will forget to make a last-minute telephone call and there will be no stomach-pumping Samaritans to run up the stairs and smash my bedroom door down and rush me off to Bellevue. I'll make it some day—I assure you of that.

THE GIRL (*Regarding him with sweet interest*) You don't look as sad as all that.

ARTHUR Oh, I have made a profession of ironic detachment. It depresses me to hear that insanity is as forlorn as anything else. I had always hoped to go crazy myself some day since I have apparently no talent for suicide.

THE GIRL I always thought life would be wonderful if I were only sane.

ARTHUR Life is merely dreary if you're sane, and unbearable if you are sensitive. I cannot think of a more meaningless sham than my own life. My parents were very poor so I spent the first twenty years of my life condemning the rich for my childhood nightmares. Oh, I was quite a Bernard Barricade when I was in college. I left the Communist Party when I discovered there were easier ways to seduce girls. I turned from reproaching society for my loneliness to reproaching my mother, and stormed out of her house to take a room for myself on the East Side. Then I fell in love—that is to say, I found living alone so unbearable I was willing to marry. She married me because all her friends were marrying somebody. Needless to say, we told each other how deeply in love we were. We wanted very much to be happy. Americans, you know, are frantic about being happy. The American nirvana is a man and his wife watching television amiably and then turning off the lights and effortless making the most ardent love to each other. Television unfortunately is a bore and ardent love is an immense drain on one's energy. I began to work day and night at my law office, and besides becoming very successful, I managed to avoid my wife entirely. For this deceit, I was called

46

ambitious and was respected by everyone including my
wife, who was quite as bored with me as I was with her.
We decided to have children because we couldn't possibly
believe we were that miserable together. All this while
I drove myself mercilessly for fear that if I paused for
just one moment, the whole slim, trembling sanity of
my life would come crashing down about my feet without the slightest sound. I went to a psychoanalyst who
wanted to know about my childhood when I could barely
remember whether I took a taxi or a bus to his office
that day. I began to drink myself into stupors, pursuing
other men's wives, and generally behaving badly. One
morning, I stared into the mirror and could barely make
out my features. Life is utterly meaningless. I have had
everything a man can get out of life—prestige, power,
money, women, children, and a handsome home only
three blocks from the Scarsdale Country Club, and all I
can think of is I want to get out of this as fast as I can.
(*He has become quite upset by now, and has to avert
his face to hide a sudden welling of tears. He takes a
moment to get a good grip on himself, readopts his sardonic air and says—*) As you see, I have quite a theatrical way when I want to.

THE GIRL (*Brightly*) Oh, I think you are wonderfully
wise.

ARTHUR Oh, it was said best by your own King Solomon,
the wisest man who ever lived, when he wrote Ecclesiastes.

THE GIRL Oh, King Solomon didn't write Ecclesiastes.
That was written by an anonymous Jewish scholar in
Alexandria. I wouldn't put too much stock in it. Weari-
ness was all the rage among the Hellenized Jews.

ARTHUR (*Staring at her*) You are an amazing kid.
(*She smiles back at him exuberantly, unabashedly showing her fondness for him. It embarrasses him, and he
turns away. He opens the door, and looks out into the*

synagogue, where the reading of the Torah has come to
an end)

THE RABBI (*Singing out*)   "Blessed art Thou, O Lord our
God, King of the Universe, who has given us the Law
of truth, and hast planted everywhere life in our midst.
Blessed art Thou, O Lord, who givest the Law."

(*There is a scattered mumbled response from the old
men in the synagogue.* ZITORSKY *now takes the Torah and
holds it up above his head and chants*)

ZITORSKY   "And this is the Law which Moses set before
the children of Israel, according to the commandment
of the Lord by the hand of Moses." (*The four men on
the platform form a small group as* ZITORSKY *marches
slowly back to the Ark carrying the Torah. A mumble
of prayers rustles through the synagogue.* ZITORSKY'S
voice rises out)   "Let them praise the name of the Lord;
for His name alone is exalted."

(*He carefully places the Torah back into the Ark. A
rumble of prayer runs through the synagogue. All the
men in the synagogue are standing now*)

ARTHUR (*Turning to* THE GIRL)   They're putting the Torah
back. Is the service over?

THE GIRL   No. I have a wonderful book I want to give
to you. Mr. Hirschman, our Community Cabalist, gave
it to me. It is called the Book of Splendor, a terribly
mystical book. And you are a mystic, you know.

ARTHUR   Oh, am I?

THE GIRL   Yes. I never met anyone who wanted to know
the meaning of life as desperately as you do. I have to
get the book for you.

(SCHLISSEL *pokes his head into the office and indicates to*
ARTHUR *that he is needed outside*)

ARTHUR   I think they need me outside.

(*He moves to the door*)

THE GIRL   Yes, we really shouldn't have been talking
during the service.

(ARTHUR *goes out of the office, closing the door behind him. He joins* SCHLISSEL, *who is a few steps away, muttering the prayers*)

ARTHUR (*Shaking his head*) What a pity, really. A lovely girl. What a pity. Now, you look like a sensible sort of man. What is all this nonsense about demons? You really should call her father or mother or whoever it is who is responsible for her.

SCHLISSEL Young man, if we called her father he would come down and take her away.

ARTHUR Yes. That would be the point, wouldn't it?

SCHLISSEL Then what happens to our exorcism?

ARTHUR What exorcism?

SCHLISSEL Listen, we've got to exorcise the dybbuk.

ARTHUR (*Aghast*) Exorcism!

(THE SEXTON *leans over the railing of the platform and admonishes them in a heavy whisper*)

THE SEXTON Sssshhhh!

(SCHLISSEL *promptly turns back to muttering his prayers.* ARTHUR *stares at him with vague disbelief*)

ARTHUR Are you serious?

(ZITORSKY'S *voice rises up loud and clear*)

ZITORSKY ". . . And it is said, and the Lord shall be king over all the earth; on that day shall the Lord be One, and His Name One."

(THE CONGREGATION, *which had been sitting, now stands again.* THE SEXTON *leans over the railing and calls to the* KESSLER *boys*)

THE SEXTON Kessler, stand up. Now is the time for your memorial prayers.

(The two KESSLER *boys nod, stand, and look unhappily down at their prayer books.* HARRIS *pokes a palsied finger onto a page to show them where to read, and the two young men now begin to read painstakingly and with no idea of what they are reading*)

KESSLER BOYS "Magnified and sanctified be His great

49

Name in the world which He hath created according to His will. May He establish His kingdom in your lifetime and in your days, and in the lifetime of all the house of Israel, speedily and at a near time; and say ye, Amen."

CONGREGATION   Amen. "Let His Great Name be blessed for ever and ever."

KESSLER BOYS   "Blessed, praised, and glorified, exalted, extolled and honored, adored, and lauded, be the Name of the Holy One, blessed be He, beyond, yea, beyond all blessings and hymns, praises and songs, which are uttered in the world, and say ye, Amen."

CONGREGATION   Amen.

(*The front door to the synagogue bursts open and* FORE-MAN *thrusts himself in, obviously much distraught; not so distraught, however, that he doesn't automatically join in the "Amen"*)

KESSLER BOYS   "May there be abundant peace from heaven, and life for us and for all Israel; and say ye, Amen."

CONGREGATION   Amen.

KESSLER BOYS   "May he who maketh peace in his high places, make peace for us and for all Israel, and say ye, Amen."

CONGREGATION   Amen.

(*The synagogue bursts into a quick mumble of prayers, except for* SCHLISSEL, *who scurries over to* FOREMAN. FOREMAN *stares at him, white with panic*)

SCHLISSEL   What happened? You got lost? You took the Long Island Railroad to Atlantic Avenue Station, and you got lost in the Atlantic Avenue Station?

FOREMAN   What Atlantic Avenue Station? I couldn't even find the Long Island Railroad!

SCHLISSEL   Idiot! You are an innocent child! Really! Services are over in a minute, and I'll take you myself. (ALPER *is leaning over the railing of the platform, making obvious gestures, as if to ask what had happened.*

50

Even ZITORSKY *looks up from his hunched position at the lectern.* SCHLISSEL *announces in a heavy whisper, as he starts to put on his coat—)* He couldn't even find the Long Island Railway Station. (ALPER *clasps his brow.* THE SEXTON *turns around to* SCHLISSEL *and admonishes him with a heavy "Ssshhh!!!"* FOREMAN *has begun walking about, mumbling the prayers by heart, automatically a part of the service again. As he passes* SCHLISSEL, *he indicates with a jerk of his head that he would like to know of the well-being of his granddaughter)* She's all right. Don't worry about her.

(FOREMAN *nods and continues mumbling his prayers. In* THE RABBI'S *office,* THE GIRL, *who has been sitting pensively, now stands, puts her coat on, goes out of the office, calmly crosses to the rear of the synagogue, and exits through the front door. Absolutely no one is aware she has gone.* THE CONGREGATION *now bursts into a loud prayer, obviously the last one of the service, since the men on the platform begin to meander off, and all those who are still wearing their phylacteries begin to strip them off, even as they say the words of the prayer)*

CONGREGATION

"He is the Lord of the Universe, who reigned ere any creature yet was formed.

At the time when all things were made by His desire, then was His name proclaimed King.

And after all things shall have had an end, He alone, the dreadest one shall reign;

Who was, who is, and who will be in glory."

(SCHLISSEL, ALPER, ZITORSKY, *and* FOREMAN *have all rattled quickly through this final paean, impatient to close off the service, while the others continue the terminal recital. The four old men form a huddled group by the front door)*

ALL FOUR (*Rattling it off*)   "And with my spirit, my body, also; the Lord is with me, and I will not fear. Amen."

ALPER   Amen, what happened?

SCHLISSEL   I'm taking him myself right away.

ZITORSKY   What happened, you got lost?

FOREMAN   I asked this fellow in the street, I said: "Could you . . ."

SCHLISSEL   (*To* ALPER, *pointing to* ARTHUR)   Listen, keep an eye on that fellow there. He wants to tell the Rabbi about the girl. All right, listen. I shall have to lead Foreman by the hand to Korpotchniker. All right, listen, we're going. Good-bye. Peace be unto you.

ALPER   Take the Long Island Railroad to the Atlantic Avenue Station. Then take the Brighton train.

SCHLISSEL   Oh, for heaven's sakes. Are you presuming to tell me how to get to Williamsburg?

ALPER   All right, go already.

SCHLISSEL   (*Muttering as he leads* FOREMAN *out the door*)   The Brighton train. If we took the Brighton train, we would spend the day in Coney Island.

(*He exits with* FOREMAN, *closing the door. The rest of the* CONGREGATION *has finally come to the end of the service*)

CONGREGATION   (*Their scattered voices rising to a coda*)   "And with my spirit, my body also; the Lord is with me, and I will not fear. Amen!"

ZITORSKY *and* ALPER   Amen!

(*There is a flurry of dispersion. The two* KESSLER *boys mumble good-byes and disappear quickly out into the street, buttoning their coats against the cold.* HARRIS, *who is slowly and tremblingly removing his phylacteries, continues slowly to dress himself again throughout the rest of the scene.* THE SEXTON *now scurries about, gathering the various phylacteries and prayer shawls and putting them back into the velvet prayer bags and then putting all the velvet bags and prayer books back into the cardboard carton they were all taken from, an activity he pursues with his usual frenetic desperation. Only* THE RABBI *and*

52

The Tenth Man

THE CABALIST *continue to say a few extra prayers: "The Thirteen Principles of Faith," etc.* THE CABALIST *reads them sitting down, hunched over his prayer book.* ALPER *and* ZITORSKY *have genuine cause for alarm concerning* ARTHUR LANDAU, *for he has ambled down to the platform, where he stands waiting for* THE RABBI *to finish his prayers. They watch* ARTHUR *guardedly.* HARRIS *suddenly decides to be communicative. He lifts his old face to* ALPER *and* ZITORSKY)

HARRIS   Ah, am I thirsty!

ALPER (*Watching* ARTHUR *carefully*)   Good.

(THE RABBI, *having finished his last prayer, now turns and starts down from the platform.* ARTHUR *steps forward to meet him*)

ARTHUR   Rabbi . . .

THE RABBI (*Walking by him*)   I'll be with you in just a moment.

(*He strides directly to his office.* ALPER *leaps to intercept him*)

ALPER   Rabbi . . .

THE RABBI (*Continuing into his office*)   I'll be with you in a minute, Alper. (*He goes into his office and closes the door.* ALPER *clasps his brow and shrugs.* ZITORSKY *mutters an involuntary "Oy." They both nod their heads and wait with the sufferance that is the badge of all their tribe.* ARTHUR *moves a few steps to* THE RABBI'S *door and also waits. In the office,* THE RABBI *sits down—all business—and dials a number. Then he speaks into the phone*)   I'd like to make a person-to-person call to Rabbi Harry Gersh in Wilmington, Delaware. The number in Wilmington is Kingswood 3-1973 . . . Thank you . . . (*He hums a snatch of the service.* ALPER *knocks lightly on the door, and, receiving no answer, opens the door and comes into the office. He stares—open-mouthed —noting the absence of* THE GIRL. *He tugs at his Vandyke beard in contemplation*)   Yes, Alper?

ALPER   Well, I'll tell you, Rabbi . . . (*He scowls, a little flustered, then turns and goes out of the office*)   Excuse me.

THE RABBI   (*On the phone*)   Locust 6-0932.

ALPER   (*To* ZITORSKY)   She's not there.

ZITORSKY   She's not there?

ALPER   I'll have to go out and look for her.

(*Frowning in contemplation,* ALPER *puts his coat on slowly and exits from the synagogue.* THE RABBI *is still on the phone. His voice rises to the pitch usually used for long-distance calls*)

THE RABBI   Harry, how are you, this is Bernard here, I'm sorry I wasn't in last night, my wife Sylvia said it was wonderful to hear your voice after all these years, how are you, Shirley, and the kids, oh, that's wonderful, I'm glad to hear it. Harry, my wife tells me you have just gotten your first congregation and you wanted some advice since I have already been fired several times . . . Good, how much are you getting? . . . Well, five thousand isn't bad for a first congregation although I always thought out-of-town paid better. And what is it, a one-year contract? . . . Well, what kind of advice can I give you? Especially you, Harry. You are a saintly, scholarly, and truly pious man, and you have no business being a rabbi. You've got to be a go-getter, Harry, unfortunately. The synagogue I am in now is in an unbelievable state of neglect and I expect to see us in prouder premises within a year. But I've got things moving now. I've started a Youth Group, a Young Married People's Club, a Theatre Club which is putting on its first production next month, *The Man Who Came to Dinner,* I'd like you to come, Harry, bring the wife, I'm sure you'll have an entertaining evening. And let me recommend that you organize a little-league baseball team. It's a marvelous gimmick, I have sixteen boys in my Sunday School now . . . Harry, listen, what do I know

about baseball? . . . Harry, let me interrupt you. How in heaven's name are you going to convey an awe of God to boys who will race out of your Hebrew classes to fly model rocket ships five hundred feet in the air exploding in three stages? To my boys, God is a retired mechanic . . . Well, I'm organizing a bazaar right now. When I hang up on you, I have to rush to the printer's to get some raffles printed, and from there I go to the Town Hall for a permit to conduct bingo games. In fact, I was so busy this morning, I almost forgot to come to the synagogue . . . (*He says gently*) Harry, with my first congregation, I also thought I was bringing the word of God. I stood up in my pulpit every Sabbath and carped at them for violating the rituals of their own religion. My congregations dwindled, and one synagogue given to my charge disappeared into a morass of mortgages. Harry, I'm afraid there are times when I don't care if they believe in God as long as they come to the synagogue . . . Of course, it's sad . . . Harry, it's been my pleasure. Have I depressed you? . . . Come and see us, Harry . . . Good luck . . . Of course. Good-bye.
(*He hangs up, stands, starts looking around for his briefcase, and strides out into the synagogue still searching for it. He is interrupted by* ARTHUR)

ARTHUR   Rabbi, I have to hurry off, but before I go I would like to talk to you about that girl in your office. These old men tell me she is possessed by a demon and I think they are intending to perform some kind of an exorcism. I must caution you that that girl should be treated only by competent psychiatrists and the most frightful harm might come to her if she is subjected to anything like— Look, do you know about this exorcism, because I cannot believe you would tolerate any . . .

THE RABBI   (*Who has been trying very hard to follow all this*)   I'm afraid you have me at a disadvantage.

ARTHUR I'm talking about the girl in your office.

THE RABBI I'm somewhat new here and don't know everybody yet by name. Please be patient with me. Now, I
take it you want to get married.

(*For a moment* ARTHUR *briefly considers the possibility
he is not really awake*)

ARTHUR (*Pensively*) This whole morning is beginning to
seem absolutely . . . Rabbi, there is a girl in your office
who is insane.

THE RABBI In my office? (THE RABBI *is suddenly distracted
by* ZITORSKY, *who has been wandering around the synagogue, looking up and down between the rows of chairs,
and is now looking into the bathroom at the upstage end
of the synagogue*) Mr. Zitorsky, what are you doing?

ZITORSKY (*To* ARTHUR, *who is moving quickly to* THE
RABBI'S *office*) Well, have you ever seen such a thing?
The girl has vanished into thin air.

(*He shuffles to* THE RABBI, *absolutely awe-struck by it
all*)

ARTHUR (*Now examining the interior of* THE RABBI'S *office*)
I suspect something more mundane, like simply walking
out the door.

(*He moves quickly to the front door, which now opens,
and* ALPER *returns, frowning with thought*)

ALPER (*To* ARTHUR) Well, is that something or isn't it?
I looked up and down, I couldn't see her.

(ARTHUR *scowls and goes out into the street, where he
stands looking up and down*)

THE RABBI Mr. Zitorsky, if you will just tell me what this
is all about.

ZITORSKY (*His eyes wide with awe*) Rabbi, Mr. Foreman
brought his granddaughter down this morning, and he
said: "She is possessed by a dybbuk!" Well, what can
you say when someone tells you something like that?

THE RABBI Oh, Mr. Foreman's granddaughter. Yes, of
course, I see.

ZITORSKY So he took us into your office where she was standing, and it spoke to us! What an experience! You cannot imagine! The voice of the dybbuk spoke to us. It was like a hollow echo of eternity, and the girl's whole body was illuminated by a frame of light! Fire flashed from her mouth. All of us were there, ask Alper here, he'll tell you. I swear this on my soul! The girl began to rise into the air!

ALPER Actually, Zitorsky is coloring the story a little.

ZITORSKY (*Riveted by the marvelousness of the fantasy*) What are you talking about? You saw it with your own eyes!

ALPER Well, it was an experience, I must say.

THE RABBI And the girl has gone now.

ZITORSKY Into the air about us.

THE RABBI And where is Mr. Foreman?

ALPER He went to Brooklyn.

THE RABBI What in heaven's name for?

ALPER To see the Korpotchniker Rabbi.

THE RABBI (*Quite impressed*) The Korpotchniker?

ZITORSKY Certainly! Maybe you don't know this, but Hirschman is his cousin.

THE RABBI Mr. Hirschman? I have to admit I didn't know that.

ZITORSKY Oh, sure. Listen, Hirschman is the first-born son of the original Korpotchniker.

ALPER I am afraid we are drifting from the point.

THE RABBI (*Frowning*) The girl probably went home. Why don't you call the girl's home, Mr. Alper, and find out if she's there? I think you are a very close friend of the family.

ARTHUR (*Who has come back into the synagogue*) Well, thank God for the first rational voice I've heard today.

ALPER (*Nodding his head sadly*) Yes, I suppose I had better call her father.

ARTHUR (*Buttoning his coat*) Fine. (*Glancing at his watch*) Gentlemen, if you don't need me for anything any more, I would like to get to my analyst. Good morning.

(*He strides to the door*)

THE RABBI Peace be unto you.

(ARTHUR *pauses at the front door, a little amused at the archaic greeting*)

ARTHUR Peace be unto you, Rabbi.

(*He opens the door and goes out*)

THE RABBI Who was that fellow?

ZITORSKY Who knows? The Sexton found him on the street.

THE RABBI (*Buttoning his own coat*) Well, I have to be down at the printer's. A dybbuk. Really. What an unusual thing. Is Mr. Foreman a mystical man? By the way, Mr. Alper—Mr. Zitorsky—you weren't at the meeting of the Brotherhood last night. I think you should take a more active interest in the synagogue. Did you receive an announcement of the meeting? Please come next time. (*He finds his briefcase*) Ah, there it is, good. (*He heads for the door*) I would like to know what the Korpotchniker said about this. Will you be here later today? I'll drop in. Let me know what happens. You better call the girl's family right away, Alper. Good morning. Peace be with you.

ALPER *and* ZITORSKY Peace be with you, Rabbi.

(THE RABBI *exits. The two old men regard each other a little balefully, and then shuffle to* THE RABBI'S *office, where* ALPER *sits down and puts his hand on the phone, resting it on the receiver, quite depressed by the turn of events. In the synagogue,* THE CABALIST *is huddled in prayer, and* THE SEXTON *has gotten a broom out and is sweeping an upstage area. A long moment of hushed silence fills the stage*)

ALPER (*His hand still on the phone*)   Zitorsky, let us reason this out.

ZITORSKY   Absolutely.

ALPER (*The Talmudic scholar*)   If I call the girl's home, there are two possibilities. Either she is home or she is not home. If she is home, why call? If she is not home, then there are two possibilities. Either her father has already called the police, or he has not called the police. If he has already called the police, then we are wasting a telephone call. If he has not called the police, he will call them. If he calls the police, then there are two possibilities. Either they will take the matter seriously or they will not. If they don't take the matter seriously, why bother calling them? If they take the matter seriously, they will rush down here to find out what we already know, so what gain will have been made? Nothing. Have I reasoned well, Zitorsky?

ZITORSKY   You have reasoned well.

ALPER   Between you and me, Zitorsky, how many people are there on the streets at this hour that we couldn't spot the girl in a minute? Why should we trouble the immense machinery of the law? We'll go out and find the girl ourselves.

(*They are both up in a minute, buttoning their coats and hurrying to the front door, where they pause*)

ZITORSKY (*Regarding* ALPER *with awe*)   Alper, what a rogue you are!

(ALPER *accepts the compliment graciously, and they both dart out into the street. Then, out of the hollow hush of the stage,* THE CABALIST'S *voice rises into a lovely chant as he rocks back and forth, his eyes closed in religious ecstasy*)

THE CABALIST (*Singing slowly and with profound conviction*)

"I believe with perfect faith in the coming of the Messiah, and though he tarry, I will wait daily for his coming.

I believe with perfect faith that there will be a resurrection of the dead

at the time when it shall please the Creator,
blessed be His name,

and exalted the remembrance of him for ever and ever."

(*The front door opens, and* THE GIRL *comes rushing in, holding a beautifully bound leather book. She looks quickly around the synagogue, now empty except for* THE SEXTON *and* THE CABALIST, *and then hurries to* THE RABBI'S *office, which is of course also empty. A kind of panic sweeps over her, and she rushes out into the synagogue again, to* THE SEXTON)

THE GIRL   Mr. Bleyer, the young man that was here, do you know . . . (*She whirls as the front door opens behind her and* ARTHUR *comes in. We have the feeling he also has been, if not running, at least walking very quickly. He and* THE GIRL *stare at each other for a moment. Then she says to him—*)   I went home to get this book for you. I wanted you to have this book I told you about.

ARTHUR (*Quietly*)   I just simply couldn't go till I knew you were all right.

(*For a moment they stand poised, staring at each other. Then she sweeps across the stage and flings herself into his arms*)

THE GIRL (*Crying out*)   Oh, I love you. I love you. I love you . . .

(*They stand, locked in embrace.* THE CABALIST'S *voice rises again in a deeply primitive chant, exquisite in its atavistic ardor*)

THE CABALIST

"For Thy salvation I hope, O Lord! I hope, O Lord, for Thy salvation. O Lord, for Thy salvation I hope!

For Thy salvation I hope, O Lord! I hope, O Lord, for
Thy salvation! O Lord, for Thy salvation I hope!"

THE CURTAIN FALLS

Scene 2

*It is now several hours later. A silent, dozing quiet has
settled over the synagogue. Indeed,* THE CABALIST *has dozed
off over a thick tome at the upstage desk on the far side of
the altar, his shawl-enshrouded head lying on his book.* THE
GIRL, *too, is napping, curled up in the worn leather armchair in* THE RABBI'S *office.* THE SEXTON *is sitting like a
cobbler on a chair stage left.* ALPER *and* ZITORSKY *sit drow-
sily on two wooden chairs, center stage. Only* ARTHUR *moves
restlessly around the synagogue. He looks into* THE RABBI'S
office, checking on THE GIRL, *studies her sleeping sweetness,
somehow deeply troubled. All is still, all is quiet.*

In the synagogue, THE CABALIST *awakens suddenly and
sits bolt upright, as if he has just had the most bizarre
dream. He stares wide-eyed at the wall in front of him. He
rises, and moves slowly downstage, his face a study in quiet
awe. Apparently, he has had a profoundly moving dream,
and he puts his hand to his brow as if to keep his thoughts
from tumbling out. An expression of exaltation spreads
across his wan, lined, bearded old face. His eyes are wide
with terror.*

THE CABALIST (*Whispering in awe*) "Blessed be the Lord.
Blessed be the Lord. Blessed be the Lord." (*He stands
now almost at the footlights, staring out over the audience, his face illuminated with ecstasy. He cries out*)
Praise ye the Lord! Hallelujah! Praise ye the Lord! Hallelujah! It is good to sing praises unto our God; for it is

pleasant and praise is seemly. Praise ye the Lord! Hallelujah! (ALPER *has watched* THE CABALIST *with drowsy interest.* THE CABALIST *turns and stares at him*) My dear friends, my dear, dear friends . . .

(*Tears fill his old eyes, and his mouth works without saying anything for a moment*)

ALPER Are you all right, Hirschman?

THE CABALIST (*Awed by an inner wonder*) I was studying the codification of the Law, especially those paragraphs beginning with the letters of my father's name—because today is my father's day of memorial. I have brought some honey cake here, in my father's memory. I have it somewhere in a paper bag. Where did I put it? I brought it here last night. It is somewhere around—and as I studied, I dozed off and my head fell upon the Book of Mishna. Oh, my dear friends, I have prayed to the Lord to send me a dream, and He has sent me a dream. I dreamt that I was bathing in a pool of the clearest mountain water. And a man of great posture appeared on the bank, and he said to me: "Rabbi, give me your blessing, for I go to make a journey." And I looked closely on the man, and it was the face of my father. And I said unto him: "My father, why do you call me Rabbi? For did I not lustfully throw away the white fringed shawl of the rabbinate and did I not mock the Lord to thy face? And have I not spent my life in prayer and penitence so that I might cleanse my soul?" And my father smiled upon me, and his bearded face glowed with gentleness, and he said unto me: "Rise from your bath, my son, and put upon you these robes of white linen which I have arrayed for you. For thy soul is cleansed and thou hast found a seat among the righteous. And the countenance of the Lord doth smile upon thee this day. So rise and rejoice and dance in the Holy Place. For thine is eternal peace and thou art among the righteous." Thus was the dream that I dreamt as my head lay on the Book of Mishna. (*He lifts his head and stares upward*) The Lord shall reign for ever. Thy God, O Zion, unto all generations. Praise ye the Lord. Hallelujah! (*He stares distractedly around him*) Where is the wine, Sexton? The wine! There was a fine new bottle on Friday! I have been given a seat among the righteous! For this day have I lived and fasted! I have been absolved! Hallelujah! Hallelujah!— Ah, the cakes! Here! Good!— (*He is beginning to laugh*) I shall dance before the Holy Ark! Sexton! Sexton! Distribute the macaroons that all may share this exalted day! The Lord hath sent me a sign, and the face of my father smiled upon me!

(*As abruptly as he had begun to laugh he begins to sob in the effusion of his joy. He sinks onto a chair and cries unashamedly*)

ALPER My dear Hirschman, how delighted we are for you.

THE SEXTON (*Offering some honey cake to* ZITORSKY) You want some cake there, Zitorsky?

ZITORSKY I'll have a little wine too as long as we're having a party.

(THE SEXTON *scurries off to the lectern, the bottom of which is a cabinet containing various sacramental things and wine*)

ARTHUR (*Who has been watching all this, rather taken by it*) What happened?

ALPER Mr. Hirschman has received a sign from God. His father has forgiven him, and his soul has been cleansed.

ARTHUR That's wonderful.

ZITORSKY (*To* THE SEXTON, *now pouring wine from a decanter*) I'll tell you, Bleyer, if you have a little whiskey, I prefer that. Wine makes me dizzy.

THE SEXTON Where would I get whiskey? This is a synagogue, not a saloon.

ZITORSKY (*Taking his glass of wine*) Happiness, Hirschman.

ALPER Some wine for our young friend here. (*To* AR-
THUR) Will you join Mr. Hirschman in his moment of
exaltation?

ARTHUR Yes, of course.

(THE SEXTON, *who is pouring the wine and sipping a
glass of his own as he pours, has begun to hum a gay
Chassidic tune. He hands* ARTHUR *his glass*)

ZITORSKY (*Handing his glass back for a refill*) Oh, will
Schlissel eat his heart out when he finds out he is missing
a party.

ALPER (*Making a toast*) Rabbi Israel, son of Isaac, I
think it is fitting we use your rabbinical title—we bow in
reverence to you.

THE CABALIST (*Deeply touched*) My dear, dear friends,
I cannot describe to you my happiness.

ZITORSKY There hasn't been a party here since that boy's
confirmation last month. Wasn't that a skimpy feast for
a confirmation? Another glass, please, Sexton. Oh, I'm
beginning to sweat. Some confirmation party that was!
The boy's father does a nice business in real estate and
all he brings down is a few pieces of sponge cake and
one bottle of whiskey. One bottle of whiskey for fifty
people! As much whiskey as I had couldn't even cure a
toothache. Oh, boy, am I getting dizzy. When I was
a boy, I could drink a whole jar of potato cider. You
remember that potato cider we used to have in Europe?
It could kill a horse. Oh, boy, what kind of wine is that?
My legs are like rubber already.

(ZITORSKY *suddenly stamps his foot and executes a few
brief Chassidic dance steps*)

ALPER This is not bad wine, you know. A pleasant bou-
quet.

ZITORSKY (*Wavering over to* ARTHUR) Have a piece of
cake, young man. What does it say in the Bible? "Go
eat your food with gladness and drink your wine with a
happy mind?" Give the boy another glass.

ARTHUR (*Smiling*)   Thank you. I'm still working on this
one.

(THE CABALIST *suddenly raises his head and bursts into
a gay Chassidic chant*)

THE CABALIST (*Bursting into song*)
"Light is sown,
sown for the righteous,
and joy for the upright,
the upright in heart.
Oh,
light is sown,
sown for the righteous . . ."

ZITORSKY (*Gaily joining in*)
"and joy for the upright,
the upright in heart.
Oh!"

(THE CABALIST *and* ZITORSKY *take each other's shoulders
and begin to dance in the formless Chassidic pattern.
They are in wonderful spirits*)
"Light is sown,
sown for the righteous . . ."

(THE SEXTON *and* ALPER *join in, clapping their hands and
eventually joining the dance so that the four old Jews
form a small ring, their arms around each other's shoulders, their old feet kicking exuberantly as they stamp
about in a sort of circular pattern*)

ALL
". . . and joy for the upright,
the upright in heart."
Oh!
Light is sown,
sown for the righteous,
and joy for the upright,
the upright in heart.

(*Round and round they stomp and shuffle, singing out
lustily, sweat forming in beads on their brows. The words*

are repeated over and over again until they degenerate, from the shortness of breath of the singers, into a "Bi-bu-bu-bi-bi-bi-bi-bi-bi-bibibi." ARTHUR *watches, delighted. Finally,* ALPER, *gasping for breath, breaks out of the ring and staggers to a chair)*

THE CABALIST   A good sixty years I haven't danced! Oh, enough! Enough! My heart feels as if it will explode!
(He staggers, laughing, from the small ring of dancers and sits down, gasping for air)

ALPER   Some more wine, Hirschman?

THE CABALIST   *(Gasping happily)*   Oh!
*(*ZITORSKY *looks up, noticing* THE GIRL, *who, awakened by the romping, has sidled out into the synagogue and has been watching the gaiety with delight.* ZITORSKY *eyes her wickedly for a moment; then advances on her, his arm outstretched, quite the old cock-of-the-walk)*

ZITORSKY   Bi-bi-bi-bi-bi-bi-bi . . .
(He seizes her in his arms and begins to twirl around, much to her delight. She dances with him, her skirts whirling and her feet twinkling, laughing at the sheer physical excitement of it all. ZITORSKY *supplies the music, a gay chant, the lyrics of which consist of: "Bi-bi-bi-bi-bi-bi-bi-bi . . .")*

THE CABALIST   The last time I danced was on the occasion of the last Day of the Holiday of Tabernacles in 1896. I was seventeen years old. *(A sudden frightened frown sweeps across his face. He mutters)*   Take heed for the girl, for the dybbuk will be upon her soon.

ALPER   *(Leaning to him)*   What did you say, Israel son of Isaac?
*(*THE CABALIST *turns to* THE GIRL *dancing with* ZITORSKY, *and stares at her)*

THE CABALIST   Let the girl rest, Zitorsky, for she struggles with the dybbuk. Behold. *(*THE GIRL *has indeed broken away from* ZITORSKY *and has begun an improvised dance of her own. The gaiety is gone from her face and is re-*

66

placed by a sullen lasciviousness. The dance she does is a patently provocative one. She dances slowly at first, and then with increasing abandon and wantonness. ZITORSKY *recoils in horror.* THE GIRL *begins to stamp her feet and to whirl more and more wildly. Her eyes grow bold and flashing and she begins to shout old Gypsy words, a mongrel Russian, Oriental in intonation.* THE CABALIST *now slowly moves to* THE GIRL, *who, when she becomes aware of his coming close, abruptly stops her dance and stands stock-still, her face a mask of extravagant pain.* THE CABALIST *regards her gently*) Lie down, my child, and rest.

(*At this quiet suggestion,* THE GIRL *begins to sway as if she is about to faint*)

THE GIRL (*Barely audible*) I feel so faint, so faint.

(*She sinks slowly to the floor, not quite in a swoon, but on the verge.* ARTHUR *races to her side*)

ARTHUR Do we have any water here?

ALPER Wine would be better. Sexton, give her some wine.

(THE SEXTON *hurries with someone's glass*)

ARTHUR (*Holding* THE GIRL's *head*) Is she a sickly girl?

ALPER (*Bending over them*) She was never sick a day in her life.

THE SEXTON Here's the wine.

ZITORSKY (*To* THE SEXTON) Did I tell you? Did I tell you?

THE GIRL I feel so faint. I feel so faint.

ARTHUR (*Bringing the glass of wine to her lips*) Sip some of this.

THE GIRL (*Murmuring*) Save me . . . save me . . .

THE CABALIST The dybbuk weakens her. I have seen this once before.

THE SEXTON (*To* ZITORSKY) When you told me about this dybbuk, I didn't believe you.

ZITORSKY So did I tell you right?

THE SEXTON Oh, boy.

ARTHUR   Help me get her onto the chair in there.

ALPER   Yes, of course.

THE SEXTON   Here, let me help a little.

(*Between them, they manage to get* THE GIRL *up and walk her slowly to* THE RABBI'S *office, where they gently help her lie down on the leather sofa*)

THE CABALIST (*To* ZITORSKY)   They haven't heard from Mr. Foreman yet?

ZITORSKY   No, we're waiting.

THE CABALIST (*Frowning*)   It is not that far to Williamsburg. Well, the girl will sleep now.

(*He walks slowly to the door of* THE RABBI'S *office, followed by a wary* ZITORSKY. ALPER *returns to the synagogue proper to join the other old men, and, for the briefest of moments,* ARTHUR *finds himself alone with* THE GIRL, *holding her head gently in his arms. Suddenly he kisses her brow and lightly strokes her hair. He rises quickly as the others return*)

ARTHUR   I think she's fallen asleep.

ALPER   Thank heavens for that.

ARTHUR   Look, I'm going to call her family. She may be quite ill. I think we'd all feel a lot better if she were in the hands of a doctor. If one of you will just give me her home telephone number . . . (*Just a little annoyed, for nobody answers him*)   Please, gentlemen, I really don't think it's wise to pursue this nonsense any longer.

THE CABALIST   It is not nonsense. I do not speak of dybbuks casually. As a young man, I saw hundreds of people come to my father claiming to be possessed, but, of all these, only two were true dybbuks. Of these two, one was a girl very much like this poor girl, and, even before the black candles and the ram's horn could be brought for the exorcism, she sank down onto the earth and died. I tell you this girl is possessed, and she will die, clutching at her throat and screaming for redemption unless the dybbuk is exorcised. (*He stares at the others and*

nods his head)   She will die. Wake the girl. I will take
her to the Korpotchniker myself.

ALPER   Zitorsky, wake the girl. I will get her coat. Sexton,
call a taxicab for Rabbi Israel. (ALPER, *who had been
reaching for* THE GIRL'S *coat, is stayed by* ARTHUR. *He
looks up at the young man*)   Young man, what are you
doing?

ARTHUR   Mr. Alper, the girl is sick. There may be something seriously wrong with her.

ALPER   Young man, Rabbi Israel says she is dying.

ARTHUR   Well, in that case certainly, let me have her home
telephone number.

ALPER (*Striding into* THE RABBI'S *office*)   You are presuming in matters that are no concern of yours.

ARTHUR (*Following*)   They are as much my concern as
they are yours. I have grown quite fond of this girl. I
want her returned to the proper authorities, right now.
If necessary, I shall call a policeman. Now, let's have no
more nonsense.

(ALPER *sinks down behind the desk, glowering. A moment of silence fills the room. Then* THE CABALIST, *who
has been standing in the rear of the office and watching
with quiet interest, says—*)

THE CABALIST   The young man doesn't believe in dybbuks?

ARTHUR   I'm afraid not. I think you are all behaving like
madmen.

(THE CABALIST *considers this answer for a moment*)

THE CABALIST   I will tell you an old Chassidic parable. A
deaf man passed by a house in which a wedding party
was going on. He looked in the window and saw all the
people there dancing and cavorting, leaping about and
laughing. However, since the man was deaf and could
not hear the music of the fiddlers, he said to himself:
"Ah, this must be a madhouse." Young man, because
you are deaf, must it follow that we are lunatics?

ARTHUR   You are quite right. I did not mean to mock your

beliefs, and I apologize for it. However, I am going to call the girl's father, and, if he wants to have the girl exorcised, that's his business. (*He sits down behind the desk, puts his hand on the receiver, and looks up at* ALPER) Well?

THE CABALIST Give him the number, Mr. Alper. (ALPER *fishes an old address book out of his vest pocket, thumbs through the pages, and hands the open book to* ARTHUR, *who begins to dial*) There is no one home in the girl's house. Her father, who wishes only to forget about the girl, has gone to his shop in the city, and, at this moment, is overeating at his lunch in a dairy restaurant. The stepmother has taken the younger children to her sister's. The girl's doctor has called the police and has gone about his rounds, and the police are diffidently riding up and down the streets of the community, looking for an old Jew and his granddaughter. (ARTHUR *says nothing, but simply waits for an answer to his ring.* THE CABALIST *sits down on the arm of the couch to contemplate. At last he says—*) I cannot understand why this young man does not believe in dybbuks.

ALPER It is symptomatic of the current generation, Rabbi Israel, to be utterly disillusioned. Historically speaking, an era of prosperity following an era of hard times usually produces a number of despairing and quietistic philosophies, for the now prosperous people have found out they are just as unhappy as when they were poor. Thus when an intelligent man of such a generation discovers that two television sets have no more meaning than one or that he gets along no better with his wife in a suburban house than he did in their small city flat, he arrives at the natural assumption that life is utterly meaningless.

THE CABALIST What an unhappy state of affairs.

(ARTHUR *returns the receiver to its cradle*)

ARTHUR (*Muttering*) Nobody home.

THE CABALIST (*To* ARTHUR) Is that true, young man, that you believe in absolutely nothing?

ARTHUR Not a damn thing.

THE CABALIST There is no truth, no beauty, no infinity, no known, no unknown.

ARTHUR Precisely.

THE CABALIST Young man, you are a fool.

ARTHUR Really. I have been reading your book—the Book of Zohar. I am sure it has lost much in the translation, but, sir, any disciple of this abracadabra is presuming when he calls anyone else a fool.

(ARTHUR *produces from his jacket the book* THE GIRL *gave him, and extends it to* THE CABALIST, *who accepts it, frowning*)

THE CABALIST You have been reading the Book of Zohar. Dear young man, one does not read the Book of Zohar, leaf through its pages, and make marginal notes. I have entombed myself in this slim volume for sixty years, raw with vulnerability to its hidden mysteries, and have sensed only a glimpse of its passion. Behind every letter of every word lies a locked image, and behind every image a sparkle of light of the ineffable brilliance of Infinity. But the concept of the Inexpressible Unknown is inconceivable to you. For you are a man possessed by the Tangible. If you cannot touch it with your fingers, it simply does not exist. Indeed, that will be the epithet of your generation—that you took everything for granted and believed in nothing. It is a very little piece of life that we know. How shall I say it? I suggest it is wiser to believe in dybbuks than in nothing at all.

ARTHUR Mr. Hirschman, a good psychiatrist—even a poor one—could strip your beliefs in ten minutes. You may think of yourself as a man with a God, but I see you as a man obsessed with guilt who has invented a God so he can be forgiven. You have invented it all—the guilt, God, forgiveness, the whole world, dybbuks, love, pas-

sion, fulfillment—the whole fantastic mess of pottage—
because it is unbearable for you to bear the pain of in-
significance. None of these things exist. You've made
them all up. The fact is, I have half a mind to let you go
through with this exorcism, for, after all the trumpetings
of rams' horns and the bellowing of incantations and
after the girl falls in a swoon on the floor—I assure you,
she will rise up again as demented as she ever was, and
I wonder what bizarre rationale and mystique you will
expound to explain all that. Now, if the disputation is at
an end, I am going to call the police.

(*He picks up the receiver again and dials the operator*)

ALPER Well, what can one say to such bitterness?

THE CABALIST (*Shrugs*) One can only say that the young
man has very little regard for psychiatrists.

(*The front door to the synagogue bursts open, and* FORE-
MAN *and* SCHLISSEL *come hurtling in, breathing heavily
and in a state of absolute confusion.* ALPER *darts out into
the synagogue proper and stares at them*)

SCHLISSEL Oh, thank God, the synagogue is still here!

ALPER Well?

SCHLISSEL (*He can hardly talk, he is so out of breath*)
Well, what?

ALPER What did the Korpotchniker say?

SCHLISSEL Who knows?! Who saw the Korpotchniker?!
We've been riding in subways for four hours! Back and
forth, in this train, in that train! I am convinced there is
no such place as Williamsburg and there is no such person as the Korpotchniker Rabbi! I tell you, twice we got
off at two different stations, just to see daylight, and, as
God is my witness, both times we were in New Jersey!

FOREMAN Oh, I tell you, I am sick from driving so much.

ALPER Idiot! You didn't take the Brighton train!

SCHLISSEL We took the Brighton train! (*He waves both
arms in a gesture of final frustration*) We took all the
trains! I haven't had a bite to eat all morning. Don't tell

72

me about Brighton trains! Don't tell me about anything! Leave me alone, and the devil take your whole capitalist economy! (ZITORSKY, THE SEXTON *and* THE CABALIST *have all come out to see what the noise is all about. Even* ARTHUR *is standing in the office doorway, listening to all this*) We asked this person, we asked that person. This person said that train. That person said this train. We went to a policeman. He puts us on a train. The conductor comes in, says: "Last stop." We get out. As God is my witness, New Jersey. We get back on that train. The conductor says: "Get off next station and take the other train." We get off the next station and take the other train. A man says: "Last stop." We get out. New Jersey!

(*In* THE RABBI'S *office,* THE GIRL *suddenly sits bolt upright, her eyes clenched tight in pain, screaming terribly, her voice shrill with anguish*)

FOREMAN (*Racing to her side*) Oh, my God! Evelyn! Evelyn! What is it?!

(THE GIRL *clutches at her throat and screams*)

THE GIRL Save me! Save me! Save me!

(ZITORSKY *and* THE SEXTON *begin to mutter rapid prayers under their breath*)

ALPER (*Putting his arm around* FOREMAN) David, she's very ill. We think she may be dying.

(ARTHUR *has raced to* THE GIRL. *He sits on the couch beside her and takes her in his arms*)

ARTHUR Call a doctor.

FOREMAN (*In panic, to* ALPER) He says I should call a doctor.

(ARTHUR *puts his hand to his brow and shakes his head as if to clear it of shock and confusion*)

ALPER (*Crossing to* THE CABALIST) Save her, Rabbi Israel. You have had your sign from God. You are among the righteous.

(ARTHUR *turns slowly and regards the silent betallithed form of the little* CABALIST)

ARTHUR (*To* THE CABALIST, *his voice cracking under emotions he was unaware he still had*) For God's sakes, perform your exorcism or whatever has to be done. I think she's dying.

(THE CABALIST *regards* ARTHUR *for a moment with the profoundest gentleness. Then he turns and, with an authoritative voice, instructs* THE SEXTON)

THE CABALIST Sexton, we shall need black candles, the ram's horn, prayer shawls of white wool, and there shall be ten Jews for a quorum to witness before God this awesome ceremony.

THE SEXTON Just plain black candles?

THE CABALIST Just plain black candles.

(THE SEXTON *is already hurrying into his coat.* ALPER *moves quietly up to* FOREMAN *standing in the office doorway, and touches his old friend's shoulder in a gesture of awe and compassion.* FOREMAN, *at the touch, begins to cry and buries his shaking old head on his friend's shoulder.* ALPER *embraces him*)

ZITORSKY (*In the synagogue, to* SCHLISSEL) I am absolutely shaking—shaking.

(ARTHUR, *having somewhat recovered his self-control, sinks down behind the desk, frowning, confused by all that is going on, and moved by a complex of feeling he cannot understand at all*)

THE CURTAIN FALLS

ACT THREE

Half an hour later.

At rise, THE GIRL *is sitting in* THE RABBI'S *office, perched on the couch, nervous, frightened, staring down at her restlessly twisting fingers.* FOREMAN *sits behind* THE RABBI'S *desk, wrapped in his own troubled thoughts. He wears over his suit a long white prayer shawl with thick black stripes, like that worn by* THE CABALIST *throughout the play.*

Indeed, all the men now wear these ankle-length white prayer shawls, except ARTHUR, *who, at rise, is also in* THE RABBI'S *office, deep in thought.*

THE CABALIST *stands downstage left, his prayer shawl hooded over his head; he is leafing through a volume, preparing the prayers for the exorcism.*

THE SEXTON *is standing by the wall phone, the receiver cradled to his ear, waiting for an answer to a call he has just put in. He is more or less surrounded by* ALPER, SCHLISSEL, *and* ZITORSKY.

ZITORSKY   How about Milsky the butcher?
ALPER   Milsky wouldn't come. Ever since they gave the seat by the East Wall to Kornblum, Milsky said he wouldn't set foot in this synagogue again. Every synagogue I have belonged to, there have always been two kosher butchers who get into a fight over who gets the favored seat by the East Wall during the High Holy

Days, and the one who doesn't abandons the congregation in a fury, and the one who does always seems to die before the next High Holy Days.

SCHLISSEL   Kornblum the butcher died? I didn't know Kornblum died.

ALPER   Sure. Kornblum died four years ago.

SCHLISSEL   Well, he had lousy meat, believe me, may his soul rest in peace.

(THE SEXTON *has hung up, recouped his dime, reinserted it, and is dialing again*)

ZITORSKY (*To* THE SEXTON)   No answer?

(THE SEXTON *shakes his head*)

THE SEXTON   I'm calling Harris.

SCHLISSEL   Harris? You tell an eighty-two-year-old man to come down and make a tenth for an exorcism, and he'll have a heart attack talking on the phone with you.

THE SEXTON (*Dialing*)   Well, what else am I to do? It is hard enough to assemble ten Jews under the best of circumstances, but in the middle of the afternoon on a Thursday it is an absolute nightmare. Aronowitz is in Miami. Klein the furrier is at his job in Manhattan. It is a workday today. Who shall I call? (*He waits for someone to answer*)   There are many things that I have to do. The tapestries on the Ark, as you see, are faded and need needlework, and the candelabras and silver goblet for the saying of the Sabbath benediction are tarnished and dull. But every second of my day seems to be taken up with an incessant search for ten Jews . . . (*On the phone*)   Hello, Harris. Harris, this is Bleyer the Sexton. We need you badly down here in the synagogue for a quorum . . . If I told you why, you wouldn't come . . . All right, I'll tell you, but, in God's name, don't tell another soul, not even your daughter-in-law . . .

SCHLISSEL   My daughter-in-law, may she grow like an onion with her head in the ground.

THE SEXTON (*On the phone*)   Hirschman is going to exorcise a dybbuk from Foreman's granddaughter . . . I said, Hirschman is . . . A dybbuk That's right, a dybbuk . . . Right here in Mineola . . . That's right. Why should Mineola be exempt from dybbuks?

ALPER (*Thinking of names*) There used to be a boy came down here every morning, about eight, nine years ago—a devout boy with forelocks and sidecurls—a pale boy, who was studying to be a rabbi at the seminary.

THE SEXTON (*On the phone*) Harris, this is not a joke.

SCHLISSEL Chwatkin.

ALPER That's right, Chwatkin. That was the boy's name. Chwatkin. Maybe we could call him. Does he still live in the community?

SCHLISSEL He's a big television actor. He's on television all the time. Pinky Sims. He's an actor.

ZITORSKY Pinky Sims? That's a name for a rabbinical student?

THE SEXTON Put on your sweater and come down.

ALPER (*To* THE SEXTON, *who has just hung up*) So Harris is coming?

THE SEXTON Yes, he's coming. So with Harris, that makes eight, and I am frankly at the end of my resources. I don't know who else to call.

ALPER This is terrible. Really. God manifests Himself in our little synagogue, and we can't even find ten Jews to say hello.

THE SEXTON I shall have to go out in the street and get two strangers. (*Putting on his coat*) Well, I don't look forward to this at all. I will have to stop people on the street, ask them if they are Jewish—which is bad enough —and then explain to them I wish them to attend the exorcism of a dybbuk—I mean, surely you can see the futility of it.

ALPER (*To* THE CABALIST, *who is crossing now en route to the office*) We can only get eight. A disgrace. Really. We shall not have the exorcism for lack of two Jews.

THE SEXTON (*On his way out*)   All right, I'm going. (*He exits*)

ZITORSKY (*To* SCHLISSEL)   In those days when I was deceiving my wife, I used to tell her I was entertaining out-of-town buyers. I once told her I was entertaining out-of-town buyers every night for almost three weeks. It was a foolhardy thing to do because even my wife could tell business was not that good. So one night she came down to my loft on Thirty-Sixth Street and walked in and caught me with—well, I'm sure I've told you this story before.

SCHLISSEL   Many times.

(THE CABALIST *enters the office. Upon his entrance,* THE GIRL *stands abruptly, obviously deeply disturbed and barely in control of herself. She turns from* THE CABALIST *and shades her eyes with her hand to hide her terror.* FOREMAN *looks up briefly. He seems to be in a state of shock.* THE CABALIST *sits down on the couch, letting his heavy prayer shawl fall back on his shoulders, and studies his hands folded patiently between his knees. After a moment, he speaks*)

THE CABALIST (*Quietly*)   Dybbuk, I am Israel son of Isaac. My father was Isaac son of Asher, and I wear his fringed shawl on my shoulders as I talk to you. (*Upon these words,* THE GIRL *suddenly contorts her form, as if seized by a violent cramp. She clutches her stomach and bends low, and soft sobs begin to come out of her*)   Reveal yourself to me.

THE GIRL (*In the voice of the dybbuk*)   I am Hannah Luchinsky.

(*In the synagogue,* ALPER, SCHLISSEL, *and* ZITORSKY *begin to edge—quite frightened—to the open office door.* ARTHUR *watches from his seat behind* THE RABBI'S *desk*)

THE CABALIST   Why do you possess this girl's body?

THE GIRL (*Twisting and contorting; in the voice of the*

dybbuk)   My soul was lost at sea, and there is no one to say the prayers for the dead over me.

THE CABALIST   I will strike a bargain with you. Leave this girl's body through her smallest finger, doing her no damage, not even a scratch, and I shall sit on wood for you for the First Seven Days of Mourning and shall plead for your soul for the First Thirty Days and shall say the prayers for the dead over you three times a day for the Eleven Months and light the Memorial Lamp each year upon the occasion of your death. I ask you to leave this girl's body.

(THE GIRL *laughs quietly*)

THE GIRL (*In the voice of the dybbuk*)   You give me short weight, for you will yourself be dead before the prayers for the new moon.

(*In the office doorway, the three old men shudder.* FORE-MAN *looks up slowly.* THE CABALIST *closes his eyes*)

THE CABALIST (*Quietly*)   How do you know this?

THE GIRL (*In the voice of the dybbuk*)   Your soul will fly straight to the Heavenly Gates and you will be embraced by the Archangel Mihoel.

THE CABALIST   Then I enjoin the Angel of Death to speed his way. Dybbuk, I order you to leave the body of this girl.

(THE GIRL'S *face suddenly flashes with malevolence*)

THE GIRL (*In the voice of the dybbuk, shouting*)   No! I seek vengeance for these forty years of limbo! I was betrayed in my youth and driven to the Evil Impulse against my will! I have suffered beyond belief, and my spirit has lived in dunghills and in piles of ashes, and I demand the soul of David son of Abram be cast through Gilgul for the space of forty years times ten to gasp for air in the sea in which I drowned . . .

FOREMAN (*Standing in terror*)   No! No!

THE GIRL (*In the voice of the dybbuk*)   . . . so that my

79

soul may have peace! A soul for a soul! That is my bargain.

FOREMAN (*Shouting*) Let it be then! Leave my granddaughter in peace and I will give my soul in exchange.

THE CABALIST (*With ringing authority*) The disposition of David son of Abram's soul will not be decided here. Its fall and ascent has been ordained by the second universe of angels. The bargain cannot be struck! Dybbuk, hear me. I order you to leave the body of this girl through her smallest finger, causing her no pain nor damage, and I give you my word, prayers will be said over you in full measure. But if you abjure these words, then must I proceed against you with malediction and anathema.

THE GIRL (*Laughs*) Raise not thy mighty arm against me, for it has no fear for me. A soul for a soul. That is my bargain.

(THE GIRL *suddenly begins to sob*)

THE CABALIST (*To* ALPER) We shall have to prepare for the exorcism.

ALPER I thought that would be the case.

THE GIRL (*Sitting down on the couch, frightened, in her own voice*) I am so afraid.

FOREMAN There is nothing to fear. It will all be over in a minute, like having a tooth pulled, and you will walk out of here a cheerful child.

SCHLISSEL (*Ambling back into the synagogue proper with* ZITORSKY *and* ALPER) I tell you, I'd feel a lot better if the Korpotchniker was doing this. If you are going to have a tooth pulled, at least let it be by a qualified dentist.

ZITORSKY I thought Hirschman handled himself very well with that dybbuk.

SCHLISSEL (*To* ALPER *and* ZITORSKY) If I tell you all something, promise you will never throw it back in my face.

ZITORSKY   What?

SCHLISSEL   I am beginning to believe she is really possessed by a dybbuk.

ZITORSKY   I'm beginning to get used to the whole thing.

(THE CABALIST *has stood and moved upstage to the rear wall of the synagogue, where he stands in meditation.* FOREMAN *is sitting again, somewhat numb, beside his granddaughter. After a moment,* THE GIRL *speaks*)

THE GIRL   I am very frightened, Arthur.

ARTHUR   (*Rises*)   Well, I spoke to my analyst, as you know, and he said he didn't think this exorcism was a bad idea at all. The point is, if you really do believe you are possessed by a dybbuk . . .

THE GIRL   Oh, I do.

ARTHUR   Well, then, he feels this exorcism might be a good form of shock treatment that will make you more responsive to psychiatric therapy and open the door to an eventual cure. Mr. Hirschman assures me it is a painless ceremony. So you really have nothing to be frightened of.

THE GIRL   Will you be here?

ARTHUR   Of course. Did you think I wouldn't?

(FOREMAN *moves slowly out into the synagogue, as if to ask something of* THE CABALIST)

THE GIRL   I always sense flight in you.

ARTHUR   Really.

THE GIRL   You are always taking to your heels, Arthur. Especially in moments like now when you want to be tender. I know that you love me or I couldn't be so happy with you, but the whole idea of love seems to terrify you, and you keep racing off to distant detachments. I feel that if I reached out for your cheek now, you would turn your head or, in some silent way, clang the iron gates shut on me. You have some strange dybbuk all of your own, some sad little turnkey, who drifts about inside of you, locking up all the little doors, and saying,

"You are dead. You are dead." You do love me, Arthur. I know that.

ARTHUR (*Gently*)   I wish you well, Evelyn. We can at least say that.

THE GIRL   I love you. I want so very much to be your wife. (*She stares at him, her face glowing with love. She says quietly*)   I will make you a good home, Arthur. You will be very happy with me. (*He regards her for a moment, caught by her wonder. He reaches forward and lightly touches her cheek. She cannot take her eyes from him*)   I adore you, Arthur.

ARTHUR (*With deep gentleness*)   You are quite mad.
(*They look at each other.* ARTHUR *stands*)

THE GIRL   You think our getting married is impractical.

ARTHUR   Yes, I would say it was at the least impractical.

THE GIRL   Because I am insane and you are suicidal.

ARTHUR   I do think those are two reasons to give one pause.

THE GIRL   Well, at least we begin with futility. Most marriages take years to arrive there.

ARTHUR   Don't be saucy, Evelyn.

THE GIRL (*Earnestly*)   Oh, Arthur, I wouldn't suggest marriage if I thought it was utterly unfeasible. I think we can make a go of it. I really do. I know you have no faith in my exorcism . . .

ARTHUR   As I say, it may be an effective shock therapy.

THE GIRL   But we could get married this minute, and I still think we could make a go of it. I'm not a dangerous schizophrenic; I just hallucinate. I could keep your house for you. I did for my father very competently before he remarried. I'm a good cook, and you do find me attractive, don't you? I love you, Arthur. You are really very good for me. I retain reality remarkably well with you. I know I could be a good wife. Many schizophrenics function quite well if one has faith in them.

82

ARTHUR (*Touched by her earnestness*) My dear Eve-lyn . . .

THE GIRL I don't ask you to have faith in dybbuks or gods or exorcisms—just in me.

(*He gently touches her cheek*)

ARTHUR How in heaven's name did we reach this point of talking marriage?

THE GIRL It is a common point of discussion between peo-ple in love.

(*He kneels before her, takes her hand between his*)

ARTHUR (*Tenderly*) I do not love you. Nor do you love me. We met five hours ago and exchanged the elemen-tary courtesy of conversation—the rest is your own in-genuousness.

THE GIRL I do not remember ever being as happy as I am this moment. I feel enchanted. (*They are terribly close now. He leans to her, his arm moving to embrace her. And then he stops, and the moment is broken. He turns away, scowls, stands*) You are in full flight again, aren't you?

ARTHUR I reserve a certain low level of morality which includes not taking advantage of incompetent minors.

THE GIRL Why can't you believe that I love you?

ARTHUR (*Angrily*) I simply do not believe anybody loves anyone. Let's have an end to this. (*He is abruptly aware that their entire love scene has been observed by the old men, who are clustered together in the open doorway of* THE RABBI'S *office, beaming at them. With a furious sigh,* ARTHUR *strides to the door and shuts it in the old men's faces. He turns back to* THE GIRL, *scowling*) Really, this is all much too fanciful. Really, it is. In an hour, you will be back to your institution, where I may or may not visit you.

(THE GIRL *sits down slowly*)

THE GIRL If I were not already insane, the thought that I might not see you again would make me so.

ARTHUR I don't know what you want of me.

THE GIRL (*One step from tears*) I want you to find the meaning of your life in me.

ARTHUR But that's insane. How can you ask such an impossible thing?

THE GIRL Because you love me.

ARTHUR (*Cries out*) I don't know what you mean by love! All it means to me is I shall buy you a dinner, take you to the theatre, and then straight to our tryst, where I shall reach under your blouse for the sake of tradition while you breathe hotly in my ear in a pretense of passion. We will mutter automatic endearments, nibbling at the sweat on each other's earlobes, all the while gracelessly fumbling with buttons and zippers, cursing under our breath the knots in our shoelaces, and telling ourselves that this whole comical business of stripping off our trousers is an act of nature like the pollination of weeds. Even in that one brief moment when our senses finally obliterate our individual alonenesses, we will hear ringing in our ears the reluctant creaking of mattress springs.

(THE GIRL *stares at him, awed by this bitter expostulation*)

THE GIRL You are possessed.

ARTHUR At your age, I suppose, one still finds theatrical charm in this ultimate of fantasies, but when you have been backstage as often as I have, you will discover love to be an altogether shabby business of cold creams and costumes.

THE GIRL (*Staring at him*) You are possessed by a dybbuk that does not allow you to love.

ARTHUR (*Crying out again in sudden anguish*) Oh, leave me alone! Let's get on with this wretched exorcism!

(*He strides to the door, suddenly turns, confused, disturbed, and would say something, but he doesn't know what. He opens the door to find the old men patiently waiting for him with beaming smiles. This disconcerts him and he turns to* THE GIRL *again and is again at a loss for words. She stares at the floor*)

THE GIRL   We could be very happy if you would have faith in me.

(*He turns and shuffles out of* THE RABBI'S *office*)

ARTHUR (*To the old men*)   It was tasteless of you to gawk at us.

(*He continues into the synagogue, trailed by the old men. He sits, and is immediately surrounded by the old men*)

FOREMAN   Are you interested in this girl, young man, because my son is not a rich man, by any means, but he will give you a fine wedding, catered by good people, with a cantor . . .

ZITORSKY   And a choir.

FOREMAN   . . . Possibly, and a dowry perhaps in the amount of five hundred dollars which, believe me, is more than he can afford. However, I am told you are a professional man, a lawyer, and the father of the bride must lay out good money for such a catch.

ALPER *and* ZITROSKY   Sure . . . Absolutely.

FOREMAN   Of course, the girl is an incompetent and you will have to apply to the courts to be appointed the committee of her person . . .

ALPER   . . . A formality, I assure you, once you have married her.

FOREMAN   As for the girl, I can tell you first hand, she is a fine Jewish girl . . .

ZITORSKY   Modest . . .

ALPER   Devout . . .

FOREMAN   . . . And she bakes first-rate pastries.

ARTHUR (*Staring at the gay old men with disbelief*)   You

85

are all mad, madder than the girl, and if I don't get out of here soon, I shall be as mad as the rest.

ZITORSKY   A beauty, young man. Listen, it is said—better a full-bosomed wife than to marry a Rothschild.

SCHLISSEL   Leave the man alone. We have all been miserably married for half a century ourselves. How can you in good faith recommend the institution?

ALPER   The girl is so obviously taken with him. It would be a good match.

FOREMAN   (*Anxiously*)   Perhaps, he is married already.

ALPER   (*To* ARTHUR)   My dear fellow, how wonderful to be in love.

ARTHUR   I love nothing!

THE CABALIST   Yes. The girl is quite right. He is possessed. He loves nothing. Love is an act of faith, and yours is a faithless generation. That is your dybbuk.

(*The front door of the synagogue opens, and* THE SEXTON *slips quickly in, quietly closing the door*)

ARTHUR   (*To* THE CABALIST)   Don't you think it's time to get on with this exorcism?

THE CABALIST   Yes.

(*He moves to the door of* THE RABBI'S *office, where he regards the supine form of* THE GIRL *on the couch*)

ALPER   (*To* THE SEXTON)   Did you get anybody?

(THE SEXTON *moves in his nervous way down into the synagogue. He has obviously been on the go since he left; sweat beads his brow, and he is breathing heavily*)

THE SEXTON   (*Unbuttoning his coat and wiping his brow*)   Gentlemen, we are in the soup.

SCHLISSEL   You couldn't find anybody?

THE SEXTON   Actually, we have nine now, but the issue of a quorum has become an academic one. Oh, let me catch my breath. The Rabbi will be here in a few minutes.

ALPER   The Rabbi?

THE SEXTON   I saw him on Woodhaven Boulevard, and he said he would join us. Harris is on his way already. I saw him coming down the hill from his house. But the whole matter is academic.

ALPER   You told the Rabbi we need him to exorcise the girl's dybbuk?

THE SEXTON   Well, what else was I to say? He asked me what I needed a quorum for at one o'clock in the afternoon, and I told him, and he thought for a moment, and he said: "All right, I'll be there in a few minutes." He is quite a nice fellow, something of a press agent perhaps, but with good intentions. Oh, I am perspiring like an animal. I shall surely have the ague tomorrow. I have been running all over looking for Jews. I even went to Friedman the tailor. He wasn't even in town. So let me tell you. I was running back here. I turned the corner on Thirty-Third Road there, and I see parked right in front of the synagogue a police patrol car.

(*The others start*)

ALPER (*Looking up*)   Oh?

THE SEXTON   That's what I mean when I say we are in the soup.

SCHLISSEL   Did they say something to you?

THE SEXTON   Sure they said something. I tell you, my heart gave such a turn when I saw that police car there. They were sitting there, those two policemen, big strapping cossacks with dark faces like avenging angels, smoking cigarettes, and with their revolvers bulging through their blue overcoats. As I walked across the street to the synagogue, my knees were knocking.

ALPER   When was this? It was just now?

THE SEXTON   Just this second. Just before I came in the door . . . Hello, Harris, how are you?

(*This last to the octogenarian, who, bundled in his heavy overcoat, muffler, and with his hat pulled down on his head, has just entered the synagogue*)

ZITORSKY (*To* THE SEXTON)   So what happened?

HARRIS (*In his high shrill voice, as he unbuttons his over-*

coat) Gentlemen! Have you heard about this dybbuk?

SCHLISSEL Harris, we were all here at the time he called you.

THE SEXTON Harris, did you see the police car outside?

SCHLISSEL So what did the policeman say?

THE SEXTON (*Unbuttoning his collar and wiping his neck with a handkerchief*) This big strapping fellow with his uniform full of buttons looks up, he says: "You know a man named David Foreman? We're looking for him and his granddaughter, a girl, eighteen years old." Well?! Eh! Well, are we in the soup or not?

(SCHLISSEL *goes to the front door, opens it a conspiratorial crack, and looks out*)

ARTHUR I don't think the police will bother you if you get your exorcism started right away. They won't interrupt a religious ceremony, especially if they don't know what it is.

THE CABALIST (*Who has made up his own mind*) Sexton, fetch the black candles, one for each man.

(THE SEXTON *scurries to* THE RABBI'S *office, where the black candles are lying on the desk, wrapped in brown grocery paper*)

ARTHUR (*Moving to the front door*) I'll stand by the door and talk to the police if they come in.

SCHLISSEL (*Closing the front door*) They're out there all right.

THE CABALIST (*He looks about the little synagogue, immensely dignified now, almost beatified in his authority. The others wait on his words*) I shall want to perform the ablutions of the Cohanim. Is there a Levite among you?

SCHLISSEL I am a Levite.

THE CABALIST You shall pour the water on my hands.

(THE SEXTON *scoots across the synagogue, carrying black candles to everyone*)

HARRIS (*Looking distractedly about*)   What are we doing now? Where is the dybbuk?

ALPER   Harris, put on a prayer shawl.

HARRIS (*Moving nervously to the office door*)   Is this actually a serious business then? Where is the dybbuk? Tell me because Bleyer the Sexton told me nothing . . .
(*His words drift off into a mumble. He enters the office, sees* THE GIRL *sitting rigidly on the chair. He starts at the sight of her, snatches a prayer shawl from the carton, and, quite in terror, darts back into the synagogue*)

THE CABALIST   There is nothing in the Book of Codes which gives the procedure for exorcism, so I have selected those passages to read that I thought most apt. For the purpose of cleansing our souls, we shall recite the Al-chait, and we shall recite that prayer of atonement which begins: "Sons of man such as sit in darkness." As you pray these prayers, let the image of God in any of His seventy-two faces rise before you.

ALPER (*Crossing into* THE RABBI'S *office*)   I'll get the books.

THE SEXTON (*Giving* SCHLISSEL *a metal bowl and a pitcher*)   Fill it with water.

SCHLISSEL   I'm an atheist. Why am I mixed up in all this?

ALPER   We do not have a quorum. Will this be valid?

THE CABALIST   We will let God decide.

THE SEXTON   When shall I blow the ram's horn?

THE CABALIST   I shall instruct you when.

HARRIS (*Putting on his shawl*)   What shall I do? Where shall I stand?

ZITORSKY (*To* HARRIS)   Stand here, and do not be afraid.
(FOREMAN *comes out of* THE RABBI'S *office carrying a long white woolen prayer shawl, which he gives to* ARTHUR)

FOREMAN (*To* ARTHUR)   I will show you how to put it on.
(*He helps* ARTHUR *enshroud himself in the prayer shawl.*

SCHLISSEL *comes out of the washroom carefully carrying his brass bowl and the pitcher filled with water. He goes to* THE CABALIST, *who holds his white hands over the basin.* SCHLISSEL *carefully pours the water over them.* THE CABALIST *speaks with great distinctness*)

THE CABALIST   "Blessed art Thou, O Lord our God, King of the Universe, who hath sanctified us by his commandments, and has commanded us to cleanse our hands."

ALL   Amen.

(*The others watch until the last of the water has been poured over his hands. A sudden silence settles over the synagogue. They are all standing about now, eight men, cloaked in white, holding their prayer books.* THE CABALIST *dries his hands on a towel handed to him by* SCHLISSEL. *He puts the towel down, rolls his sleeves down, takes his long shawl and, with a sweep of his arms, raises it over his head, lifts his face, and cries out—*)

THE CABALIST   "Thou knowest the secrets of eternity and the most hidden mysteries of all living. Thou searchest the innermost recesses, and tryest the reins and the heart. Nought is concealed from thee, or hidden from thine eyes. May it then be thy will, O Lord our God and God of our fathers, to forgive us for all our sins, to pardon us for all our iniquities, and to grant us remission for all our transgressions."

(*As one, the other old men sweep their shawls over their heads and begin the ancient recital of their sins. They all face the Ark, standing in their places, bending and twisting at the knees and beating upon their breasts with the clenched fists of their right hands. They all pray individually, lifting their voices in a wailing of the spirit.* ARTHUR *remains silent*)

ALL

"For the sin which we have committed before thee under compulsion, or of our own will;

And for the sin which we have committed before thee in hardening of the heart!

For the sin which we have committed before thee unknowingly":

ZITORSKY

"And for the sin which we have committed before thee with utterance of the lips."

FOREMAN

"For the sin which we have committed before thee by unchastity";

SCHLISSEL

"For the sin which we have committed before thee by scoffing";

HARRIS

"For the sin which we have committed before thee by slander;

And for the sin which we have committed before thee by the stretched-forth neck of pride":

(*It is a deadly serious business, this gaunt confessional. The spectacle of the eight men, cloaked in white, crying out into the air the long series of their sins and their pleas for remission, has a suggestion of the fearsome barbarism of the early Hebrews. They stand, eyes closed, and in the fervor of communication with God, their faces pained with penitence. The last of the old men,* HARRIS, *finally cries out the last lines of supplication, his thin voice all alone in the hush of the synagogue*)

"And also for the sins for which we are liable to any of the four death penalties inflicted by the court—stoning, burning, beheading, and strangling; for thou art the forgiver of Israel and the pardoner of the tribes of Jeshurun in every generation and beside thee we have no king, who pardoneth and forgiveth."

(*Again, the silence falls over the stage*)

THE CABALIST "Children of men, such as sit in darkness and in the shadow of death, being bound in affliction and iron, He brought them out of darkness, and the shadow of death."

THE OTHERS "Children of men, such as sit in darkness and in the shadow of death, being bound in affliction and iron, He brought them out of darkness, and the shadow of death."

THE CABALIST "Fools because of their transgressions, and because of their iniquities are afflicted."

THE OTHERS "Fools because of their transgressions and because of their iniquities are afflicted."

THE CABALIST "They cry unto The Lord in their trouble, and He saveth them out of their distress."

(*The repetition of the lines has its cumulative effect on* ARTHUR. *His lips begin to move involuntarily, and soon, he has joined the others, quietly muttering the words*)

ARTHUR *and* THE OTHERS "They cry unto The Lord in their trouble, and He saveth them out of their distress."

THE CABALIST "Then He is gracious unto him and saith":

ARTHUR *and* THE OTHERS "Then He is gracious unto him and saith":

THE CABALIST "Deliver him from going down to the pit; I have found a ransom."

ARTHUR *and* THE OTHERS "Deliver him from going down to the pit; I have found a ransom."

THE CABALIST Amen.

ARTHUR *and* THE OTHERS Amen.

THE CABALIST Bring the girl in, Mr. Foreman.

(FOREMAN *nods and goes into* THE RABBI'S *office*)

ALPER (*To* SCHLISSEL) I don't like it. Even if the Rabbi comes, there will only be nine of us. I am a traditionalist. Without a quorum of ten, it won't work.

SCHLISSEL (*Muttering*) So what do you want me to do?

(*In* THE RABBI'S *office,* FOREMAN *touches* THE GIRL'S *shoulder, and she starts from her comalike state and looks at him*)

FOREMAN Come. It is time.

(*She nods nervously and sits up. There is a vacuous look about her, the vague, distracted look of the insane*)

THE GIRL (*Quite numbly*)   Where are you taking me? My mother is in Rome. They put the torch to her seven sons, and they hold her hostage. (*She rises in obedience to her grandfather's arm as he gently escorts her out of the office into the synagogue proper. All the while she maintains a steady drone of rattling gibberish*)   Where were you yesterday? I asked everybody about you. You should have been here. We had a lot of fun. We had a party, and there were thousands of people, Calebites and Bedouins, dancing like gypsies.

(*She suddenly lapses into a sullen silence, staring at the ground, her shoulders jerking involuntarily. The others regard her uneasily*)

THE SEXTON   Shall I take the ram's horn out?

THE CABALIST   Yes.

(THE SEXTON *produces the horn-shaped trumpet from the base of the pulpit. The front door of the synagogue now opens, and a tall, strapping young* POLICEMAN, *heavy with the authority of his thick blue overcoat, steps one step into the synagogue. He stands in the open doorway, one hand on the latch of the door, his attitude quite brusque—as if he could not possibly get his work done if he had to be polite*)

THE POLICEMAN   Is Rabbi Marks here?

(ALPER *throws up his arms in despair. The others alternately stare woodenly at* THE POLICEMAN *or down at the floor.* ARTHUR, *still deeply disturbed, rubs his brow.* THE CABALIST *begins to pray silently, only his lips moving in rapid supplication*)

THE SEXTON   No, he's not.

THE POLICEMAN   I'm looking for a girl named Evelyn Foreman. Is that the girl?

(*He indicates* THE GIRL)

ALPER (*Moving away, muttering*)   Is there any need, Officer, to be so brusque or to stand in an open doorway so that we all chill to our bones?

THE POLICEMAN (*Closing the door behind him*) Sorry.

SCHLISSEL (*To* ZITORSKY) A real cossack, eh? What a brute. He will take us all to the station house and beat us with night sticks.

THE POLICEMAN (*A little more courteously*) A girl named Evelyn Foreman. Her father has put out a call for her. She's missing from her home. He said she might be here with her grandfather. Is there a Mr. David Foreman here?

(*Nobody says anything*)

ALPER You are interrupting a service, Officer.

THE POLICEMAN I'm sorry. Just tell me, is that the girl? I'll call in and tell them we found her.

(SCHLISSEL *suddenly advances on* THE POLICEMAN)

SCHLISSEL First of all, where do you come to walk in here like you were raiding a poolroom? This is a synagogue, you animal. Have a little respect.

THE POLICEMAN All right, all right, I'm sorry. I happen to be Jewish myself.

(ALPER *looks up quickly*)

ALPER You're Jewish? (ALPER *turns slowly to* THE SEXTON) Sexton, our tenth man.

THE SEXTON Alper, are you crazy?

ALPER A fine, strapping Jewish boy. (*To* THE POLICEMAN) Listen, we need a tenth. You'll help us out, won't you?

SCHLISSEL (*Strolling nervously past* ALPER) Alper, what are you doing, for God's sakes?

ALPER We have to have ten men.

SCHLISSEL What kind of prank is this? You are an impossible rogue, do you know that?

ALPER (*Taking* SCHLISSEL *aside*) What are you getting so excited about? He doesn't have to know what it is. We'll tell him it's a wedding. I think it's funny.

SCHLISSEL   Well, we will see how funny it is when they take us to the basement of the police station and beat us with their night sticks.

ALPER   Night sticks. Really, Schlissel, you are a romantic. (*Advancing on* THE POLICEMAN)   I tell you, Officer, it would really help us out if you would stay ten or fifteen minutes. This girl—if you really want to know—is about to be married, and what is going on here is the Ritual of Shriving.

ZITORSKY   Shriving?

ALPER   A sort of ceremony of purification. It is a ritual not too commonly practiced any more, and I suggest you will find it quite interesting.

HARRIS (*To* SCHLISSEL)   What is he talking about?

SCHLISSEL   Who knows?

(THE POLICEMAN *opens the door and calls to his colleague outside*)

THE POLICEMAN   I'll be out in about ten minutes, Tommy, all right? (*He opens the door wider for* THE RABBI, *who now comes hurrying into the synagogue, still carrying his briefcase*)   Hello, Rabbi, how are you?

(THE RABBI *frowns, a little confused at* THE POLICEMAN'S *presence*)

THE RABBI   Hello, Officer, what are you doing here?

(*He moves quickly to his office, taking stock of everything as he goes: the seven old men and* ARTHUR *in their white shawls, and* THE GIRL *standing woodenly in the center of the synagogue.* ALPER *and* ZITORSKY *greet him with hellos, at which he nods back*)

THE POLICEMAN   They've asked me to make a tenth for the shriving.

THE RABBI (*Frowning as he darts into his office*)   Shriving? (*He opens his desk to get out his own large white shawl, unbuttoning his coat as he does. He notes* ALPER, *who has followed him to the doorway*)   What is the policeman doing here?

ALPER We needed a tenth.

(*In the synagogue,* THE POLICEMAN *speaks amiably to* ZITORSKY)

THE POLICEMAN This is the girl, isn't it? (ZITORSKY *nods his head bleakly*) What's really going on here?

(*In* THE RABBI'S *office,* THE RABBI *sweeps his large shawl over his shoulders*)

ALPER We have said Al-chait and a prayer of atonement, and we are waiting now just for you.

(THE RABBI *frowns in troubled thought, slips his skullcap on as he slips his fedora off. In the synagogue,* ZITORSKY *shuffles to* SCHLISSEL)

ZITORSKY (*Indicating* THE POLICEMAN *with his head, he mutters*) He knows, he knows.

SCHLISSEL Of course. Did Alper expect to get away with such a collegiate prank?

(*In* THE RABBI'S *office,* THE RABBI *finishes a rapid, silent prayer, standing with his eyes closed. He looks up at* ALPER *now*)

THE RABBI I would rather not take any active role in this exorcism. I am not quite sure of my rabbinical position. But it would please me a great deal to believe once again in a God of dybbuks. (*He walks quickly past* ALPER *out into the synagogue.* ALPER *follows*) Well, we are ten.

(*A silence falls upon the gathered men*)

FOREMAN May God look upon us with the eye of mercy and understanding and may He forgive us if we sin in our earnestness.

THE OTHERS Amen.

THE CABALIST Sexton, light the candles. (THE SEXTON *lights each man's candle.* THE CABALIST *advances slowly to* THE GIRL, *who stands slackly, her body making small occasional jerking movements, apparently in a schizophrenic state.* THE CABALIST *slowly draws a line before* THE GIRL *with the flat of his toe. He speaks quietly*) Dybbuk, I draw this line beyond which you may not come. You may not do harm to anyone in this room. (*The old men shift nervously in their various positions around the synagogue.* THE CABALIST *turns to* THE SEXTON) Open the Ark. (THE SEXTON *moves quickly up to the altar and opens the brown sliding doors of the Ark, exposing the several scrolls within, standing in their handsome velvet coverings.* THE CABALIST *moves slowly back to his original position; he says quietly—*) Dybbuk, you are in the presence of God and His Holy Scrolls. (THE GIRL *gasps*) I plead with you one last time to leave the body of this girl. (*There is no answer*) Then I will invoke the curse of excommunication upon your pitiable soul. Sexton, blow Tekiah. (THE SEXTON *raises the ram's horn to his lips, and the eerie, frightening tones shrill out into the hushed air*) Sexton, blow Shevurim. (*Again,* THE SEXTON *raises the ram's horn and blows a variation of the first hollow tones*) Sexton, blow Teruah. (*A third time,* THE SEXTON *blows a variation of the original tones*) Sexton, blow the Great Tekiah, and, upon the sound of these tones, dybbuk, you will be wrenched from the girl's body and there will be cast upon you the final anathema of excommunication from all the world of the living and from all the world of the dead. Sexton, blow the Great Tekiah.

(*For the fourth time,* THE SEXTON *raises the ram's horn to his lips and blows a quick succession of loud blasts. A silence falls heavily on the gathered men, the notes fading into the air. Nothing happens.* THE GIRL *remains as she was, standing slackly, her hands making involuntary little movements.* FOREMAN'S *head sinks slowly on his chest, and an expression of deep pain covers his face.* THE CABALIST *stares steadily at* THE GIRL. *Suddenly,* ARTHUR *begins to moan softly, and then with swift violence a horrible scream tears out of his throat. He staggers one brief step forward. At the peak of his scream, he falls heavily down on the floor of the synagogue in a complete faint. The echoes of his scream tingle momentarily in the high corners of the air in the synagogue. The others stand petrified for a moment, staring at his slack body on the floor)*

ALPER My God. I think what has happened is that we have exorcised the wrong dybbuk.

(THE POLICEMAN *starts toward* ARTHUR'S *limp body)*

THE POLICEMAN All right, don't crowd around. Let him breathe.

THE CABALIST He will be all right in a moment.

ZITORSKY If I didn't see this with my own eyes, I wouldn't believe it.

THE RABBI Mr. Hirschman, will he be all right?

THE CABALIST Yes.

SCHLISSEL (*With simple devoutness*) Praise be to the Lord, for His compassion is everywhere.

(HARRIS *sinks down onto a chair, exhausted and terrified by the whole experience.* THE RABBI *moves slowly down and stares at* ARTHUR *as* SCHLISSEL, ZITORSKY *and* ALPER *help him to a chair)*

ALPER How are you, my dear fellow?

ARTHUR (*Still in a state of shock*) I don't know.

THE SEXTON (*Coming forward with some wine*) Would you like a sip of wine?

ARTHUR (*Taking the goblet*) Yes, thank you very much. (*Turning to look at* THE GIRL) How is she?

(*Her schizophrenic state is quite obvious.* ARTHUR *turns back, his face furrowed and his eyes closed now in a mask of pain)*

SCHLISSEL Was it a painful experience, my friend?

ARTHUR I don't know. I feel beyond pain. (*Indeed, his hands are visibly trembling as if from cold; his face is rigid and masklike. Words become more difficult to say*) I feel as if I have been reduced to the moment of birth, as if the universe has become one hunger.

(*He seems to be almost on the verge of collapse)*

ALPER   A hunger for what?

ARTHUR (*Whispering*)   I don't know.

THE CABALIST   For life.

(*At these words,* ARTHUR *sinks back into his chair, exhausted*)

ARTHUR   Yes, for life. I want to live. (*He opens his eyes and begins to pray quietly*)   God of my fathers, you have exorcised all truth as I knew it out of me. You have taken away my reason and definition. Give me then a desire to wake in the morning, a passion for the things of life, a pleasure in work, a purpose to sorrow . . . (*He slowly stands, for a reason unknown even to himself, and turns to regard the slouched figure of* THE GIRL)   Give me all of these things in one—give me the ability to love. (*In a hush of the scene, he moves slowly to* THE GIRL *and stands before her crouched slack figure*)   Dybbuk, hear me. I will cherish this girl, and give her a home. I will tend to her needs and hold her in my arms when she screams out with your voice. Her soul is mine now—her soul, her charm, her beauty—even you, her insanity, are mine. If God will not exorcise you, dybbuk, I will. (*To* THE GIRL)   Evelyn, I will get your coat. We have a lot of things to do this afternoon. (*He turns to the others*)   It is not a simple matter to get somebody released from an institution in New York. (*He starts briskly across to* THE RABBI'S *office and pauses at the door*)   Officer, why don't you just call in and say you have located the girl and she is being brought to her father. (*To* MR. FOREMAN)   You'd better come along with us. Would somebody get my coat? We will need her father's approval. We shall have to stop off at my office and have my secretary draw some papers.

(MR. FOREMAN *has hurriedly gotten* THE GIRL'S *coat,* ARTHUR'S *coat, and his own. In this rather enchanted state, these three drift to the exit door*)

THE POLICEMAN   Rabbi, is this all right?

99

THE RABBI   Yes, quite all right.

ARTHUR (*Pausing at the door, bemused, enchanted*)   Oh
—thank you all. Good-bye.

ALL   Good-bye.

ZITORSKY   Go in good health.

ALPER   Come back and make a tenth for us sometime.
(ARTHUR *smiles and herds* THE GIRL *and* FOREMAN *out of
the synagogue. The door closes behind them*)

SCHLISSEL (*Sitting with a deep sigh*)   Well, what is one to
say? An hour ago, he didn't believe in God; now he's
exorcising dybbuks.

ALPER (*Pulling up a chair*)   He still doesn't believe in
God. He simply wants to love. (ZITORSKY *joins the other
two*)   And when you stop and think about it, gentlemen, is there any difference? Let us make a supposi-
tion . . .
(*As the curtain falls, life as it was slowly returns to the
synagogue. The three old men engage in disputation,*
THE CABALIST *returns to his isolated studies,* THE RABBI
moves off into his office, THE SEXTON *finds a chore for
himself, and* THE POLICEMAN *begins to button his coat*)

THE CURTAIN FALLS

Lorraine Hansberry

A Raisin in the Sun

What happens to a dream deferred?
Does it dry up
Like a raisin in the sun?
Or fester like a sore—
And then run?
Does it stink like rotten meat?
Or crust and sugar over—
Like a syrupy sweet?

Maybe it just sags
Like a heavy load.

Or does it explode?

—LANGSTON HUGHES

TO MAMA:
IN GRATITUDE FOR THE DREAM

A Raisin in the Sun was first presented by Philip Rose and
David J. Cogan at the Ethel Barrymore Theatre, New York
City, March 11, 1959, with the following cast:

(*In order of appearance*)

RUTH YOUNGER	Ruby Dee
TRAVIS YOUNGER	Glyn Turman
WALTER LEE YOUNGER (BROTHER)	Sidney Poitier
BENEATHA YOUNGER	Diana Sands
LENA YOUNGER (MAMA)	Claudia McNeil
JOSEPH ASAGAI	Ivan Dixon
GEORGE MURCHISON	Louis Gossett
KARL LINDNER	John Fiedler
BOBO	Lonne Elder III
MOVING MEN	Ed Hall, Douglas Turner

DIRECTED BY Lloyd Richards
DESIGNED AND LIGHTED BY Ralph Alswang
COSTUMES BY Virginia Volland

The action of the play is set in Chicago's Southside, sometime between World War II and the present.

ACT ONE

Scene 1. Friday morning.
Scene 2. The following morning.

ACT TWO

Scene 1. Later, the same day.
Scene 2. Friday night, a few weeks later.
Scene 3. Moving day, one week later.

ACT THREE

An hour later.

ACT · ONE

Scene One

The YOUNGER *living room would be a comfortable and well-ordered room if it were not for a number of indestructible contradictions to this state of being. Its furnishings are typical and undistinguished and their primary feature now is that they have clearly had to accommodate the living of too many people for too many years—and they are tired. Still, we can see that at some time, a time probably no longer remembered by the family (except perhaps for* MAMA), *the furnishings of this room were actually selected with care and love and even hope—and brought to this apartment and arranged with taste and pride.*

That was a long time ago. Now the once loved pattern of the couch upholstery has to fight to show itself from under acres of crocheted doilies and couch covers which have themselves finally come to be more important than the upholstery. And here a table or a chair has been moved to disguise the worn places in the carpet; but the carpet has fought back by showing its weariness, with depressing uniformity, elsewhere on its surface.

Weariness has, in fact, won in this room. Everything has been polished, washed, sat on, used, scrubbed too often. All pretenses but living itself have long since vanished from the very atmosphere of this room.

Moreover, a section of this room, for it is not really a room unto itself, though the landlord's lease would make

*it seem so, slopes backward to provide a small kitchen area,
where the family prepares the meals that are eaten in the
living room proper, which must also serve as dining room.
The single window that has been provided for these "two"
rooms is located in this kitchen area. The sole natural light
the family may enjoy in the course of a day is only that
which fights its way through this little window.*

*At left, a door leads to a bedroom which is shared by
MAMA and her daughter, BENEATHA. At right, opposite, is
a second room (which in the beginning of the life of this
apartment was probably a breakfast room) which serves
as a bedroom for WALTER and his wife, RUTH.*

*Time: Sometime between World War II and the present.
Place: Chicago's Southside.*

*At rise: It is morning dark in the living room. TRAVIS is
asleep on the make-down bed at center. An alarm clock
sounds from within the bedroom at right, and presently
RUTH enters from that room and closes the door behind
her. She crosses sleepily toward the window. As she passes
her sleeping son she reaches down and shakes him a little.
At the window she raises the shade and a dusky Southside
morning light comes in feebly. She fills a pot with water
and puts it on to boil. She calls to the boy, between yawns,
in a slightly muffled voice.*

*RUTH is about thirty. We can see that she was a pretty
girl, even exceptionally so, but now it is apparent that life
has been little that she expected, and disappointment has
already begun to hang in her face. In a few years, before
thirty-five even, she will be known among her people as a
"settled woman."*

*She crosses to her son and gives him a good, final, rous-
ing shake.*

106

RUTH Come on now, boy, it's seven thirty! (*Her son sits up at last, in a stupor of sleepiness*) I say hurry up, Travis! You ain't the only person in the world got to use a bathroom! (*The child, a sturdy, handsome little boy of ten or eleven, drags himself out of the bed and almost blindly takes his towels and "today's clothes" from drawers and a closet and goes out to the bathroom, which is in an outside hall and which is shared by another family or families on the same floor.* RUTH *crosses to the bedroom door at right and opens it and calls in to her husband*) Walter Lee! . . . It's after seven thirty! Lemme see you do some waking up in there now! (*She waits*) You better get up from there, man! It's after seven thirty I tell you. (*She waits again*) All right, you just go ahead and lay there and next thing you know Travis be finished and Mr. Johnson'll be in there and you'll be fussing and cussing round here like a mad man! And be late too! (*She waits, at the end of patience*) *Walter Lee—it's time for you to get up!*

(*She waits another second and then starts to go into the bedroom, but is apparently satisfied that her husband has begun to get up. She stops, pulls the door to, and returns to the kitchen area. She wipes her face with a moist cloth and runs her fingers through her sleep-disheveled hair in a vain effort and ties an apron around her housecoat. The bedroom door at right opens and her husband stands in the doorway in his pajamas, which are rumpled and mismated. He is a lean, intense young man in his middle thirties, inclined to quick nervous movements and erratic speech habits—and always in his voice there is a quality of indictment*)

WALTER Is he out yet?

RUTH What you mean *out?* He ain't hardly got in there good yet.

WALTER (*Wandering in, still more oriented to sleep than to a new day*) Well, what was you doing all that yelling for if I can't even get in there yet? (*Stopping and thinking*) Check coming today?

RUTH They *said* Saturday and this is just Friday and I hopes to God you ain't going to get up here first thing this morning and start talking to me 'bout no money— 'cause I 'bout don't want to hear it.

WALTER Something the matter with you this morning?

RUTH No—I'm just sleepy as the devil. What kind of eggs you want?

WALTER Not scrambled. (RUTH *starts to scramble eggs*) Paper come? (RUTH *points impatiently to the rolled up* Tribune *on the table, and he gets it and spreads it out and vaguely reads the front page*) Set off another bomb yesterday.

RUTH (*Maximum indifference*) Did they?

WALTER (*Looking up*) What's the matter with you?

RUTH Ain't nothing the matter with me. And don't keep asking me that this morning.

WALTER Ain't nobody bothering you. (*Reading the news of the day absently again*) Say Colonel McCormick is sick.

RUTH (*Affecting tea-party interest*) Is he now? Poor thing.

WALTER (*Sighing and looking at his watch*) Oh, me. (*He waits*) Now what is that boy doing in that bathroom all this time? He just going to have to start getting up earlier. I can't be being late to work on account of him fooling around in there.

RUTH (*Turning on him*) Oh, no he ain't going to be getting up no earlier no such thing! It ain't his fault that he can't get to bed no earlier nights 'cause he got a bunch of crazy good-for-nothing clowns sitting up running their mouths in what is supposed to be his bedroom after ten o'clock at night . . .

WALTER That's what you mad about, ain't it? The things

108

I want to talk about with my friends just couldn't be important in your mind, could they?

(*He rises and finds a cigarette in her handbag on the table and crosses to the little window and looks out, smoking and deeply enjoying this first one*)

RUTH (*Almost matter of factly, a complaint too automatic to deserve emphasis*) Why you always got to smoke before you eat in the morning?

WALTER (*At the window*) Just look at 'em down there . . . Running and racing to work . . . (*He turns and faces his wife and watches her a moment at the stove, and then, suddenly*) You look young this morning, baby.

RUTH (*Indifferently*) Yeah?

WALTER Just for a second—stirring them eggs. It's gone now—just for a second it was—you looked real young again. (*Then, drily*) It's gone now—you look like yourself again.

RUTH Man, if you don't shut up and leave me alone.

WALTER (*Looking out to the street again*) First thing a man ought to learn in life is not to make love to no colored woman first thing in the morning. You all some evil people at eight o'clock in the morning.

(TRAVIS *appears in the hall doorway, almost fully dressed and quite wide awake now, his towels and pajamas across his shoulders. He opens the door and signals for his father to make the bathroom in a hurry*)

TRAVIS (*Watching the bathroom*) Daddy, come on!

(WALTER *gets his bathroom utensils and flies out to the bathroom*)

RUTH Sit down and have your breakfast, Travis.

TRAVIS Mama, this is Friday. (*Gleefully*) Check coming tomorrow, huh?

RUTH You get your mind off money and eat your breakfast.

TRAVIS (*Eating*) This is the morning we supposed to bring the fifty cents to school.

RUTH Well, I ain't got no fifty cents this morning.

TRAVIS Teacher say we have to.

RUTH I don't care what teacher say. I ain't got it. Eat your breakfast, Travis.

TRAVIS I *am* eating.

RUTH Hush up now and just eat!

(*The boy gives her an exasperated look for her lack of understanding, and eats grudgingly*)

TRAVIS You think Grandmama would have it?

RUTH No! And I want you to stop asking your grandmother for money, you hear me?

TRAVIS (*Outraged*) Gaaaleee! I don't ask her, she just gimme it sometimes!

RUTH Travis Willard Younger—I got too much on me this morning to be—

TRAVIS Maybe Daddy—

RUTH *Travis!*

(*The boy hushes abruptly. They are both quiet and tense for several seconds*)

TRAVIS (*Presently*) Could I maybe go carry some groceries in front of the supermarket for a little while after school then?

RUTH Just hush, I said. (TRAVIS *jabs his spoon into his cereal bowl viciously, and rests his head in anger upon his fists*) If you through eating, you can get over there and make up your bed.

(*The boy obeys stiffly and crosses the room, almost mechanically, to the bed and more or less carefully folds the covering. He carries the bedding into his mother's room and returns with his books and cap*)

TRAVIS (*Sulking and standing apart from her unnaturally*) I'm gone.

RUTH (*Looking up from the stove to inspect him automatically*) Come here. (*He crosses to her and she*

110

studies his head)   If you don't take this comb and fix
this here head, you better! (TRAVIS *puts down his books
with a great sigh of oppression, and crosses to the mirror. His mother mutters under her breath about his
"stubbornness"*)   'Bout to march out of here with that
head looking just like chickens slept in it! I just don't
know where you get your slubborn ways . . . And get
your jacket, too. Looks chilly out this morning.

TRAVIS (*With conspicuously brushed hair and jacket*)   I'm
gone.

RUTH   Get carfare and milk money— (*Waving one finger*)
—and not a single penny for no caps, you hear me?

TRAVIS (*With sullen politeness*)   Yes'm.

(*He turns in outrage to leave. His mother watches after
him as in his frustration he approaches the door almost
comically. When she speaks to him, her voice has become
a very gentle tease*)

RUTH (*Mocking; as she thinks he would say it*)   Oh,
Mama makes me so mad sometimes, I don't know what
to do! (*She waits and continues to his back as he stands
stock-still in front of the door*)   I wouldn't kiss that
woman good-bye for nothing in this world this morning!
(*The boy finally turns around and rolls his eyes at her,
knowing the mood has changed and he is vindicated; he
does not, however, move toward her yet*)   Not for nothing in this world! (*She finally laughs aloud at him and
holds out her arms to him and we see that it is a way
between them, very old and practiced. He crosses to her
and allows her to embrace him warmly but keeps his
face fixed with masculine rigidity. She holds him back
from her presently and looks at him and runs her fingers
over the features of his face. With utter gentleness—*)
Now—whose little old angry man are you?

TRAVIS (*The masculinity and gruffness start to fade at last*)
Aw gaalee—Mama . . .

RUTH (*Mimicking*)   Aw—gaaaaalleeeee, Mama! (*She

111

*pushes him, with rough playfulness and finality, toward
the door)* Get on out of here or you going to be late.

TRAVIS *(In the face of love, new aggressiveness)* Mama,
could I *please* go carry groceries?

RUTH Honey, it's starting to get so cold evenings.

WALTER *(Coming in from the bathroom and drawing a
make-believe gun from a make-believe holster and shoot-
ing at his son)* What is it he wants to do?

RUTH Go carry groceries after school at the supermarket.

WALTER Well, let him go . . .

TRAVIS *(Quickly, to the ally)* I *have* to—she won't gimme
the fifty cents . . .

WALTER *(To his wife only)* Why not?

RUTH *(Simply, and with flavor)* 'Cause we don't have it.

WALTER *(To RUTH only)* What you tell the boy things
like that for? *(Reaching down into his pants with a
rather important gesture)* Here, son—

*(He hands the boy the coin, but his eyes are directed to
his wife's. TRAVIS takes the money happily)*

TRAVIS Thanks, Daddy.

*(He starts out. RUTH watches both of them with murder
in her eyes. WALTER stands and stares back at her with
defiance, and suddenly reaches into his pocket again on
an afterthought)*

WALTER *(Without even looking at his son, still staring hard
at his wife)* In fact, here's another fifty cents . . . Buy
yourself some fruit today—or take a taxi cab to school
or something!

TRAVIS Whoopee—

*(He leaps up and clasps his father around the middle
with his legs, and they face each other in mutual appreciation; slowly WALTER LEE peeks around the boy to
catch the violent rays from his wife's eyes and draws his
head back as if shot)*

WALTER You better get down now—and get to school,
man.

TRAVIS (*At the door*)   O.K. Good-bye.
(*He exits*)

WALTER (*After him, pointing with pride*)   That's *my* boy.
(*She looks at him in disgust and turns back to her work*)
You know what I was thinking 'bout in the bathroom
this morning?

RUTH   No.

WALTER   How come you always try to be so pleasant!

RUTH   What is there to be pleasant 'bout!

WALTER   You want to know what I was thinking 'bout in
the bathroom or not!

RUTH   I know what you was thinking 'bout.

WALTER (*Ignoring her*)   'Bout what me and Willy Harris
was talking about last night.

RUTH (*Immediately—a refrain*)   Willy Harris is a good-
for-nothing loud mouth.

WALTER   Anybody who talks to me has got to be a good-
for-nothing loud mouth, ain't he? And what you know
about who is just a good-for-nothing loud mouth? Charlie
Atkins was just a "good-for-nothing loud mouth" too,
wasn't he! When he wanted me to go in the dry-cleaning
business with him. And now—he's grossing a hundred
thousand a year. A hundred thousand dollars a year!
You still call *him* a loud mouth!

RUTH (*Bitterly*)   Oh, Walter Lee . . .
(*She folds her head on her arms over on the table*)

WALTER (*Rising and coming to her and standing over her*)
You tired, ain't you? Tired of everything. Me, the boy,
the way we live—this beat-up hole—everything. Ain't
you? (*She doesn't look up, doesn't answer*)   So tired—
moaning and groaning all the time, but you wouldn't do
nothing to help, would you? You couldn't be on my side
that long for nothing, could you?

RUTH   Walter, please leave me alone.

WALTER   A man needs for a woman to back him up . . .

RUTH   Walter—

WALTER   Mama would listen to you. You know she listen
to you more than she do me and Bennie. She think more
of you. All you have to do is just sit down with her when
you drinking your coffee one morning and talking 'bout
things like you do and— (*He sits down beside her and
demonstrates graphically what he thinks her methods and
tone should be*)   —you just sip your coffee, see, and say
easy like that you been thinking 'bout that deal Walter
Lee is so interested in, 'bout the store and all, and sip
some more coffee, like what you saying ain't really that
important to you— And the next thing you know, she
be listening good and asking you questions and when I
come home—I can tell her the details. This ain't no fly-
by-night proposition, baby. I mean we figured it out, me
and Willy and Bobo.

RUTH   (*With a frown*)   Bobo?

WALTER   Yeah. You see, this little liquor store we got in
mind cost seventy-five thousand and we figured the initial
investment on the place be 'bout thirty thousand, see.
That be ten thousand each. Course, there's a couple of
hundred you got to pay so's you don't spend your life
just waiting for them clowns to let your license get approved—

RUTH   You mean graft?

WALTER   (*Frowning impatiently*)   Don't call it that. See
there, that just goes to show you what women understand about the world. Baby, don't *nothing* happen for
you in this world 'less you pay *somebody* off!

RUTH   Walter, leave me alone! (*She raises her head and
stares at him vigorously—then says, more quietly*)   Eat
your eggs, they gonna be cold.

WALTER (*Straightening up from her and looking off*)
That's it. There you are. Man say to his woman: I got
me a dream. His woman say: Eat your eggs. (*Sadly, but
gaining in power*)   Man say: I got to take hold of this

114

here world, baby! And a woman will say: Eat your eggs and go to work. (*Passionately now*) Man say: I got to change my life, I'm choking to death, baby! And his woman say— (*In utter anguish as he brings his fists down on his thighs*) —Your eggs is getting cold!

RUTH (*Softly*) Walter, that ain't none of our money.

WALTER (*Not listening at all or even looking at her*) This morning, I was lookin' in the mirror and thinking about it . . . I'm thirty-five years old; I been married eleven years and I got a boy who sleeps in the living room— (*Very, very quietly*) —and all I got to give him is stories about how rich white people live . . .

RUTH Eat your eggs, Walter.

WALTER *Damn my eggs . . . damn all the eggs that ever was!*

RUTH Then go to work.

WALTER (*Looking up at her*) See—I'm trying to talk to you 'bout myself— (*Shaking his head with the repetition*) —and all you can say is eat them eggs and go to work.

RUTH (*Wearily*) Honey, you never say nothing new. I listen to you every day, every night and every morning, and you never say nothing new. (*Shrugging*) So you would rather *be* Mr. Arnold than be his chauffeur. So— I would *rather* be living in Buckingham Palace.

WALTER That is just what is wrong with the colored woman in this world . . . Don't understand about building their men up and making 'em feel like they somebody. Like they can do something.

RUTH (*Drily, but to hurt*) There *are* colored men who do things.

WALTER No thanks to the colored woman.

RUTH Well, being a colored woman, I guess I can't help myself none.

(*She rises and gets the ironing board and sets it up and*

attacks a huge pile of rough-dried clothes, sprinkling them in preparation for the ironing and then rolling them into tight fat balls)

WALTER (*Mumbling*) We one group of men tied to a race of women with small minds.

(*His sister* BENEATHA *enters. She is about twenty, as slim and intense as her brother. She is not as pretty as her sister-in-law, but her lean, almost intellectual face has a handsomeness of its own. She wears a bright-red flannel nightie, and her thick hair stands wildly about her head. Her speech is a mixture of many things; it is different from the rest of the family's insofar as education has permeated her sense of English—and perhaps the Midwest rather than the South has finally—at last—won out in her inflection; but not altogether, because over all of it is a soft slurring and transformed use of vowels which is the decided influence of the Southside. She passes through the room without looking at either* RUTH *or* WALTER *and goes to the outside door and looks, a little blindly, out to the bathroom. She sees that it has been lost to the Johnsons. She closes the door with a sleepy vengeance and crosses to the table and sits down a little defeated)*

BENEATHA   I am going to start timing those people.

WALTER   You should get up earlier.

BENEATHA (*Her face in her hands. She is still fighting the urge to go back to bed*)   Really—would you suggest dawn? Where's the paper?

WALTER (*Pushing the paper across the table to her as he studies her almost clinically, as though he has never seen her before*)   You a horrible-looking chick at this hour.

BENEATHA (*Drily*)   Good morning, everybody.

WALTER (*Senselessly*)   How is school coming?

BENEATHA (*In the same spirit*)   Lovely. Lovely. And you know, biology is the greatest. (*Looking up at him*)   I dissected something that looked just like you yesterday.

WALTER   I just wondered if you've made up your mind and everything.

BENEATHA (*Gaining in sharpness and impatience*)   And what did I answer yesterday morning—and the day before that?

RUTH (*From the ironing board, like someone disinterested and old*)   Don't be so nasty, Bennie.

BENEATHA (*Still to her brother*)   And the day before that and the day before that!

WALTER (*Defensively*)   I'm interested in you. Something wrong with that? Ain't many girls who decide—

WALTER *and* BENEATHA (*In unison*)   —"to be a doctor." (*Silence*)

WALTER   Have we figured out yet just exactly how much medical school is going to cost?

RUTH   Walter Lee, why don't you leave that girl alone and get out of here to work?

BENEATHA (*Exits to the bathroom and bangs on the door*) Come on out of there, please!
(*She comes back into the room*)

WALTER (*Looking at his sister intently*)   You know the check is coming tomorrow.

BENEATHA (*Turning on him with a sharpness all her own*) That money belongs to Mama, Walter, and it's for her to decide how she wants to use it. I don't care if she wants to buy a house or a rocket ship or just nail it up somewhere and look at it. It's hers. Not ours—*hers.*

WALTER (*Bitterly*)   Now ain't that fine! You just got your mother's interest at heart, ain't you, girl? You such a nice girl—but if Mama got that money she can always take a few thousand and help you through school too—can't she?

BENEATHA   I have never asked anyone around here to do anything for me!

WALTER   No! And the line between asking and just accepting when the time comes is big and wide—ain't it!

BENEATHA (*With fury*) What do you want from me, Brother—that I quit school or just drop dead, which!

WALTER I don't want nothing but for you to stop acting holy 'round here. Me and Ruth done made some sacrifices for you—why can't you do something for the family?

RUTH Walter, don't be dragging me in it.

WALTER You are in it— Don't you get up and go work in somebody's kitchen for the last three years to help put clothes on her back?

RUTH Oh, Walter—that's not fair . . .

WALTER It ain't that nobody expects you to get on your knees and say thank you, Brother; thank you, Ruth; thank you, Mama—and thank you, Travis, for wearing the same pair of shoes for two semesters—

BENEATHA (*Dropping to her knees*) Well—I *do*—all right?—thank everybody . . . and forgive me for ever wanting to be anything at all . . . forgive me, forgive me!

RUTH Please stop it! Your mama'll hear you.

WALTER Who the hell told you you had to be a doctor? If you so crazy 'bout messing 'round with sick people—then go be a nurse like other women—or just get married and be quiet . . .

BENEATHA Well—you finally got it said . . . It took you three years but you finally got it said. Walter, give up; leave me alone—it's Mama's money.

WALTER *He was my father, too!*

BENEATHA So what? He was mine, too—and Travis' grandfather—but the insurance money belongs to Mama. Picking on me is not going to make her give it to you to invest in any liquor stores— (*Underbreath, dropping into a chair*) —and I for one say, God bless Mama for that!

WALTER (*To* RUTH) See—did you hear? Did you hear!

RUTH Honey, please go to work.

WALTER   Nobody in this house is ever going to understand me.

BENEATHA   Because you're a nut.

WALTER   Who's a nut?

BENEATHA   You—you are a nut. Thee is mad, boy.

WALTER (*Looking at his wife and his sister from the door, very sadly*)   The world's most backward race of people, and that's a fact.

BENEATHA (*Turning slowly in her chair*)   And then there are all those prophets who would lead us out of the wilderness— (WALTER *slams out of the house*)   —into the swamps!

RUTH   Bennie, why you always gotta be pickin' on your brother? Can't you be a little sweeter sometimes? (*Door opens.* WALTER *walks in*)

WALTER (*To* RUTH)   I need some money for carfare.

RUTH (*Looks at him, then warms; teasing, but tenderly*) Fifty cents? (*She goes to her bag and gets money*) Here, take a taxi.

(WALTER *exits.* MAMA *enters. She is a woman in her early sixties, full-bodied and strong. She is one of those women of a certain grace and beauty who wear it so unobtrusively that it takes a while to notice. Her dark-brown face is surrounded by the total whiteness of her hair, and, being a woman who has adjusted to many things in life and overcome many more, her face is full of strength. She has, we can see, wit and faith of a kind that keep her eyes lit and full of interest and expectancy. She is, in a word, a beautiful woman. Her bearing is perhaps most like the noble bearing of the women of the Hereros of Southwest Africa—rather as if she imagines that as she walks she still bears a basket or a vessel upon her head. Her speech, on the other hand, is as careless as her carriage is precise—she is inclined to slur everything—but her voice is perhaps not so much quiet as simply soft*)

119

MAMA   Who that 'round here slamming doors at this hour?
(*She crosses through the room, goes to the window, opens
it, and brings in a feeble little plant growing doggedly
in a small pot on the window sill. She feels the dirt and
puts it back out*)

RUTH   That was Walter Lee. He and Bennie was at it
again.

MAMA   My children and they tempers. Lord, if this little
old plant don't get more sun than it's been getting it ain't
never going to see spring again. (*She turns from the window*)   What's the matter with you this morning, Ruth?
You looks right peaked. You aiming to iron all them
things? Leave some for me. I'll get to 'em this afternoon.
Bennie honey, it's too drafty for you to be sitting 'round
half dressed. Where's your robe?

BENEATHA   In the cleaners.

MAMA   Well, go get mine and put it on.

BENEATHA   I'm not cold, Mama, honest.

MAMA   I know—but you so thin . . .

BENEATHA (*Irritably*)   Mama, I'm not cold.

MAMA (*Seeing the make-down bed as* TRAVIS *has left it*)
Lord have mercy, look at that poor bed. Bless his heart
—he tries, don't he?
(*She moves to the bed* TRAVIS *has sloppily made up*)

RUTH   No—he don't half try at all 'cause he knows you
going to come along behind him and fix everything.
That's just how come he don't know how to do nothing
right now—you done spoiled that boy so.

MAMA   Well—he's a little boy. Ain't supposed to know
'bout housekeeping. My baby, that's what he is. What
you fix for his breakfast this morning?

RUTH (*Angrily*)   I feed my son, Lena!

MAMA   I ain't meddling— (*Underbreath; busy-bodyish*)
I just noticed all last week he had cold cereal, and when
it starts getting this chilly in the fall a child ought to have

120

some hot grits or something when he goes out in the cold—

RUTH (*Furious*) I gave him hot oats—is that all right!

MAMA I ain't meddling. (*Pause*) Put a lot of nice butter on it? (RUTH *shoots her an angry look and does not reply*) He likes lots of butter.

RUTH (*Exasperated*) Lena—

MAMA (*To* BENEATHA. MAMA *is inclined to wander conversationally sometimes*) What was you and your brother fussing 'bout this morning?

BENEATHA It's not important, Mama.

(*She gets up and goes to look out at the bathroom, which is apparently free, and she picks up her towels and rushes out*)

MAMA What was they fighting about?

RUTH Now you know as well as I do.

MAMA (*Shaking her head*) Brother still worrying hisself sick about that money?

RUTH You know he is.

MAMA You had breakfast?

RUTH Some coffee.

MAMA Girl, you better start eating and looking after yourself better. You almost thin as Travis.

RUTH Lena—

MAMA Un-hunh?

RUTH What are you going to do with it?

MAMA Now don't you start, child. It's too early in the morning to be talking about money. It ain't Christian.

RUTH It's just that he got his heart set on that store—

MAMA You mean that liquor store that Willy Harris want him to invest in?

RUTH Yes—

MAMA We ain't no business people, Ruth. We just plain working folks.

RUTH Ain't nobody business people till they go into business. Walter Lee say colored people ain't never going to start getting ahead till they start gambling on some different kinds of things in the world—investments and things.

MAMA   What done got into you, girl? Walter Lee done finally sold you on investing.

RUTH   No. Mama, something is happening between Walter and me. I don't know what it is—but he needs something —something I can't give him any more. He needs this chance, Lena.

MAMA   (*Frowning deeply*)   But liquor, honey—

RUTH   Well—like Walter say—I spec people going to always be drinking themselves some liquor.

MAMA   Well—whether they drinks it or not ain't none of my business. But whether I go into business selling it to 'em *is,* and I don't want that on my ledger this late in life. (*Stopping suddenly and studying her daughter-in-law*)   Ruth Younger, what's the matter with you today? You look like you could fall over right there.

RUTH   I'm tired.

MAMA   Then you better stay home from work today.

RUTH   I can't stay home. She'd be calling up the agency and screaming at them, "My girl didn't come in today— send me somebody! My girl didn't come in!" Oh, she just have a fit . . .

MAMA   Well, let her have it. I'll just call her up and say you got the flu—

RUTH   (*Laughing*)   Why the flu?

MAMA   'Cause it sounds respectable to 'em. Something white people get, too. They know 'bout the flu. Otherwise they think you been cut up or something when you tell 'em you sick.

RUTH   I got to go in. We need the money.

MAMA   Somebody would of thought my children done all but starved to death the way they talk about money here late. Child, we got a great big old check coming tomorrow.

RUTH (*Sincerely, but also self-righteously*) Now that's your money. It ain't got nothing to do with me. We all feel like that—Walter and Bennie and me—even Travis.

MAMA (*Thoughtfully, and suddenly very far away*) Ten thousand dollars—

RUTH Sure is wonderful.

MAMA Ten thousand dollars.

RUTH You know what you should do, Miss Lena? You should take yourself a trip somewhere. To Europe or South America or someplace—

MAMA (*Throwing up her hands at the thought*) Oh, child!

RUTH I'm serious. Just pack up and leave! Go on away and enjoy yourself some. Forget about the family and have yourself a ball for once in your life—

MAMA (*Drily*) You sound like I'm just about ready to die. Who'd go with me? What I look like wandering 'round Europe by myself?

RUTH Shoot—these here rich white women do it all the time. They don't think nothing of packing up their suitcases and piling on one of them big steamships and—swoosh!—they gone, child.

MAMA Something always told me I wasn't no rich white woman.

RUTH Well—what are you going to do with it then?

MAMA I ain't rightly decided. (*Thinking. She speaks now with emphasis*) Some of it got to be put away for Beneatha and her schoolin'—and ain't nothing going to touch that part of it. Nothing. (*She waits several seconds, trying to make up her mind about something, and looks at* RUTH *a little tentatively before going on*) Been thinking that we maybe could meet the notes on a little old two-story somewhere, with a yard where Travis could play in the summertime, if we use part of the insurance for a down payment and everybody kind of pitch in. I could maybe take on a little day work again, few days a week—

RUTH (*Studying her mother-in-law furtively and concentrating on her ironing, anxious to encourage without seeming to*)   Well, Lord knows, we've put enough rent into this here rat trap to pay for four houses by now . . .

MAMA (*Looking up at the words "rat trap" and then looking around and leaning back and sighing—in a suddenly reflective mood—*)   "Rat trap"—yes, that's all it is. (*Smiling*)   I remember just as well the day me and Big Walter moved in here. Hadn't been married but two weeks and wasn't planning on living here no more than a year. (*She shakes her head at the dissolved dream*) We was going to set away, little by little, don't you know, and buy a little place out in Morgan Park. We had even picked out the house. (*Chuckling a little*)   Looks right dumpy today. But Lord, child, you should know all the dreams I had 'bout buying that house and fixing it up and making me a little garden in the back— (*She waits and stops smiling*)   And didn't none of it happen.
(*Dropping her hands in a futile gesture*)

RUTH (*Keeps her head down, ironing*)   Yes, life can be a barrel of disappointments, sometimes.

MAMA   Honey, Big Walter would come in here some nights back then and slump down on that couch there and just look at the rug, and look at me and look at the rug and then back at me—and I'd know he was down then . . . really down. (*After a second very long and thoughtful pause; she is seeing back to times that only she can see*) And then, Lord, when I lost that baby—little Claude—I almost thought I was going to lose Big Walter too. Oh, that man grieved hisself! He was one man to love his children.

RUTH   Ain't nothin' can tear at you like losin' your baby.

MAMA   I guess that's how come that man finally worked hisself to death like he done. Like he was fighting his own war with this here world that took his baby from him.

RUTH   He sure was a fine man, all right. I always liked
Mr. Younger.

MAMA   Crazy 'bout his children! God knows there was
plenty wrong with Walter Younger—hard-headed, mean,
kind of wild with women—plenty wrong with him. But
he sure loved his children. Always wanted them to have
something—be something. That's where Brother gets all
these notions, I reckon. Big Walter used to say, he'd get
right wet in the eyes sometimes, lean his head back with
the water standing in his eyes and say, "Seem like God
didn't see fit to give the black man nothing but dreams
—but He did give us children to make them dreams seem
worth while." (*She smiles*)   He could talk like that,
don't you know.

RUTH   Yes, he sure could. He was a good man, Mr.
Younger.

MAMA   Yes, a fine man—just couldn't never catch up with
his dreams, that's all.

(BENEATHA *comes in, brushing her hair and looking up
to the ceiling, where the sound of a vacuum cleaner has
started up*)

BENEATHA   What could be so dirty on that woman's rugs
that she has to vacuum them every single day?

RUTH   I wish certain young women 'round here who I
could name would take inspiration about certain rugs in
a certain apartment I could also mention.

BENEATHA (*Shrugging*)   How much cleaning can a house
need, for Christ's sakes.

MAMA (*Not liking the Lord's name used thus*)   Bennie!

RUTH   Just listen to her—just listen!

BENEATHA   Oh, God!

MAMA   If you use the Lord's name just one more time—

BENEATHA (*A bit of a whine*)   Oh, Mama—

RUTH   Fresh—just fresh as salt, this girl!

BENEATHA (*Drily*)   Well—if the salt loses its savor—

MAMA   Now that will do. I just ain't going to have you

125

'round here reciting the scriptures in vain—you hear me?

BENEATHA   How did I manage to get on everybody's wrong side by just walking into a room?

RUTH   If you weren't so fresh—

BENEATHA   Ruth, I'm twenty years old.

MAMA   What time you be home from school today?

BENEATHA   Kind of late. (*With enthusiasm*)   Madeline is going to start my guitar lessons today.

(MAMA *and* RUTH *look up with the same expression*)

MAMA   Your *what* kind of lessons?

BENEATHA   Guitar.

RUTH   Oh, Father!

MAMA   How come you done taken it in your mind to learn to play the guitar?

BENEATHA   I just want to, that's all.

MAMA   (*Smiling*)   Lord, child, don't you know what to do with yourself? How long it going to be before you get tired of this now—like you got tired of that little play-acting group you joined last year? (*Looking at* RUTH) And what was it the year before that?

RUTH   The horseback-riding club for which she bought that fifty-five-dollar riding habit that's been hanging in the closet ever since!

MAMA   (*To* BENEATHA)   Why you got to flit so from one thing to another, baby?

BENEATHA   (*Sharply*)   I just want to learn to play the guitar. Is there anything wrong with that?

MAMA   Ain't nobody trying to stop you. I just wonders sometimes why you has to flit so from one thing to another all the time. You ain't never done nothing with all that camera equipment you brought home—

BENEATHA   I don't flit! I—I experiment with different forms of expression—

RUTH   Like riding a horse?

BENEATHA   —People have to express themselves one way or another.

126

MAMA   What is it you want to express?

BENEATHA (*Angrily*)   Me! (MAMA *and* RUTH *look at each other and burst into raucous laughter*)   Don't worry—I don't expect you to understand.

MAMA (*To change the subject*)   Who you going out with tomorrow night?

BENEATHA (*With displeasure*)   George Murchison again.

MAMA (*Pleased*)   Oh—you getting a little sweet on him?

RUTH   You ask me, this child ain't sweet on nobody but herself— (*Underbreath*)   Express herself!
(*They laugh*)

BENEATHA   Oh—I like George all right, Mama. I mean I like him enough to go out with him and stuff, but—

RUTH (*For devilment*)   What does *and stuff* mean?

BENEATHA   Mind your own business.

MAMA   Stop picking at her now, Ruth. (*A thoughtful pause, and then a suspicious sudden look at her daughter as she turns in her chair for emphasis*)   What *does* it mean?

BENEATHA (*Wearily*)   Oh, I just mean I couldn't ever really be serious about George. He's—he's so shallow.

RUTH   Shallow—what do you mean he's shallow? He's *Rich!*

MAMA   Hush, Ruth.

BENEATHA   I know he's rich. He knows he's rich, too.

RUTH   Well—what other qualities a man got to have to satisfy you, little girl?

BENEATHA   You wouldn't even begin to understand. Anybody who married Walter could not possibly understand.

MAMA (*Outraged*)   What kind of way is that to talk about your brother?

BENEATHA   Brother is a flip—let's face it.

MAMA (*To* RUTH, *helplessly*)   What's a flip?

RUTH (*Glad to add kindling*)   She's saying he's crazy.

BENEATHA   Not crazy. Brother isn't really crazy yet—he—he's an elaborate neurotic.

MAMA   Hush your mouth!

BENEATHA   As for George. Well. George looks good—he's
got a beautiful car and he takes me to nice places and,
as my sister-in-law says, he is probably the richest boy I
will ever get to know and I even like him sometimes—
but if the Youngers are sitting around waiting to see if
their little Bennie is going to tie up the family with the
Murchisons, they are wasting their time.

RUTH   You mean you wouldn't marry George Murchison
if he asked you someday? That pretty, rich thing? Honey,
I knew you was odd—

BENEATHA   No I would not marry him if all I felt for him
was what I feel now. Besides, George's family wouldn't
really like it.

MAMA   Why not?

BENEATHA   Oh, Mama—the Murchisons are honest-to-
God-real-*live*-rich colored people, and the only people in
the world who are more snobbish than rich white people
are rich colored people. I thought everybody knew that.
I've met Mrs. Murchison. She's a scene!

MAMA   You must not dislike people 'cause they well off,
honey.

BENEATHA   Why not? It makes just as much sense as dis-
liking people 'cause they are poor, and lots of people do
that.

RUTH   (*A wisdom-of-the-ages manner. To* MAMA) Well,
she'll get over some of this—

BENEATHA   Get over it? What are you talking about, Ruth?
Listen, I'm going to be a doctor. I'm not worried about
who I'm going to marry yet—if I ever get married.

MAMA *and* RUTH   *If!*

MAMA   Now, Bennie—

BENEATHA   Oh, I probably will . . . but first I'm going to
be a doctor, and George, for one, still thinks that's pretty
funny. I couldn't be bothered with that. I am going to be

128

a doctor and everybody around here better understand
that!

MAMA (*Kindly*) 'Course you going to be a doctor, honey,
God willing.

BENEATHA (*Drily*) God hasn't got a thing to do with it.

MAMA Beneatha—that just wasn't necessary.

BENEATHA Well—neither is God. I get sick of hearing
about God.

MAMA Beneatha!

BENEATHA I mean it! I'm just tired of hearing about God
all the time. What has He got to do with anything? Does
he pay tuition?

MAMA You 'bout to get your fresh little jaw slapped!

RUTH That's just what she needs, all right!

BENEATHA Why? Why can't I say what I want to around
here, like everybody else?

MAMA It don't sound nice for a young girl to say things
like that—you wasn't brought up that way. Me and your
father went to trouble to get you and Brother to church
every Sunday.

BENEATHA Mama, you don't understand. It's all a matter
of ideas, and God is just one idea I don't accept. It's not
important. I am not going out and be immoral or commit crimes because I don't believe in God. I don't even
think about it. It's just that I get tired of Him getting
credit for all the things the human race achieves through
its own stubborn effort. There simply is no blasted God
—there is only man and it is he who makes miracles!

(MAMA *absorbs this speech, studies her daughter and rises
slowly and crosses to* BENEATHA *and slaps her powerfully
across the face. After, there is only silence and the daughter drops her eyes from her mother's face, and* MAMA *is
very tall before her*)

MAMA Now—you say after me, in my mother's house
there is still God. (*There is a long pause and* BENEATHA

129

stares at the floor wordlessly. MAMA *repeats the phrase with precision and cool emotion*)   In my mother's house there is still God.

BENEATHA   In my mother's house there is still God.

(*A long pause*)

MAMA (*Walking away from* BENEATHA, *too disturbed for triumphant posture. Stopping and turning back to her daughter*)   There are some ideas we ain't going to have in this house. Not long as I am at the head of this family.

BENEATHA   Yes, ma'am.

(MAMA *walks out of the room*)

RUTH (*Almost gently, with profound understanding*)   You think you a woman, Bennie—but you still a little girl. What you did was childish—so you got treated like a child.

BENEATHA   I see. (*Quietly*)   I also see that everybody thinks it's all right for Mama to be a tyrant. But all the tyranny in the world will never put a God in the heavens! (*She picks up her books and goes out*)

RUTH (*Goes to* MAMA's *door*)   She said she was sorry.

MAMA (*Coming out, going to her plant*)   They frightens me, Ruth. My children.

RUTH   You got good children, Lena. They just a little off sometimes—but they're good.

MAMA   No—there's something come down between me and them that don't let us understand each other and I don't know what it is. One done almost lost his mind thinking 'bout money all the time and the other done commence to talk about things I can't seem to understand in no form or fashion. What is it that's changing, Ruth?

RUTH (*Soothingly, older than her years*)   Now . . . you taking it all too seriously. You just got strong-willed children and it takes a strong woman like you to keep 'em in hand.

130

MAMA (*Looking at her plant and sprinkling a little water on it*) They spirited all right, my children. Got to admit they got spirit—Bennie and Walter. Like this little old plant that ain't never had enough sunshine or nothing—and look at it . . .

(*She has her back to* RUTH, *who has had to stop ironing and lean against something and put the back of her hand to her forehead*)

RUTH (*Trying to keep* MAMA *from noticing*) You . . . sure . . . loves that little old thing, don't you? . . .

MAMA Well, I always wanted me a garden like I used to see sometimes at the back of the houses down home. This plant is close as I ever got to having one. (*She looks out of the window as she replaces the plant*) Lord, ain't nothing as dreary as the view from this window on a dreary day, is there? Why ain't you singing this morning, Ruth? Sing that "No Ways Tired." That song always lifts me up so— (*She turns at last to see that* RUTH *has slipped quietly into a chair, in a state of semiconsciousness*) Ruth! Ruth honey—what's the matter with you . . . Ruth!

CURTAIN

Scene Two

It is the following morning; a Saturday morning, and house cleaning is in progress at the YOUNGERS. *Furniture has been shoved hither and yon and* MAMA *is giving the kitchen-area walls a washing down.* BENEATHA, *in dungarees, with a handkerchief tied around her face, is spraying insecticide into the cracks in the walls. As they work, the radio is on and a Southside disk-jockey program is inappropriately filling the house with a rather exotic saxophone blues.* TRAVIS, *the sole idle one, is leaning on his arms, looking out of the window.*

TRAVIS   Grandmama, that stuff Bennie is using smells awful. Can I go downstairs, please?

MAMA   Did you get all them chores done already? I ain't seen you doing much.

TRAVIS   Yes'm—finished early. Where did Mama go this morning?

MAMA   (*Looking at* BENEATHA)   She had to go on a little errand.

TRAVIS   Where?

MAMA   To tend to her business.

TRAVIS   Can I go outside then?

MAMA   Oh, I guess so. You better stay right in front of the house, though . . . and keep a good lookout for the postman.

TRAVIS   Yes'm. (*He starts out and decides to give his* AUNT BENEATHA *a good swat on the legs as he passes her*) Leave them poor little old cockroaches alone, they ain't bothering you none.
(*He runs as she swings the spray gun at him both viciously and playfully.* WALTER *enters from the bedroom and goes to the phone*)

MAMA   Look out there, girl, before you be spilling some of that stuff on that child!

TRAVIS   (*Teasing*)   That's right—look out now!
(*He exits*)

BENEATHA   (*Drily*)   I can't imagine that it would hurt him —it has never hurt the roaches.

MAMA   Well, little boys' hides ain't as tough as Southside roaches.

WALTER   (*Into phone*)   Hello—let me talk to Willy Harris.

MAMA   You better get over there behind the bureau. I seen one marching out of there like Napoleon yesterday.

132

WALTER   Hello, Willy? It ain't come yet. It'll be here in a few minutes. Did the lawyer give you the papers?

BENEATHA   There's really only one way to get rid of them, Mama—

MAMA   How?

BENEATHA   Set fire to this building.

WALTER   Good. Good. I'll be right over.

BENEATHA   Where did Ruth go, Walter?

WALTER   I don't know.

   (*He exits abruptly*)

BENEATHA   Mama, where did Ruth go?

MAMA (*Looking at her with meaning*)   To the doctor, I think.

BENEATHA   The doctor? What's the matter? (*They exchange glances*)   You don't think—

MAMA (*With her sense of drama*)   Now I ain't saying what I think. But I ain't never been wrong 'bout a woman neither.

   (*The phone rings*)

BENEATHA (*At the phone*)   Hay-lo . . . (*Pause, and a moment of recognition*)   Well—when did you get back! . . . And how was it? . . . Of course I've missed you —in my way . . . This morning? No . . . house cleaning and all that and Mama hates it if I let people come over when the house is like this . . . You *have?* Well, that's different . . . What is it— Oh, what the hell, come on over . . . Right, see you then.

   (*She hangs up*)

MAMA (*Who has listened vigorously, as is her habit*)   Who is that you inviting over here with this house looking like this? You ain't got the pride you was born with!

BENEATHA   Asagai doesn't care how houses look, Mama— he's an intellectual.

MAMA   *Who?*

BENEATHA   Asagai—Joseph Asagai. He's an African boy

I met on campus. He's been studying in Canada all summer.

MAMA   What's his name?

BENEATHA   Asagai, Joseph. Ah-sah-guy . . . He's from Nigeria.

MAMA   Oh, that's the little country that was founded by slaves way back . . .

BENEATHA   No, Mama—that's Liberia.

MAMA   I don't think I never met no African before.

BENEATHA   Well, do me a favor and don't ask him a whole lot of ignorant questions about Africans. I mean, do they wear clothes and all that—

MAMA   Well, now, I guess if you think we so ignorant 'round here maybe you shouldn't bring your friends here—

BENEATHA   It's just that people ask such crazy things. All anyone seems to know about when it comes to Africa is Tarzan—

MAMA   (*Indignantly*)   Why should I know anything about Africa?

BENEATHA   Why do you give money at church for the missionary work?

MAMA   Well, that's to help save people.

BENEATHA   You mean save them from *heathenism*—

MAMA   (*Innocently*)   Yes.

BENEATHA   I'm afraid they need more salvation from the British and the French.

(RUTH *comes in forlornly and pulls off her coat with dejection. They both turn to look at her*)

RUTH   (*Dispiritedly*)   Well, I guess from all the happy faces—everybody knows.

BENEATHA   You pregnant?

MAMA   Lord have mercy, I sure hope it's a little old girl. Travis ought to have a sister.

(BENEATHA *and* RUTH *give her a hopeless look for this grandmotherly enthusiasm*)

134

BENEATHA How far along are you?

RUTH Two months.

BENEATHA Did you mean to? I mean did you plan it or was it an accident?

MAMA What do you know about planning or not planning?

BENEATHA Oh, Mama.

RUTH (*Wearily*) She's twenty years old, Lena.

BENEATHA Did you plan it, Ruth?

RUTH Mind your own business.

BENEATHA It is my business—where is he going to live, on the *roof*? (*There is silence following the remark as the three women react to the sense of it*) Gee—I didn't mean that, Ruth, honest. Gee, I don't feel like that at all. I—I think it is wonderful.

RUTH (*Dully*) Wonderful.

BENEATHA Yes—really.

MAMA (*Looking at* RUTH, *worried*) Doctor say everything going to be all right?

RUTH (*Far away*) Yes—she says everything is going to be fine . . .

MAMA (*Immediately suspicious*) "She"— What doctor you went to? (RUTH *folds over, near hysteria.* MAMA *worriedly hovers over her*) Ruth honey—what's the matter with you—you sick?

(RUTH *has her fists clenched on her thighs and is fighting hard to suppress a scream that seems to be rising in her*)

BENEATHA What's the matter with her, Mama?

MAMA (*Working her fingers in* RUTH'S *shoulder to relax her*) She be all right. Women gets right depressed sometimes when they get her way. (*Speaking softly, expertly, rapidly*) Now you just relax. That's right . . . just lean back, don't think 'bout nothing at all . . . nothing at all—

RUTH I'm all right . . .

(*The glassy-eyed look melts and then she collapses into
a fit of heavy sobbing. The bell rings*)

BENEATHA   Oh, my God—that must be Asagai.

MAMA (*To* RUTH)   Come on now, honey. You need to lie
down and rest awhile . . . then have some nice hot
food.

(*They exit,* RUTH'S *weight on her mother-in-law.* BE-
NEATHA, *herself profoundly disturbed, opens the door to
admit a rather dramatic-looking young man with a large
package*)

ASAGAI   Hello, Alaiyo—

BENEATHA (*Holding the door open and regarding him with
pleasure*)   Hello . . . (*Long pause*)   Well—come in.
And please excuse everything. My mother was very upset
about my letting anyone come here with the place like
this.

ASAGAI (*Coming into the room*)   You look disturbed too
. . . Is something wrong?

BENEATHA (*Still at the door, absently*)   Yes . . . we've
all got acute ghetto-itus. (*She smiles and comes toward
him, finding a cigarette and sitting*)   So—sit down! How
was Canada?

ASAGAI (*A sophisticate*)   Canadian.

BENEATHA (*Looking at him*)   I'm very glad you are back.

ASAGAI (*Looking back at her in turn*)   Are you really?

BENEATHA   Yes—very.

ASAGAI   Why—you were quite glad when I went away.
What happened?

BENEATHA   You went away.

ASAGAI   Ahhhhhhhh.

BENEATHA   Before—you wanted to be so serious before
there was time.

ASAGAI   How much time must there be before one knows
what one feels?

BENEATHA (*Stalling this particular conversation. Her hands*

136

pressed together, in a deliberately childish gesture)
What did you bring me?

ASAGAI (*Handing her the package*)   Open it and see.

BENEATHA (*Eagerly opening the package and drawing out
some records and the colorful robes of a Nigerian
woman*)   Oh, Asagai! . . . You got them for me! . . .
How beautiful . . . and the records too!
(*She lifts out the robes and runs to the mirror with them
and holds the drapery up in front of herself*)

ASAGAI (*Coming to her at the mirror*)   I shall have to
teach you how to drape it properly. (*He flings the material about her for the moment and stands back to look
at her*)   Ah— Oh-pay-gay-day, oh-gbah-mu-shay. (*A
Yoruba exclamation for admiration*)   You wear it well
. . . very well . . . mutilated hair and all.

BENEATHA (*Turning suddenly*)   My hair—what's wrong
with my hair?

ASAGAI (*Shrugging*)   Were you born with it like that?

BENEATHA (*Reaching up to touch it*)   No . . . of course
not.
(*She looks back to the mirror, disturbed*)

ASAGAI (*Smiling*)   How then?

BENEATHA   You know perfectly well how . . . as crinkly
as yours . . . that's how.

ASAGAI   And it is ugly to you that way?

BENEATHA (*Quickly*)   Oh, no—not ugly . . . (*More
slowly, apologetically*)   But it's so hard to manage when
it's, well—raw.

ASAGAI   And so to accommodate that—you mutilate it
every week?

BENEATHA   It's not mutilation!

ASAGAI (*Laughing aloud at her seriousness*)   Oh . . .
please! I am only teasing you because you are so very
serious about these things. (*He stands back from her and
folds his arms across his chest as he watches her pulling*

at her hair and frowning in the mirror) Do you remember the first time you met me at school? . . . (*He laughs*) You came up to me and you _said—and I thought you were the most serious little thing I had ever seen—you said: (*He imitates her*) "Mr. Asagai—I want very much to talk with you. About Africa. You see, Mr. Asagai, I am looking for my *identity!*" (*He laughs*)

BENEATHA (*Turning to him, not laughing*) Yes— (*Her face is quizzical, profoundly disturbed*)

ASAGAI (*Still teasing and reaching out and taking her face in his hands and turning her profile to him*) Well . . . it is true that this is not so much a profile of a Hollywood queen as perhaps a queen of the Nile— (*A mock dismissal of the importance of the question*) But what does it matter? Assimilationism is so popular in your country.

BENEATHA (*Wheeling, passionately, sharply*) I am not an assimilationist!

ASAGAI (*The protest hangs in the room for a moment and ASAGAI studies her, his laughter fading*) Such a serious one. (*There is a pause*) So—you like the robes? You must take excellent care of them—they are from my sister's personal wardrobe.

BENEATHA (*With incredulity*) You—you sent all the way home—for me?

ASAGAI (*With charm*) For you—I would do much more . . . Well, that is what I came for. I must go.

BENEATHA Will you call me Monday?

ASAGAI Yes . . . We have a great deal to talk about. I mean about identity and time and all that.

BENEATHA Time?

ASAGAI Yes. About how much time one needs to know what one feels.

BENEATHA You never understood that there is more than one kind of feeling which can exist between a man and a woman—or, at least, there should be.

ASAGAI (*Shaking his head negatively but gently*)   No. Between a man and a woman there need be only one kind of feeling. I have that for you . . . Now even . . . right this moment . . .

BENEATHA   I know—and by itself—it won't do. I can find that anywhere.

ASAGAI   For a woman it should be enough.

BENEATHA   I know—because that's what it says in all the novels that men write. But it isn't. Go ahead and laugh— but I'm not interested in being someone's little episode in America or— (*With feminine vengeance*)   —one of them! (ASAGAI *has burst into laughter again*)   That's funny as hell, huh!

ASAGAI   It's just that every American girl I have known has said that to me. White—black—in this you are all the same. And the same speech, too!

BENEATHA   (*Angrily*)   Yuk, yuk, yuk!

ASAGAI   It's how you can be sure that the world's most liberated women are not liberated at all. You all talk about it too much!

(MAMA *enters and is immediately all social charm because of the presence of a guest*)

BENEATHA   Oh—Mama—this is Mr. Asagai.

MAMA   How do you do?

ASAGAI (*Total politeness to an elder*)   How do you do, Mrs. Younger. Please forgive me for coming at such an outrageous hour on a Saturday.

MAMA   Well, you are quite welcome. I just hope you understand that our house don't always look like this. (*Chatterish*)   You must come again. I would love to hear all about— (*Not sure of the name*)   —your country. I think it's so sad the way our American Negroes don't know nothing about Africa 'cept Tarzan and all that. And all that money they pour into these churches when they ought to be helping you people over there drive out them French and Englishmen done taken away your land.

Lorraine Hansberry

(*The mother flashes a slightly superior look at her daughter upon completion of the recitation*)

ASAGAI (*Taken aback by this sudden and acutely unrelated expression of sympathy*) Yes . . . yes . . .

MAMA (*Smiling at him suddenly and relaxing and looking him over*) How many miles is it from here to where you come from?

ASAGAI Many thousands.

MAMA (*Looking at him as she would* WALTER) I bet you don't half look after yourself, being away from your mama either. I spec you better come 'round here from time to time and get yourself some decent home-cooked meals . . .

ASAGAI (*Moved*) Thank you. Thank you very much. (*They are all quiet, then—*) Well . . . I must go. I will call you Monday, Alaiyo.

MAMA What's that he call you?

ASAGAI Oh—"Alaiyo." I hope you don't mind. It is what you would call a nickname, I think. It is a Yoruba word. I am a Yoruba.

MAMA (*Looking at* BENEATHA) I—I thought he was from—

ASAGAI (*Understanding*) Nigeria is my country. Yoruba is my tribal origin—

BENEATHA You didn't tell us what Alaiyo means . . . for all I know, you might be calling me Little Idiot or something . . .

ASAGAI Well . . . let me see . . . I do not know how just to explain it . . . The sense of a thing can be so different when it changes languages.

BENEATHA You're evading.

ASAGAI No—really it is difficult . . . (*Thinking*) It means . . . it means One for Whom Bread—Food—Is Not Enough. (*He looks at her*) Is that all right?

BENEATHA (*Understanding, softly*) Thank you.

MAMA (*Looking from one to the other and not understand-*

140

ing any of it)   Well . . . that's nice . . . You must
come to see us again—Mr.—

ASAGAI   Ah-sah-guy . . .

MAMA   Yes . . . Do come again.

ASAGAI   Good-bye.

(*He exits*)

MAMA (*After him*)   Lord, that's a pretty thing just went
out here! (*Insinuatingly, to her daughter*)   Yes, I guess
I see why we done commence to get so interested in
Africa 'round here. Missionaries my aunt Jenny!

(*She exits*)

BENEATHA   Oh, Mama! . . .

(*She picks up the Nigerian dress and holds it up to her
in front of the mirror again. She sets the headdress on
haphazardly and then notices her hair again and clutches
at it and then replaces the headdress and frowns at herself. Then she starts to wriggle in front of the mirror as
she thinks a Nigerian woman might.* TRAVIS *enters and
regards her*)

TRAVIS   You cracking up?

BENEATHA   Shut up.

(*She pulls the headdress off and looks at herself in the
mirror and clutches at her hair again and squinches her
eyes as if trying to imagine something. Then, suddenly,
she gets her raincoat and kerchief and hurriedly prepares
for going out*)

MAMA (*Coming back into the room*)   She's resting now.
Travis, baby, run next door and ask Miss Johnson to
please let me have a little kitchen cleanser. This here can
is empty as Jacob's kettle.

TRAVIS   I just came in.

MAMA   Do as you told. (*He exits and she looks at her
daughter*)   Where are you going?

BENEATHA (*Halting at the door*)   To become a queen of
the Nile!

(*She exits in a breathless blaze of glory.* RUTH *appears in the bedroom doorway*)

MAMA   Who told you to get up?

RUTH   Ain't nothing wrong with me to be lying in no bed for. Where did Bennie go?

MAMA   (*Drumming her fingers*)   Far as I could make out —to Egypt. (RUTH *just looks at her*)   What time is it getting to?

RUTH   Ten twenty. And the mailman going to ring that bell this morning just like he done every morning for the last umpteen years.

(TRAVIS *comes in with the cleanser can*)

TRAVIS   She say to tell you that she don't have much.

MAMA   (*Angrily*)   Lord, some people I could name sure is tight-fisted! (*Directing her grandson*)   Mark two cans of cleanser down on the list there. If she that hard up for kitchen cleanser, I sure don't want to forget to get her none!

RUTH   Lena—maybe the woman is just short on cleanser—

MAMA   (*Not listening*)   —Much baking powder as she done borrowed from me all these years, she could of done gone into the baking business!

(*The bell sounds suddenly and sharply and all three are stunned—serious and silent—mid-speech. In spite of all the other conversations and distractions of the morning, this is what they have been waiting for, even* TRAVIS, *who looks helplessly from his mother to his grandmother.* RUTH *is the first to come to life again*)

RUTH   (*To* TRAVIS)   *Get down them steps, boy!*

(TRAVIS *snaps to life and flies out to get the mail*)

MAMA   (*Her eyes wide, her hand to her breast*)   You mean it done really come?

RUTH   (*Excited*)   Oh, Miss Lena!

MAMA   (*Collecting herself*)   Well . . . I don't know what we all so excited about 'round here for. We known it was coming for months.

142

RUTH   That's a whole lot different from having it come and
being able to hold it in your hands . . . a piece of paper
worth ten thousand dollars . . . (TRAVIS *bursts back
into the room. He holds the envelope high above his head,
like a little dancer, his face is radiant and he is breathless. He moves to his grandmother with sudden slow
ceremony and puts the envelope into her hands. She accepts it, and then merely holds it and looks at it*)   Come
on! Open it . . . Lord have mercy, I wish Walter Lee
was here!

TRAVIS   Open it, Grandmama!

MAMA (*Staring at it*)   Now you all be quiet. It's just a
check.

RUTH   Open it . . .

MAMA (*Still staring at it*)   Now don't act silly . . . We
ain't never been no people to act silly 'bout no money—

RUTH (*Swiftly*)   We ain't never had none before—*open
it!*

(MAMA *finally makes a good strong tear and pulls out
the thin blue slice of paper and inspects it closely. The
boy and his mother study it raptly over* MAMA'S *shoulders*)

MAMA   Travis! (*She is counting off with doubt*)   Is that
the right number of zeros.

TRAVIS   Yes'm . . . ten thousand dollars. Gaalee, Grandmama, you rich.

MAMA (*She holds the check away from her, still looking at
it. Slowly her face sobers into a mask of unhappiness*)
Ten thousand dollars. (*She hands it to* RUTH)   Put it
away somewhere, Ruth. (*She does not look at* RUTH;
*her eyes seem to be seeing something somewhere very
far off*)   Ten thousand dollars they give you. Ten thousand dollars.

TRAVIS (*To his mother, sincerely*)   What's the matter with
Grandmama—don't she want to be rich?

RUTH (*Distractedly*)   You go on out and play now, baby.

(TRAVIS *exits.* MAMA *starts wiping dishes absently, humming intently to herself.* RUTH *turns to her, with kind exasperation*)   You've gone and got yourself upset.

MAMA (*Not looking at her*)   I spec if it wasn't for you all . . . I would just put that money away or give it to the church or something.

RUTH   Now what kind of talk is that. Mr. Younger would just be plain mad if he could hear you talking foolish like that.

MAMA (*Stopping and staring off*)   Yes . . . he sure would. (*Sighing*)   We got enough to do with that money, all right. (*She halts then, and turn and looks at her daughter-in-law hard;* RUTH *avoids her eyes and* MAMA *wipes her hands with finality and starts to speak firmly to* RUTH)   Where did you go today, girl?

RUTH   To the doctor.

MAMA (*Impatiently*)   Now, Ruth . . . you know better than that. Old Doctor Jones is strange enough in his way but there ain't nothing 'bout him make somebody slip and call him "she"—like you done this morning.

RUTH   Well, that's what happened—my tongue slipped.

MAMA   You went to see that woman, didn't you?

RUTH (*Defensively, giving herself away*)   What woman you talking about?

MAMA (*Angrily*)   That woman who—
(WALTER *enters in great excitement*)

WALTER   Did it come?

MAMA (*Quietly*)   Can't you give people a Christian greeting before you start asking about money?

WALTER (*To* RUTH)   Did it come? (RUTH *unfolds the check and lays it quietly before him, watching him intently with thoughts of her own.* WALTER *sits down and grasps it close and counts off the zeros*)   Ten thousand dollars— (*He turns suddenly, frantically to his mother and draws some papers out of his breast pocket*)   Mama —look. Old Willy Harris put everything on paper—

144

MAMA Son—I think you ought to talk to your wife . . .
I'll go on out and leave you alone if you want—

WALTER I can talk to her later—Mama, look—

MAMA Son—

WALTER WILL SOMEBODY PLEASE LISTEN TO ME
TODAY!

MAMA (*Quietly*) I don't 'low no yellin' in this house,
Walter Lee, and you know it— (WALTER *stares at them
in frustration and starts to speak several times*) And
there ain't going to be no investing in no liquor stores. I
don't aim to have to speak on that again.
(*A long pause*)

WALTER Oh—so you don't aim to have to speak on that
again? So *you* have decided . . . (*Crumpling his papers*)
Well, *you* tell that to my boy tonight when you put him
to sleep on the living-room couch . . . (*Turning to*
MAMA *and speaking directly to her*) Yeah—and tell it
to my wife, Mama, tomorrow when she has to go out
of here to look after somebody else's kids. And tell it to
me, Mama, every time we need a new pair of curtains
and I have to watch *you* go out and work in somebody's
kitchen. Yeah, you tell me then!
(WALTER *starts out*)

RUTH Where you going?

WALTER I'm going out!

RUTH Where?

WALTER Just out of this house somewhere—

RUTH (*Getting her coat*) I'll come too.

WALTER I don't want you to come!

RUTH I got something to talk to you about, Walter.

WALTER That's too bad.

MAMA (*Still quietly*) Walter Lee— (*She waits and he
finally turns and looks at her*) Sit down.

WALTER I'm a grown man, Mama.

MAMA Ain't nobody said you wasn't grown. But you still

145

in my house and my presence. And as long as you are—
you'll talk to your wife civil. Now sit down.

RUTH (*Suddenly*)   Oh, let him go on out and drink himself to death! He makes me sick to my stomach! (*She
flings her coat against him*)

WALTER (*Violently*)   And you turn mine too, baby! (RUTH
goes into their bedroom and slams the door behind her)
That was my greatest mistake—

MAMA (*Still quietly*)   Walter, what is the matter with you?

WALTER   Matter with me? Ain't nothing the matter with
me!

MAMA·   Yes there is. Something eating you up like a crazy
man. Something more than me not giving you this money.
The past few years I been watching it happen to you.
You get all nervous acting and kind of wild in the eyes—
(WALTER *jumps up impatiently at her words*)   I said sit
there now, I'm talking to you!

WALTER   Mama—I don't need no nagging at me today.

MAMA   Seem like you getting to a place where you always
tied up in some kind of knot about something. But if
anybody ask you 'bout it you just yell at 'em and bust out
of the house and go out and drink somewheres. Walter
Lee, people can't live with that. Ruth's a good, patient
girl in her way—but your getting to be too much. Boy,
don't make the mistake of driving that girl away from
you.

WALTER   Why—what she do for me?

MAMA   She loves you.

WALTER   Mama—I'm going out. I want to go off somewhere and be by myself for a while.

MAMA   I'm sorry 'bout your liquor store, son. It just wasn't
the thing for us to do. That's what I want to tell you
about—

WALTER   I got to go out, Mama—
(*He rises*)

MAMA   It's dangerous, son.

146

WALTER   What's dangerous?

MAMA   When a man goes outside his home to look for peace.

WALTER (*Beseechingly*)   Then why can't there never be no peace in this house then?

MAMA   You done found it in some other house?

WALTER   No—there ain't no woman! Why do women always think there's a woman somewhere when a man gets restless (*Coming to her*)   Mama—Mama—I want so many things . . .

MAMA   Yes, son—

WALTER   I want so many things that they are driving me kind of crazy . . . Mama—look at me.

MAMA   I'm looking at you. You a good-looking boy. You got a job, a nice wife, a fine boy and—

WALTER   A job. (*Looks at her*)   Mama, a job? I open and close car doors all day long. I drive a man around in his limousine and I say, "Yes, sir; no, sir; very good, sir; shall I take the Drive, sir?" Mama, that ain't no kind of job . . . that ain't nothing at all. (*Very quietly*) Mama, I don't know if I can make you understand.

MAMA   Understand what, baby?

WALTER (*Quietly*)   Sometimes it's like I can see the future stretched out in front of me—just plain as day. The future, Mama. Hanging over there at the edge of my days. Just waiting for me—a big, looming blank space— full of *nothing*. Just waiting for *me*. (*Pause*)   Mama— sometimes when I'm downtown and I pass them cool, quiet-looking restaurants where them white boys are sitting back and talking 'bout things . . . sitting there turning deals worth millions of dollars . . . sometimes I see guys don't look much older than me—

MAMA   Son—how come you talk so much 'bout money?

WALTER (*With immense passion*)   Because it is life, Mama!

MAMA (*Quietly*)   Oh— (*Very quietly*)   So now it's life. Money is life. Once upon a time freedom used to be life

147

—now it's money. I guess the world really do change . . .

WALTER   No—it was always money, Mama. We just didn't know about it.

MAMA   No . . . something has changed. (*She looks at him*)   You something new, boy. In my time we was worried about not being lynched and getting to the North if we could and how to stay alive and still have a pinch of dignity too . . . Now here come you and Beneatha —talking 'bout things we ain't never even thought about hardly, me and your daddy. You ain't satisfied or proud of nothing we done. I mean that you had a home; that we kept you out of trouble till you was grown; that you don't have to ride to work on the back of nobody's street-car— You my children—but how different we done become.

WALTER   You just don't understand, Mama, you just don't understand.

MAMA   Son—do you know your wife is expecting another baby? (WALTER *stands, stunned, and absorbs what his mother has said*)   That's what she wanted to talk to you about. (WALTER *sinks down into a chair*)   This ain't for me to be telling—but you ought to know. (*She waits*) I think Ruth is thinking 'bout getting rid of that child.

WALTER (*Slowly understanding*)   No—no—Ruth wouldn't do that.

MAMA   When the world gets ugly enough—a woman will do anything for her family. *The part that's already living.*

WALTER   You don't know Ruth, Mama, if you think she would do that.

(RUTH *opens the bedroom door and stands there a little limp*)

RUTH (*Beaten*)   Yes I would too, Walter. (*Pause*)   I gave her a five-dollar down payment.

(*There is total silence as the man stares at his wife and the mother stares at her son*)

MAMA (*Presently*)   Well—(*Tightly*)   Well—son, I'm waiting to hear you say something . . . I'm waiting to hear how you be your father's son. Be the man he was . . . (*Pause*)   Your wife say she going to destroy your child. And I'm waiting to hear you talk like him and say we a people who give children life, not who destroys them— (*She rises*)   I'm waiting to see you stand up and look like your daddy and say we done give up one baby to poverty and that we ain't going to give up nary another one . . . I'm waiting.

WALTER   Ruth—

MAMA   If you a son of mine, tell her! (WALTER *turns, looks at her and can say nothing. She continues, bitterly*) You . . . you are a disgrace to your father's memory. Somebody get me my hat.

CURTAIN

ACT TWO

Scene One

Time: Later the same day.

    At rise: RUTH *is ironing again. She has the radio going. Presently* BENEATHA'S *bedroom door opens and* RUTH'S *mouth falls and she puts down the iron in fascination.*

RUTH   What have we got on tonight!

BENEATHA (*Emerging grandly from the doorway so that we can see her thoroughly robed in the costume Asagai brought*) You are looking at what a well-dressed Nigerian woman wears— (*She parades for* RUTH, *her hair completely hidden by the headdress; she is coquettishly fanning herself with an ornate oriental fan, mistakenly more like Butterfly than any Nigerian that ever was*) Isn't it beautiful? (*She promenades to the radio and, with an arrogant flourish, turns off the good loud blues that is playing*) Enough of this assimilationist junk! (RUTH *follows her with her eyes as she goes to the phonograph and puts on a record and turns and waits ceremoniously for the music to come up. Then, with a shout—*) OCOMOGOSIAY!

    (RUTH *jumps. The music comes up, a lovely Nigerian melody.* BENEATHA *listens, enraptured, her eyes far away —"back to the past." She begins to dance.* RUTH *is dumfounded*)

RUTH   What kind of dance is that?

BENEATHA   A folk dance.

RUTH (*Pearl Bailey*) What kind of folks do that, honey?

BENEATHA   It's from Nigeria. It's a dance of welcome.

RUTH   Who you welcoming?

BENEATHA   The men back to the village.

RUTH   Where they been?

BENEATHA   How should I know—out hunting or something. Anyway, they are coming back now . . .

RUTH   Well, that's good.

BENEATHA   (*With the record*)

Alundi, alundi
Alundi alunya
Jop pu a jeepua
Ang gu soooooooooo

Ai yai yae . . .
Ayehaye—alundi . . .

(WALTER *comes in during this performance; he has obviously been drinking. He leans against the door heavily and watches his sister, at first with distaste. Then his eyes look off—"back to the past"—as he lifts both his fists to the roof, screaming*)

WALTER   YEAH . . . AND ETHIOPIA STRETCH FORTH HER HANDS AGAIN! . . .

RUTH (*Drily, looking at him*)   Yes—and Africa sure is claiming her own tonight.

(*She gives them both up and starts ironing again*)

WALTER (*All in a drunken, dramatic shout*)   Shut up! . . . I'm digging them drums . . . them drums move me! . . . (*He makes his weaving way to his wife's face and leans in close to her*)   In my *heart of hearts*— (*He thumps his chest*)   —I am much warrior!

RUTH (*Without even looking up*)   In your heart of hearts you are much drunkard.

WALTER (*Coming away from her and starting to wander around the room, shouting*)   Me and Jomo . . . (*Intently, in his sister's face. She has stopped dancing to watch him in this unknown mood*)   That's my man,

Kenyatta. (*Shouting and thumping his chest*) FLAM-
ING SPEAR! HOT DAMN! (*He is suddenly in poses-
sion of an imaginary spear and actively spearing enemies all over the room*) OCOMOGOSIAY . . . THE
LION IS WAKING . . . OWIMOWEH! (*He pulls
his shirt open and leaps up on a table and gestures with
his spear. The bell rings.* RUTH *goes to answer*)

BENEATHA (*To encourage* WALTER, *thoroughly caught up
with this side of him*) *OCOMOGOSIAY, FLAMING
SPEAR!*

WALTER (*On the table, very far gone, his eyes pure glass
sheets. He sees what we cannot, that he is a leader of his
people, a great chief, a descendant of Chaka, and that the
hour to march has come*) Listen, my black brothers—

BENEATHA OCOMOGOSIAY!

WALTER —Do you hear the waters rushing against the
shores of the coastlands—

BENEATHA OCOMOGOSIAY!

WALTER —Do you hear the screeching of the cocks in
yonder hills beyond where the chiefs meet in council for
the coming of the mighty war—

BENEATHA OCOMOGOSIAY!

WALTER —Do you hear the beating of the wings of the
birds flying low over the mountains and the low places
of our land—

(RUTH *opens the door.* GEORGE MURCHISON *enters*)

BENEATHA OCOMOGOSIAY!

WALTER —Do you hear the singing of the women, singing
the war songs of our fathers to the babies in the great
houses . . . singing the sweet war songs? OH, DO YOU
HEAR, MY BLACK BROTHERS!

BENEATHA (*Completely gone*) We hear you, Flaming
Spear—

WALTER Telling us to prepare for the greatness of the
time—(*To* GEORGE) Black Brother!

(*He extends his hand for the fraternal clasp*)

A Raisin in the Sun

GEORGE   Black Brother, hell!

RUTH (*Having had enough, and embarrassed for the family*) Beneatha you got company—what's the matter with you? Walter Lee Younger, get down off that table and stop acting like a fool . . .

(WALTER *comes down off the table suddenly and makes a quick exit to the bathroom*)

RUTH   He's had a little to drink . . . I don't know what her excuse is.

GEORGE (*To* BENEATHA)   Look honey, we're going *to* the theatre—we're not going to be *in* it . . . so go change, huh?

RUTH   You expect this boy to go out with you looking like that?

BENEATHA (*Looking at* GEORGE)   That's up to George. If he's ashamed of his heritage—

GEORGE   Oh, don't be so proud of yourself, Bennie—just because you look eccentric.

BENEATHA   How can something that's natural be eccentric?

GEORGE   That's what being eccentric means—being natural. Get dressed.

BENEATHA   I don't like that, George.

RUTH   Why must you and your brother make an argument out of everything people say?

BENEATHA   Because I hate assimilationist Negroes!

RUTH   Will somebody please tell me what assimila-who-ever means!

GEORGE   Oh, it's just a college girl's way of calling people Uncle Toms—but that isn't what it means at all.

RUTH   Well, what does it mean?

BENEATHA (*Cutting* GEORGE *off and staring at him as she replies to* RUTH)   It means someone who is willing to give up his own culture and submerge himself completely in the dominant, and in this case, *oppressive* culture!

GEORGE   Oh, dear, dear, dear! Here we go! A lecture on
the African past! On our Great West African Heritage!
In one second we will hear all about the great Ashanti
empires; the great Songhay civilizations; and the great
sculpture of Bénin—and then some poetry in the Bantu
—and the whole monologue will end with the word
heritage! (*Nastily*)   Let's face it, baby, your heritage is
nothing but a bunch of raggedy-assed spirituals and some
grass huts!

BENEATHA   *Grass huts!* (RUTH *crosses to her and forcibly
pushes her toward the bedroom*)   See there . . . you
are standing there in your splendid ignorance talking
about people who were the first to smelt iron on the
face of the earth! (RUTH *is pushing her through the
door*)   The Ashanti were performing surgical opera-
tions when the English— (RUTH *pulls the door to, with*
BENEATHA *on the other side, and smiles graciously at*
GEORGE. BENEATHA *opens the door and shouts the end of
the sentence defiantly at* GEORGE)   —were still tatooing
themselves with blue dragons . . .
(*She goes back inside*)

RUTH   Have a seat, George. (*They both sit.* RUTH *folds
her hands rather primly on her lap, determined to dem-
onstrate the civilization of the family*)   Warm, ain't it?
I mean for September. (*Pause*)   Just like they always
say about Chicago weather: If it's too hot or cold for
you, just wait a minute and it'll change. (*She smiles happily at this cliché of clichés*)   Everybody say it's got to
do with them bombs and things they keep setting off.
(*Pause*)   Would you like a nice cold beer?

GEORGE   No, thank you. I don't care for beer. (*He looks
at his watch*)   I hope she hurries up.

RUTH   What time is the show?

GEORGE   It's an eight-thirty curtain. That's just Chicago,
though. In New York standard curtain time is eight
forty.

154

(*He is rather proud of this knowledge*)

RUTH (*Properly appreciating it*) You get to New York a lot?

GEORGE (*Offhand*) Few times a year.

RUTH Oh—that's nice. I've never been to New York. (WALTER *enters. We feel he has relieved himself, but the edge of unreality is still with him*)

WALTER New York ain't got nothing Chicago ain't. Just a bunch of hustling people all squeezed up together—being "Eastern."

(*He turns his face into a screw of displeasure*)

GEORGE Oh—you've been?

WALTER *Plenty* of times.

RUTH (*Shocked at the lie*) Walter Lee Younger!

WALTER (*Staring her down*) Plenty! (*Pause*) What we got to drink in this house? Why don't you offer this man some refreshment. (*To* GEORGE) They don't know how to entertain people in this house, man.

GEORGE Thank you—I don't really care for anything.

WALTER (*Feeling his head; sobriety coming*) Where's Mama?

RUTH She ain't come back yet.

WALTER (*Looking* MURCHISON *over from head to toe, scrutinizing his carefully casual tweed sports jacket over cashmere V-neck sweater over soft eyelet shirt and tie, and soft slacks, finished off with white buckskin shoes*) Why all you college boys wear them fairyish-looking white shoes?

RUTH Walter Lee!

(GEORGE MURCHISON *ignores the remark*)

WALTER (*To* RUTH) Well, they look crazy as hell—white shoes, cold as it is.

RUTH (*Crushed*) You have to excuse him—

WALTER No he don't! Excuse me for what? What you always excusing me for! I'll excuse myself when I needs to be excused! (*A pause*) They look as funny as them black knee socks Beneatha wears out of here all the time.

RUTH   It's the college *style,* Walter.

WALTER   Style, hell. She looks like she got burnt legs or something!

RUTH   Oh, Walter—

WALTER   (*An irritable mimic*)   Oh, Walter! Oh, Walter! (*To* MURCHISON)   How's your old man making out? I understand you all going to buy that big hotel on the Drive? (*He finds a beer in the refrigerator, wanders over to* MURCHISON, *sipping and wiping his lips with the back of his hand, and straddling a chair backwards to talk to the other man*)   Shrewd move. Your old man is all right, man. (*Tapping his head and half winking for emphasis*)   I mean he knows how to operate. I mean he thinks *big,* you know what I mean, I mean for a *home,* you know? But I think he's kind of running out of ideas now. I'd like to talk to him. Listen, man, I got some plans that could turn this city upside down. I mean I think like he does. *Big.* Invest big, gamble big, hell, lose *big* if you have to, you know what I mean. It's hard to find a man on this whole Southside who understands my kind of thinking—you dig? (*He scrutinizes* MUR-CHISON *again, drinks his beer, squints his eyes and leans in close, confidential, man to man*)   Me and you ought to sit down and talk sometimes, man. Man, I got me some ideas . . . ,

MURCHISON   (*With boredom*)   Yeah—sometimes we'll have to do that, Walter.

WALTER   (*Understanding the indifference, and offended*)   Yeah—well, when you get the time, man. I know you a busy little boy.

RUTH   Walter, please—

WALTER   (*Bitterly, hurt*)   I know ain't nothing in this world as busy as you colored college boys with your fraternity pins and white shoes . . .

156

RUTH (*Covering her face with humiliation*)   Oh, Walter
Lee—

WALTER   I see you all all the time—with the books tucked
under your arms—going to your (*British A—a mimic*)
"clahsses." And for what! What the hell you learning
over there? Filling up your heads— (*Counting off on his
fingers*)   —with the sociology and the psychology—but
they teaching you how to be a man? How to take over
and run the world? They teaching you how to run a rubber plantation or a steel mill? Naw—just to talk proper
and read books and wear white shoes . . .

GEORGE (*Looking at him with distaste, a little above it all*)
You're all wacked up with bitterness, man.

WALTER (*Intently, almost quietly, between the teeth, glar-
ing at the boy*)   And you—ain't you bitter, man? Ain't
you just about had it yet? Don't you see no stars gleam-
ing that you can't reach out and grab? You happy?—
you contented son-of-a-bitch—you happy? You got it
made? Bitter? Man, I'm a volcano. Bitter? Here I am a
giant—surrounded by ants! Ants who can't even understand what it is the giant is talking about.

RUTH (*Passionately and suddenly*)   Oh, Walter—ain't you
with nobody!

WALTER (*Violently*)   No! 'Cause ain't nobody with me!
Not even my own mother!

RUTH   Walter, that's a terrible thing to say!
   (BENEATHA *enters, dressed for the evening in a cocktail
   dress and earrings*)

GEORGE   Well—hey, you look great.

BENEATHA   Let's go, George. See you all later.

RUTH   Have a nice time.

GEORGE   Thanks. Good night. (*To* WALTER, *sarcastically*)
Good night, *Prometheus.*
   (BENEATHA *and* GEORGE *exit*)

WALTER (*To* RUTH)   Who is Prometheus?

RUTH   I don't know. Don't worry about it.

WALTER   (*In fury, pointing after* GEORGE)   See there—they get to a point where they can't insult you man to man— they got to go talk about something ain't nobody never heard of!

RUTH   How you know it was an insult? (*To humor him*) Maybe Prometheus is a nice fellow.

WALTER   Prometheus! I bet there ain't even no such thing! I bet that simple-minded clown—

RUTH   Walter—

(*She stops what she is doing and looks at him*)

WALTER   (*Yelling*)   Don't start!

RUTH   Start what?

WALTER   Your nagging! Where was I? Who was I with? How much money did I spend?

RUTH   (*Plaintively*)   Walter Lee—why don't we just try to talk about it . . .

WALTER   (*Not listening*)   I been out talking with people who understand me. People who care about the things I got on my mind.

RUTH   (*Wearily*)   I guess that means people like Willy Harris.

WALTER   Yes, people like Willy Harris.

RUTH   (*With a sudden flash of impatience*)   Why don't you all just hurry up and go into the banking business and stop talking about it!

WALTER   Why? You want to know why? 'Cause we all tied up in a race of people that don't know how to do nothing but moan, pray and have babies!

(*The line is too bitter even for him and he looks at her and sits down*)

RUTH   Oh, Walter . . . (*Softly*)   Honey, why can't you stop fighting me?

WALTER   (*Without thinking*)   Who's fighting you? Who even cares about you?

(*This line begins the retardation of his mood*)

RUTH Well— (*She waits a long time, and then with resignation starts to put away her things*) I guess I might as well go on to bed . . . (*More or less to herself*) I don't know where we lost it . . . but we have . . . (*Then, to him*) I—I'm sorry about this new baby, Walter. I guess maybe I better go on and do what I started . . . I guess I just didn't realize how bad things was with us . . . I guess I just didn't really realize— (*She starts out to the bedroom and stops*) You want some hot milk?

WALTER Hot milk?

RUTH Yes—hot milk.

WALTER Why hot milk?

RUTH 'Cause after all that liquor you come home with you ought to have something hot in your stomach.

WALTER I don't want no milk.

RUTH You want some coffee then?

WALTER No, I don't want no coffee. I don't want nothing hot to drink. (*Almost plaintively*) Why you always trying to give me something to eat?

RUTH (*Standing and looking at him helplessly*) What else can I give you, Walter Lee Younger?
(*She stands and looks at him and presently turns to go out again. He lifts his head and watches her going away from him in a new mood which began to emerge when he asked her "Who cares about you?"*)

WALTER It's been rough, ain't it, baby? (*She hears and stops but does not turn around and he continues to her back*) I guess between two people there ain't never as much understood as folks generally thinks there is. I mean like between me and you— (*She turns to face him*) How we gets to the place where we scared to talk softness to each other. (*He waits, thinking hard himself*) Why you think it got to be like that? (*He is thoughtful, almost as a child would be*) Ruth, what is it gets into people ought to be close?

159

RUTH   I don't know, honey. I think about it a lot.

WALTER   On account of you and me, you mean? The way things are with us. The way something done come down between us.

RUTH   There ain't so much between us, Walter . . . Not when you come to me and try to talk to me. Try to be with me . . . a little even.

WALTER (*Total honesty*) Sometimes . . . sometimes . . . I don't even know how to try.

RUTH   Walter—

WALTER   Yes?

RUTH (*Coming to him, gently and with misgiving, but coming to him*) Honey . . . life don't have to be like this. I mean sometimes people can do things so that things are better . . . You remember how we used to talk when Travis was born . . . about the way we were going to live . . . the kind of house . . . (*She is stroking his head*) Well, it's all starting to slip away from us . . .

(MAMA *enters, and* WALTER *jumps up and shouts at her*)

WALTER   Mama, where have you been?

MAMA   My—them steps is longer than they used to be. Whew! (*She sits down and ignores him*) How you feeling this evening, Ruth?

(RUTH *shrugs, disturbed some at having been prematurely interrupted and watching her husband knowingly*)

WALTER   Mama, where have you been all day?

MAMA (*Still ignoring him and leaning on the table and changing to more comfortable shoes*) Where's Travis?

RUTH   I let him go out earlier and he ain't come back yet. Boy, is he going to get it!

WALTER   Mama!

MAMA (*As if she has heard him for the first time*) Yes, son?

WALTER   Where did you go this afternoon?

MAMA   I went down town to tend to some business that I had to tend to.

WALTER   What kind of business?

MAMA   You know better than to question me like a child, Brother.

WALTER   (*Rising and bending over the table*)   Where were you, Mama? (*Bringing his fists down and shouting*) Mama, you didn't go do something with that insurance money, something crazy?

(*The front door opens slowly, interrupting him, and* TRAVIS *peeks his head in, less than hopefully*)

TRAVIS   (*To his mother*)   Mama, I—

RUTH   "Mama I" nothing! You're going to get it, boy! Get on in that bedroom and get yourself ready!

TRAVIS   But I—

MAMA   Why don't you all never let the child explain himself.

RUTH   Keep out of it now, Lena.

(MAMA *clamps her lips together, and* RUTH *advances toward her son menacingly*)

RUTH   A thousand times I have told you not to go off like that—

MAMA   (*Holding out her arms to her grandson*)   Well—at least let me tell him something. I want him to be the first one to hear . . . Come here, Travis. (*The boy obeys, gladly*) Travis— (*She takes him by the shoulders and looks into his face*)   —you know that money we got in the mail this morning?

TRAVIS   Yes'm—

MAMA   Well—what you think your grandmama gone and done with that money?

TRAVIS   I don't know, Grandmama.

MAMA   (*Putting her finger on his nose for emphasis*)   She went out and she bought you a house! (*The explosion comes from* WALTER *at the end of the revelation and he*

161

jumps up and turns away from all of them in a fury.
MAMA *continues, to* TRAVIS) You glad about the house?
It's going to be yours when you get to be a man.

TRAVIS Yeah—I always wanted to live in a house.

MAMA All right, gimme some sugar then— (TRAVIS *puts
his arms around her neck as she watches her son over
the boy's shoulder. Then, to* TRAVIS, *after the embrace*)
Now when you say your prayers tonight, you thank God
and your grandfather—'cause it was him who give you
the house—in his way.

RUTH (*Taking the boy from* MAMA *and pushing him toward the bedroom*) Now you get out of here and get
ready for your beating.

TRAVIS Aw, Mama—

RUTH Get on in there— (*Closing the door behind him
and turning radiantly to her mother-in-law*) So you
went and did it!

MAMA (*Quietly, looking at her son with pain*) Yes, I did.

RUTH (*Raising both arms classically*) Praise God!
(*Looks at* WALTER *a moment, who says nothing. She
crosses rapidly to her husband*) Please, honey—let me
be glad . . . you be glad too. (*She has laid her hands
on his shoulders, but he shakes himself free of her
roughly, without turning to face her*) Oh, Walter . . .
a home . . . *a home.* (*She comes back to* MAMA)
Well—where is it? How big is it? How much it going to
cost?

MAMA Well—

RUTH When we moving?

MAMA (*Smiling at her*) First of the month.

RUTH (*Throwing back her head with jubilance*) Praise
God!

MAMA (*Tentatively, still looking at her son's back turned
against her and* RUTH) It's—it's a nice house too . . .
(*She cannot help speaking directly to him. An imploring
quality in her voice, her manner, makes her almost like*

162

a girl now) Three bedrooms—nice big one for you and Ruth. . . . Me and Beneatha still have to share our room, but Travis have one of his own—and— (*With difficulty*) I figures if the—new baby—is a boy, we could get one of them double-decker outfits . . . And there's a yard with a little patch of dirt where I could maybe get to grow me a few flowers . . . And a nice big basement . . .

RUTH Walter honey, be glad—

MAMA (*Still to his back, fingering things on the table*) 'Course I don't want to make it sound fancier than it is . . . It's just a plain little old house—but it's made good and solid—and it will be *ours*. Walter Lee—it makes a difference in a man when he can walk on floors that belong to *him* . . .

RUTH Where is it?

MAMA (*Frightened at this telling*) Well—well—it's out there in Clybourne Park—

(RUTH's *radiance fades abruptly, and* WALTER *finally turns slowly to face his mother with incredulity and hostility*)

RUTH Where?

MAMA (*Matter-of-factly*) Four o six Clybourne Street, Clybourne Park.

RUTH Clybourne Park? Mama, there ain't no colored people living in Clybourne Park.

MAMA (*Almost idiotically*) Well, I guess there's going to be some now.

WALTER (*Bitterly*) So that's the peace and comfort you went out and bought for us today!

MAMA (*Raising her eyes to meet his finally*) Son—I just tried to find the nicest place for the least amount of money for my family.

RUTH (*Trying to recover from the shock*) Well—well—'course I ain't one never been 'fraid of no crackers, mind you—but—well, wasn't there no other houses nowhere?

MAMA   Them houses they put up for colored in them areas way out all seem to cost twice as much as other houses. I did the best I could.

RUTH   (*Struck senseless with the news, in its various degrees of goodness and trouble, she sits a moment, her fists propping her chin in thought, and then she starts to rise, bringing her fists down with vigor, the radiance spreading from cheek to cheek again*)   Well—well!— All I can say is—if this is my time in life—*my time*—to say good-bye— (*And she builds with momentum as she starts to circle the room with an exuberant, almost tearfully happy release*)   —to these Goddamned cracking walls!— (*She pounds the walls*)   and these marching roaches!— (*She wipes at an imaginary army of marching roaches*)   —and this cramped little closet which ain't now or never was no kitchen! . . . then I say it loud and good, *Hallelujah! and good-bye misery . . . I don't never want to see your ugly face again!* (*She laughs joyously, having practically destroyed the apartment, and flings her arms up and lets them come down happily, slowly, reflectively, over her abdomen, aware for the first time perhaps that the life therein pulses with happiness and not despair*)   Lena?

MAMA   (*Moved, watching her happiness*)   Yes, honey?

RUTH   (*Looking off*)   Is there—is there a whole lot of sunlight?

MAMA   (*Understanding*)   Yes, child, there's a whole lot of sunlight.

(*Long pause*)

RUTH   (*Collecting herself and going to the door of the room* TRAVIS *is in*)   Well—I guess I better see 'bout Travis. (*To* MAMA)   Lord, I sure don't feel like whipping nobody today!

(*She exits*)

MAMA   (*The mother and son are left alone now and the mother waits a long time, considering deeply, before she speaks*)   Son—you—you understand what I done, **don't** you? (WALTER *is silent and sullen*)   I—I just seen my family falling apart today . . . just falling to pieces in front of my eyes . . . We couldn't of gone on like we was today. We was going backwards 'stead of forwards— talking 'bout killing babies and wishing each other was dead . . . When it gets like that in life—you just got to do something different, push on out and do something bigger . . . (*She waits*)   I wish you say something, son . . . I wish you'd say how deep inside you you think I done the right thing—

WALTER (*Crossing slowly to his bedroom door and finally turning there and speaking measuredly*)   What you need me to say you done right for? *You* the head of this family. You run our lives like you want to. It was your money and you did what you wanted with it. So what you need for me to say it was all right for? (*Bitterly, to hurt her as deeply as he knows is possible*)   So you butchered up a dream of mine—you—who always talk- ing 'bout your children's dreams . . .

MAMA   Walter Lee—

(*He just closes the door behind him.* MAMA *sits alone, thinking heavily*)

CURTAIN

Scene Two

Time: Friday night. A few weeks later.

   At rise: Packing crates mark the intention of the family to move. BENEATHA *and* GEORGE *come in, presumably from an evening out again.*

GEORGE   O.K. . . . O.K., whatever you say . . . (*They both sit on the couch. He tries to kiss her. She moves away*)   Look, we've had a nice evening; let's not spoil it, huh? . . .

(*He again turns her head and tries to nuzzle in and she turns away from him, not with distaste but with momentary lack of interest; in a mood to pursue what they were talking about*)

BENEATHA   I'm *trying* to talk to you.

GEORGE   We always talk.

BENEATHA   Yes—and I love to talk.

GEORGE   (*Exasperated; rising*)   I know it and I don't mind it sometimes . . . I want you to cut it out, see—The moody stuff, I mean. I don't like it. You're a nice-looking girl . . . all over. That's all you need, honey, forget the atmosphere. Guys aren't going to go for the atmosphere —they're going to go for what they see. Be glad for that. Drop the Garbo routine. It doesn't go with you. As for myself, I want a nice— (*Groping*) —simple— (*Thoughtfully*) —sophisticated girl . . . not a poet— O.K.?

(*She rebuffs him again and he starts to leave*)

BENEATHA   Why are you angry?

GEORGE   Because this is stupid! I don't go out with you to discuss the nature of "quiet desperation" or to hear all about your thoughts—because the world will ·go on thinking what it thinks regardless—

BENEATHA   Then why read books? Why go to school?

GEORGE   (*With artificial patience, counting on his fingers*)   It's simple. You read books—to learn facts—to get grades—to pass the course—to get a degree. That's all— it has nothing to do with thoughts.

(*A long pause*)

BENEATHA   I see. (*A longer pause as she looks at him*) Good night, George.

(GEORGE *looks at her a little oddly, and starts to exit. He meets* MAMA *coming in*)

GEORGE Oh—hello, Mrs. Younger.

MAMA Hello, George, how you feeling?

GEORGE Fine—fine, how are you?

MAMA Oh, a little tired. You know them steps can get you after a day's work. You all have a nice time tonight?

GEORGE Yes—a fine time. Well, good night.

MAMA Good night. (*He exits.* MAMA *closes the door behind her*) Hello, honey. What you sitting like that for?

BENEATHA I'm just sitting.

MAMA Didn't you have a nice time?

BENEATHA No.

MAMA No? What's the matter?

BENEATHA Mama, George is a fool—honest. (*She rises*)

MAMA (*Hustling around unloading the packages she has entered with. She stops*) Is he, baby?

BENEATHA Yes.

(BENEATHA *makes up* TRAVIS' *bed as she talks*)

MAMA You sure?

BENEATHA Yes.

MAMA Well—I guess you better not waste your time with no fools.

(BENEATHA *looks up at her mother, watching her put groceries in the refrigerator. Fnally she gathers up her things and starts into the bedroom. At the door she stops and looks at her mother*)

BENEATHA Mama—

MAMA Yes, baby—

BENEATHA Thank you.

MAMA For what?

BENEATHA For understanding me this time.

(*She exits quickly and the mother stands, smiling a little, looking at the place where* BENEATHA *just stood.* RUTH *enters*)

RUTH Now don't you fool with any of this stuff, Lena—
MAMA Oh, I just thought I'd sort a few things out.

(*The phone rings.* RUTH *answers*)

RUTH (*At the phone*) Hello—Just a minute. (*Goes to door*) Walter, it's Mrs. Arnold. (*Waits. Goes back to the phone. Tense*) Hello. Yes, this is his wife speaking . . . He's lying down now. Yes . . . well, he'll be in tomorrow. He's been very sick. Yes—I know we should have called, but we were so sure he'd be able to come in today. Yes—yes, I'm very sorry. Yes . . . Thank you very much. (*She hangs up.* WALTER *is standing in the doorway of the bedroom behind her*) That was Mrs. Arnold.

WALTER (*Indifferently*) Was it?

RUTH She said if you don't come in tomorrow that they are getting a new man . . .

WALTER Ain't that sad—ain't that crying sad.

RUTH She said Mr. Arnold has had to take a cab for three days . . . Walter, you ain't been to work for three days! (*This is a revelation to her*) Where you been, Walter Lee Younger? (WALTER *looks at her and starts to laugh*) You're going to lose your job.

WALTER That's right . . .

RUTH Oh, Walter, and with your mother working like a dog every day—

WALTER That's sad too—Everything is sad.

MAMA What you been doing for these three days, son?

WALTER Mama—you don't know all the things a man what got leisure can find to do in this city . . . What's this—Friday night? Well—Wednesday I borrowed Willy Harris' car and I went for a drive . . . just me and myself and I drove and drove . . . Way out . . . way past South Chicago, and I parked the car and I sat and looked at the steel mills all day long. I just sat in the car and looked at them big black chimneys for hours. Then I drove back and I went to the Green Hat. (*Pause*) And

Thursday—Thursday I borrowed the car again and I got in it and I pointed it the other way and I drove the other way—for hours—way, way up to Wisconsin, and I looked at the farms. I just drove and looked at the farms. Then I drove back and I went to the Green Hat. (*Pause*) And today—today I didn't get the car. Today I just walked. All over the Southside. And I looked at the Negroes and they looked at me and finally I just sat down on the curb at Thirty-ninth and South Parkway and I just sat there and watched the Negroes go by. And then I went to the Green Hat. You all sad? You all depressed? And you know where I am going right now— (RUTH *goes out quietly*)

MAMA   Oh, Big Walter, is this the harvest of our days?

WALTER   You know what I like about the Green Hat? (*He turns the radio on and a steamy, deep blues pours into the room*)   I like this little cat they got there who blows a sax . . . He blows. He talks to me. He ain't but 'bout five feet tall and he's got a conked head and his eyes is always closed and he's all music—

MAMA (*Rising and getting some papers out of her hand-bag*)   Walter—

WALTER   And there's this other guy who plays the piano . . . and they got a sound. I mean they can work on some music . . . They got the best little combo in the world in the Green Hat . . . You can just sit there and drink and listen to them three men play and you realize that don't nothing matter worth a damn, but just being there—

MAMA   I've helped do it to you, haven't I, son? Walter, I been wrong.

WALTER   Naw—you ain't never been wrong about nothing, Mama.

MAMA   Listen to me, now. I say I been wrong, son. That I been doing to you what the rest of the world been doing to you. (*She stops and he looks up slowly at her and she*

169

meets his eyes pleadingly) Walter—what you ain't never understood is that I ain't got nothing, don't own nothing, ain't never really wanted nothing that wasn't for you. There ain't nothing as precious to me . . . There ain't nothing worth holding on to, money, dreams, nothing else—if it means—if it means it's going to destroy my boy. (*She puts her papers in front of him and he watches her without speaking or moving*) I paid the man thirty-five hundred dollars down on the house. That leaves sixty-five hundred dollars. Monday morning I want you to take this money and take three thousand dollars and put it in a savings account for Beneatha's medical schooling. The rest you put in a checking account—with your name on it. And from now on any penny that comes out of it or that go in it is for you to look after. For you to decide. (*She drops her hands a little helplessly*) It ain't much, but it's all I got in the world and I'm putting in your hands. I'm telling you to be the head of this family from now on like you supposed to be.

WALTER (*Stares at the money*) You trust me like that, Mama?

MAMA I ain't never stop trusting you. Like I ain't never stop loving you.

(*She goes out, and* WALTER *sits looking at the money on the table as the music continues in its idiom, pulsing in the room. Finally, in a decisive gesture, he gets up and, in a furious action, flings the bedclothes wildly from his son's makeshift bed to all over the floor—with a cry of desperation. Then he picks up the money and goes out in a hurry*)

CURTAIN

Scene Three

Time: Saturday, moving day, one week later.

Before the curtain rises, RUTH'S *voice, a strident, dramatic church alto, cuts through the silence.*

It is, in the darkness, a triumphant surge, a penetrating statement of expectation: "Oh, Lord, I don't feel no ways tired! Children, oh, glory halleujah!"

As the curtain rises we see that RUTH *is alone in the living room, finishing up the family's packing. It is moving day. She is nailing crates and tying cartons.* BENEATHA *enters, carrying a guitar case, and watches her exuberant sister-in-law.*

RUTH Hey!

BENEATHA (*Putting away the case*) Hi.

RUTH (*Pointing at a package*) Honey—look in that package there and see what I found on sale this morning at the South Center. (RUTH *gets up and moves to the package and draws out some curtains*) Lookahere—hand-turned hems!

BENEATHA How do you know the window size out there?

RUTH (*Who hadn't thought of that*) Oh—Well, they bound to fit something in the whole house. Anyhow, they was too good a bargain to pass us. (RUTH *slaps her head, suddenly remembering something*) Oh, Bennie—I meant to put a special note on that carton over there. That's your mama's good china and she wants 'em to be very careful with it.

BENEATHA I'll do it.

(BENEATHA *finds a piece of paper and starts to draw large letters on it*)

RUTH You know what I'm going to do soon as I get in that new house?

BENEATHA What?

RUTH Honey—I'm going to run me a tub of water up to here . . . (*With her fingers practically up to her nostrils*) And I'm going to get in it—and I am going to sit . . . and sit . . . and sit in that hot water and the first person who knocks to tell *me* to hurry up and come out—

BENEATHA Gets shot at sunrise.

RUTH (*Laughing happily*) You said it, sister! (*Noticing how large* BENEATHA *is absent-mindedly making the note*) Honey, they ain't going to read that from no airplane.

BENEATHA (*Laughing herself*) I guess I always think things have more emphasis if they are big, somehow.

RUTH (*Looking up at her and smiling*) You and your brother seem to have that as a philosophy of life. Lord, that man—done changed so 'round here. You know—you know what we did last night? Me and Walter Lee?

BENEATHA What?

RUTH (*Smiling to herself*) We went to the movies. (*Looking at* BENEATHA *to see if she understands*) We went to the movies. You know the last time me and Walter went to the movies together?

BENEATHA No.

RUTH Me neither. That's how long it been. (*Smiling again*) But we went last night. The picture wasn't much good, but that didn't seem to matter. We went— and we held hands.

BENEATHA Oh, Lord!

RUTH We held hands—and you know what?

BENEATHA What?

RUTH When we come out of the show it was late and dark

172

and all the stores and things was closed up . . . and it was kind of chilly and there wasn't many people on the streets . . . and we was still holding hands, me and Walter.

BENEATHA   You're killing me.

(WALTER *enters with a large package. His happiness is deep in him; he cannot keep still with his new-found exuberance. He is singing and wiggling and snapping his fingers. He puts his package in a corner and puts a phonograph record, which he has brought in with him, on the record player. As the music comes up he dances over to* RUTH *and tries to get her to dance with him. She gives in at last to his raunchiness and in a fit of giggling allows herself to be drawn into his mood and together they deliberately burlesque an old social dance of their youth*)

BENEATHA   (*Regarding them a long time as they dance, then drawing in her breath for a deeply exaggerated comment which she does not particularly mean*)   Talk about—olddddddddddd-fashioneddddddddd—Negroes!

WALTER   (*Stopping momentarily*)   What kind of Negroes? (*He says this in fun. He is not angry with her today, nor with anyone. He starts to dance with his wife again*)

BENEATHA   Old-fashioned.

WALTER   (*As he dances with* RUTH)   You know, when these *New Negroes* have their convention— (*Pointing at his sister*)   —that is going to be the chairman of the Committee on Unending Agitation. (*He goes on dancing, then stops*)   Race, race, race! . . . Girl, I do believe you are the first person in the history of the entire human race to successfully brainwash yourself. (BENEATHA *breaks up and he goes on dancing. He stops again, enjoying his tease*)   Damn, even the N double A C P takes a holiday sometimes! (BENEATHA *and* RUTH *laugh. He dances with* RUTH *some more and starts to laugh and stops and pantomimes someone over an oper-*

ating table)   I can just see that chick someday looking down at some poor cat on an operating table before she starts to slice him, saying . . . (*Pulling his sleeves back maliciously*)   "By the way, what are your views on civil rights down there? . . ."

(*He laughs at her again and starts to dance happily. The bell sounds*)

BENEATHA   Sticks and stones may break my bones but . . . words will never hurt me!

(BENEATHA *goes to the door and opens it as* WALTER *and* RUTH *go on with the clowning.* BENEATHA *is somewhat surprised to see a quiet-looking middle-aged white man in a business suit holding his hat and a briefcase in his hand and consulting a small piece of paper*)

MAN   Uh—how do you do, miss. I am looking for a Mrs.— (*He looks at the slip of paper*)   Mrs. Lena Younger?

BENEATHA   (*Smoothing her hair with slight embarrassment*) Oh—yes, that's my mother. Excuse me. (*She closes the door and turns to quiet the other two*)   Ruth! Brother! Somebody's here. (*Then she opens the door. The man casts a curious quick glance at all of them*)   Uh—come in please.

MAN   (*Coming in*)   Thank you.

BENEATHA   My mother isn't here just now. Is it business?

MAN   Yes . . . well, of a sort.

WALTER   (*Freely, the Man of the House*)   Have a seat. I'm Mrs. Younger's son. I look after most of her business matters.

(RUTH *and* BENEATHA *exchange amused glances*)

MAN   (*Regarding* WALTER, *and sitting*)   Well—My name is Karl Lindner . . .

WALTER   (*Stretching out his hand*)   Walter Younger. This is my wife— (RUTH *nods politely*)   —and my sister.

LINDNER   How do you do.

WALTER   (*Amiably, as he sits himself easily on a chair,*

leaning with interest forward on his knees and looking expectantly into the newcomer's face) What can we do for you, Mr. Lindner!

LINDNER (*Some minor shuffling of the hat and briefcase on his knees*) Well—I am a representative of the Clybourne Park Improvement Association—

WALTER (*Pointing*) Why don't you sit your things on the floor?

LINDNER Oh—yes. Thank you. (*He slides the briefcase and hat under the chair*) And as I was saying—I am from the Clybourne Park Improvement Association and we have had it brought to our attention at the last meeting that you people—or at least your mother—has bought a piece of residential property at— (*He digs for the slip of paper again*) —four o six Clybourne Street . . .

WALTER That's right. Care for something to drink? Ruth, get Mr. Lindner a beer.

LINDNER (*Upset for some reason*) Oh—no, really. I mean thank you very much, but no thank you.

RUTH (*Innocently*) Some coffee?

LINDNER Thank you, nothing at all.

(BENEATHA *is watching the man carefully*)

LINDNER Well, I don't know how much you folks know about our organization. (*He is a gentle man; thoughtful and somewhat labored in his manner*) It is one of these community organizations set up to look after—oh, you know, things like block upkeep and special projects and we also have what we call our New Neighbors Orientation Committee . . .

BENEATHA (*Drily*) Yes—and what do they do?

LINDNER (*Turning a little to her and then returning the main force to* WALTER) Well—it's what you might call a sort of welcoming committee, I guess. I mean they, we, I'm the chairman of the committee—go around and see the new people who move into the neighborhood and

sort of give them the lowdown on the way we do things
out in Clybourne Park.

BENEATHA (*With appreciation of the two meanings, which
escape* RUTH *and* WALTER)   Un-huh.

LINDNER   And we also have the category of what the
association calls— (*He looks elsewhere*)   —uh—special community problems . . .

BENEATHA   Yes—and what are some of those?

WALTER   Girl, let the man talk.

LINDNER (*With understated relief*)   Thank you. I would
sort of like to explain this thing in my own way. I mean
I want to explain to you in a certain way.

WALTER   Go ahead.

LINDNER   Yes. Well. I'm going to try to get right to the
point. I'm sure we'll all appreciate that in the long run.

BENEATHA   Yes.

WALTER   Be still now!

LINDNER   Well—

RUTH (*Still innocently*)   Would you like another chair—
you don't look comfortable.

LINDNER (*More frustrated than annoyed*)   No, thank you
very much. Please. Well—to get right to the point I—
(*A great breath, and he is off at last*)   I am sure you
people must be aware of some of the incidents which
have happened in various parts of the city when colored
people have moved into certain areas— (BENEATHA *ex-
hales heavily and starts tossing a piece of fruit up and
down in the air*)   Well—because we have what I think
is going to be a unique type of organization in American
community life—not only do we deplore that kind of
thing—but we are trying to do something about it.
(BENEATHA *stops tossing and turns with a new and
quizzical interest to the man*)   We feel— (*gaining con-
fidence in his mission because of the interest in the faces
of the people he is talking to*)   —we feel that most of
the trouble in this world, when you come right down to

it— (*He hits his knee for emphasis*) —most of the trouble exists because people just don't sit down and talk to each other.

RUTH (*Nodding as she might in church, pleased with the remark*) You can say that again, mister.

LINDNER (*More encouraged by such affirmation*) That we don't try hard enough in this world to understand the other fellow's problem. The other guy's point of view.

RUTH Now that's right.

(BENEATHA *and* WALTER *merely watch and listen with genuine interest*)

LINDNER Yes—that's the way we feel out in Clybourne Park. And that's why I was elected to come here this afternoon and talk to you people. Friendly like, you know, the way people should talk to each other and see if we couldn't find some way to work this thing out. As I say, the whole business is a matter of *caring* about the other fellow. Anybody can see that you are a nice family of folks, hard working and honest I'm sure. (BENEATHA *frowns slightly, quizzically, her head tilted regarding him*) Today everybody knows what it means to be on the outside of *something*. And of course, there is always somebody who is out to take the advantage of people who don't always understand.

WALTER What do you mean?

LINDNER Well—you see our community is made up of people who've worked hard as the dickens for years to build up that little community. They're not rich and fancy people; just hard-working, honest people who don't really have much but those little homes and a dream of the kind of community they want to raise their children in. Now, I don't say we are perfect and there is a lot wrong in some of the things they want. But you've got to admit that a man, right or wrong, has the right to want to have the neighborhood he lives in a certain kind of way. And at the moment the overwhelming majority of our people out there feel that people get along better, take more of a common interest in the life of the community, when they share a common background. I want you to believe me when I tell you that race prejudice simply doesn't enter into it. It is a matter of the people of Clybourne Park believing, rightly or wrongly, as I say, that for the happiness of all concerned that our Negro families are happier when they live in their *own* communities.

BENEATHA (*With a grand and bitter gesture*) This, friends, is the Welcoming Committee!

WALTER (*Dumfounded, looking at* LINDNER) Is this what you came marching all the way over here to tell us?

LINDNER Well, now we've been having a fine conversation. I hope you'll hear me all the way through.

WALTER (*Tightly*) Go ahead, man.

LINDNER You see—in the face of all things I have said, we are prepared to make your family a very generous offer . . .

BENEATHA Thirty pieces and not a coin less!

WALTER Yeah?

LINDNER (*Putting on his glasses and drawing a form out of the briefcase*) Our association is prepared, through the collective effort of our people, to buy the house from you at a financial gain to your family.

RUTH Lord have mercy, ain't this the living gall!

WALTER All right, you through?

LINDNER Well, I want to give you the exact terms of the financial arrangement—

WALTER We don't want to hear no exact terms of no arrangements. I want to know if you got any more to tell us 'bout getting together?

LINDNER (*Taking off his glasses*) Well—I don't suppose that you feel . . .

WALTER Never mind how I feel—you got any more to

say 'bout how people ought to sit down and talk to each other? . . . Get out of my house, man.

(*He turns his back and walks to the door*)

LINDNER (*Looking around at the hostile faces and reaching and assembling his hat and briefcase*) Well—I don't understand why you people are reacting this way. What do you think you are going to gain by moving into a neighborhood where you just aren't wanted and where some elements—well—people can get awful worked up when they feel that their whole way of life and everything they've ever worked for is threatened.

WALTER Get out.

LINDNER (*At the door, holding a small card*) Well—I'm sorry it went like this.

WALTER Get out.

LINDNER (*Almost sadly regarding* WALTER) You just can't force people to change their hearts, son.

(*He turns and puts his card on a table and exits.* WALTER *pushes the door to with stinging hatred, and stands looking at it.* RUTH *just sits and* BENEATHA *just stands. They say nothing.* MAMA *and* TRAVIS *enter*)

MAMA Well—this all the packing got done since I left out of here this morning. I testify before God that my children got all the energy of the dead. What time the moving men due?

BENEATHA Four o'clock. You had a caller, Mama.

(*She is smiling, teasingly*)

MAMA Sure enough—who?

BENEATHA (*Her arms folded saucily*) The Welcoming Committee.

(WALTER *and* RUTH *giggle*)

MAMA (*Innocently*) Who?

BENEATHA The Welcoming Committee. They said they're sure going to be glad to see you when you get there.

WALTER (*Devilishly*) Yeah, they said they can't hardly wait to see your face.

(*Laughter*)

MAMA (*Sensing their facetiousness*) What's the matter with you all?

WALTER Ain't nothing the matter with us. We just telling you 'bout the gentleman who came to see you this afternoon. From the Clybourne Park Improvement Association.

MAMA What he want?

RUTH (*In the same mood as* BENEATHA *and* WALTER) To welcome you, honey.

WALTER He said they can't hardly wait. He said the one thing they don't have, that they just *dying* to have out there is a fine family of colored people! (*To* RUTH *and* BENEATHA) Ain't that right!

RUTH *and* BENEATHA (*Mockingly*) Yeah! He left his card in case—

(*They indicate the card, and* MAMA *picks it up and throws it on the floor—understanding and looking off as she draws her chair up to the table on which she has put her plant and some sticks and some cord*)

MAMA Father, give us strength. (*Knowingly—and without fun*) Did he threaten us?

BENEATHA Oh—Mama—they don't do it like that any more. He talked Brotherhood. He said everybody ought learn how to sit down and hate each other with good Christian fellowship.

(*She and* WALTER *shake hands to ridicule the remark*)

MAMA (*Sadly*) Lord, protect us . . .

RUTH You should hear the money those folks raised to buy the house from us. All we paid and then some.

BENEATHA What they think we going to do—eat 'em?

RUTH No, honey, marry 'em.

MAMA (*Shaking her head*) Lord, Lord, Lord . . .

RUTH Well—that's the way the crackers crumble. Joke.

BENEATHA (*Laughingly noticing what her mother is doing*) Mama, what are you doing?

MAMA   Fixing my plant so it won't get hurt none on the way . . .

BENEATHA   Mama, you going to take *that* to the new house?

MAMA   Un-huh—

BENEATHA   That raggedy-looking old thing?

MAMA (*Stopping and looking at her*)   It expresses *me*.

RUTH (*With delight, to* BENEATHA)   So there, Miss Thing! (WALTER *comes to* MAMA *suddenly and bends down behind her and squeezes her in his arms with all his strength. She is overwhelmed by the suddenness of it and, though delighted, her manner is like that of* RUTH *with* TRAVIS)

MAMA   Look out now, boy! You make me mess up my thing here!

WALTER (*His face lit, he slips down on his knees beside her, his arms still about he*r)   Mama . . . you know what it means to climb up in the chariot?

MAMA (*Gruffly, very happy*)   Get on away from me now . . .

RUTH (*Near the gift-wrapped package, trying to catch* WALTER'S *eye*)   Psst—

WALTER   What the old song say, Mama . . .

RUTH   Walter—Now?
(*She is pointing at the package*)

WALTER (*Speaking the lines, sweetly, playfully, in his mother's face*)
I got wings . . . you got wings . . .
All God's children got wings . . .

MAMA   Boy—get out of my face and do some work . . .

WALTER
When I get to heaven gonna put on my wings,
Gonna fly all over God's heaven . . .

BENEATHA (*Teasingly, from across the room*)   Everybody talking 'bout heaven ain't going there!

WALTER (*To* RUTH, *who is carrying the box across to*

them) I don't know, you think we ought to give her that . . . Seems to me she ain't been very appreciative around here.

MAMA (*Eying the box, which is obviously a gift*) What is that?

WALTER (*Taking it from* RUTH *and putting it on the table in front of* MAMA) Well—what you all think. Should we give it to her?

RUTH Oh—she was pretty good today.

MAMA I'll good you—
(*She turns her eyes to the box again*)

BENEATHA Open it, Mama.
(*She stands up, looks at it, turns and looks at all of them, and then presses her hands together and does not open the package*)

WALTER (*Sweetly*) Open it, Mama. It's for you. (MAMA *looks in his eyes. It is the first present in her life without its being Christmas. Slowly she opens her package and lifts out, one by one, a brand-new sparkling set of gardening tools.* WALTER *continues, prodding*) Ruth made up the note—read it . . .

MAMA (*Picking up the card and adjusting her glasses*) "To our own Mrs. Miniver—Love from Brother, Ruth and Beneatha." Ain't that lovely . . .

TRAVIS (*Tugging at his father's sleeve*) Daddy, can I give her mine now?

WALTER All right, son. (TRAVIS *flies to get his gift*) Travis didn't want to go in with the rest of us, Mama. He got his own. (*Somewhat amused*) We don't know what it is . . .

TRAVIS (*Racing back in the room with a large hatbox and putting it in front of his grandmother*) Here!

MAMA Lord have mercy, baby. You done gone and bought your grandmother a hat?

TRAVIS (*Very proud*) Open it!
(*She does and lifts out an elaborate, but very elaborate,*

182

wide gardening hat, and all the adults break up at the sight of it)

RUTH Travis, honey, what is that?

TRAVIS *(Who thinks it is beautiful and appropriate)* It's a gardening hat! Like the ladies always have on in the magazines when they work in their gardens.

BENEATHA *(Giggling fiercely)* Travis—we were trying to make Mama Mrs. Miniver—not Scarlet O'Hara!

MAMA *(Indignantly)* What's the matter with you all! This here is a beautiful hat! *(Absurdly)* I always wanted me one just like it!

(She pops it on her head to prove it to her grandson, and the hat is ludicrous and considerably oversized)

RUTH Hot dog! Go, Mama!

WALTER *(Doubled over with laughter)* I'm sorry, Mama —but you look like you ready to go out and chop you some cotton sure enough!

(They all laugh except MAMA, out of deference to TRAVIS' feelings)

MAMA *(Gathering the boy up to her)* Bless your heart— this is the prettiest hat I ever owned— (WALTER, RUTH *and* BENEATHA *chime in—noisily, festively and insincerely congratulating* TRAVIS *on his gift)* What are we all standing around here for? We ain't finished packin' yet. Bennie, you ain't packed one book.

(The bell rings)

BENEATHA That couldn't be the movers . . . it's not hardly two good yet—

(BENEATHA goes into her room. MAMA starts for door)

WALTER *(Turning, stiffening)* Wait—wait—I'll get it.

(He stands and looks at the door)

MAMA You expecting company, son?

WALTER *(Just looking at the door)* Yeah—yeah . . .

(MAMA looks at RUTH, and they exchange innocent and unfrightened glances)

MAMA *(Not understanding)* Well, let them in, son.

BENEATHA (*From her room*)   We need some more string.

MAMA   Travis—you run to the hardware and get me some
string cord.

(MAMA *goes out and* WALTER *turns and looks at* RUTH.
TRAVIS *goes to a dish for money*)

RUTH   Why don't you answer the door, man?

WALTER (*Suddenly bounding across the floor to her*)
'Cause sometimes it hard to let the future begin! (*Stoop-
ing down in her face*)
I got wings!
You got wings!
All God's children got wings!
(*He crosses to the door and throws it open. Standing
there is a very slight little man in a not too prosperous
business suit and with haunted frightened eyes and a hat
pulled down tightly, brim up, around his forehead.* TRAVIS
passes between the men and exits. WALTER *leans deep in
the man's face, still in his jubilance*)
When I get to heaven gonna put on my wings,
Gonna fly all over God's heaven . . .
(*The little man just stares at him*)
Heaven—
(*Suddenly he stops and looks past the little man into the
empty hallway*)   Where's Willy, man?

BOBO   He ain't with me.

WALTER (*Not disturbed*)   Oh—come on in. You know
my wife.

BOBO (*Dumbly, taking off his hat*)   Yes—h'you, Miss
Ruth.

RUTH (*Quietly, a mood apart from her husband already,
seeing* BOBO)   Hello, Bobo.

WALTER   You right on time today . . . Right on time.
That's the way! (*He slaps* BOBO *on his back*)   Sit down
. . . lemme hear.

(RUTH *stands stiffly and quietly in back of them, as*

184

though somehow she senses death, her eyes fixed on her husband)

BOBO (*His frightened eyes on the floor, his hat in his hands*) Could I please get a drink a water, before I tell you about it, Walter Lee?

(WALTER *does not take his eyes off the man.* RUTH *goes blindly to the tap and gets a glass of water and brings it to* BOBO)

WALTER There ain't nothing wrong, is there?

BOBO Lemme tell you—

WALTER Man—didn't nothing go wrong?

BOBO Lemme tell you—Walter Lee. (*Looking at* RUTH *and talking to her more than to* WALTER) You know how it was. I got to tell you how it was. I mean first I got to tell you how it was all the way . . . I mean about the money I put in, Walter Lee . . .

WALTER (*With taut agitation now*) What about the money you put in?

BOBO Well—it wasn't much as we told you—me and Willy— (*He stops*) I'm sorry, Walter. I got a bad feeling about it. I got a real bad feeling about it . . .

WALTER Man, what you telling me about all this for? . . . Tell me what happened in Springfield . . .

BOBO Springfield.

RUTH (*Like a dead woman*) What was supposed to happen in Springfield?

BOBO (*To her*) This deal that me and Walter went into with Willy—Me and Willy was going to go down to Springfield and spread some money 'round so's we wouldn't have to wait so long for the liquor license . . . That's what we were going to do. Everybody said that was the way you had to do, you understand, Miss Ruth?

WALTER Man—what happened down there?

BOBO (*A pitiful man, near tears*) I'm trying to tell you, Walter.

WALTER (*Screaming at him suddenly*) THEN TELL ME, GODDAMNIT . . . WHAT'S THE MATTER WITH YOU?

BOBO Man . . . I didn't go to no Springfield, yesterday.

WALTER (*Halted, life hanging in the moment*) Why not?

BOBO (*The long way, the hard way to tell*) 'Cause I didn't have no reasons to . . .

WALTER Man, what are you talking about!

BOBO I'm talking about the fact that when I got to the train station yesterday morning—eight o'clock like we planned . . . Man—*Willy didn't never show up.*

WALTER Why . . . where was he . . . where is he?

BOBO That's what I'm trying to tell you . . . I don't know . . . I waited six hours . . . I called his house . . . and I waited . . . six hours . . . I waited in that train station six hours . . . (*Breaking into tears*) That was all the extra money I had in the world . . . (*Looking up at* WALTER *with the tears running down his face*) Man, *Willy is gone.*

WALTER Gone, what you mean Willy is gone? Gone where? You mean he went by himself. You mean he went off to Springfield by himself—to take care of getting the license— (*Turns and looks anxiously at* RUTH) You mean maybe he didn't want too many people in on the business down there? (*Looks to* RUTH *again, as before*) You know Willy got his own ways. (*Looks back to* BOBO) Maybe you was late yesterday and he just went on down there without you. Maybe—maybe—he's been callin' you at home tryin' to tell you what happened or something. Maybe—maybe—he just got sick. He's somewhere—he's got to be somewhere. We just got to find him—me and you got to find him. (*Grabs* BOBO *senselessly by the collar and starts to shake him*) We got to!

BOBO (*In sudden angry, frightened agony*) What's the

matter with you, Walter! *When a cat take off with your money he don't leave you no maps!*

WALTER (*Turning madly, as though he is looking for* WILLY *in the very room*) Willy! . . . Willy . . . don't do it . . . Please don't do it . . . Man, not with that money . . . Man, please, not with that money . . . Oh, God . . . Don't let it be true . . . (*He is wandering around, crying out for Willy and looking for him or perhaps for help from God*) Man . . . I trusted you . . . Man, I put my life in your hands . . . (*He starts to crumple down on the floor as* RUTH *just covers her face in horror.* MAMA *opens the door and comes into the room, with* BENEATHA *behind her*) Man . . . (*He starts to pound the floor with his fists, sobbing wildly*) *That money is made out of my father's flesh* . . .

BOBO (*Standing over him helplessly*) I'm sorry, Walter . . . (*Only* WALTER'S *sobs reply.* BOBO *puts on his hat*) I had my life staked on this deal, too . . . (*He exits*)

MAMA (*To* WALTER) Son— (*She goes to him, bends down to him, talks to his bent head*) Son . . . Is it gone? Son, I gave you sixty-five hundred dollars. Is it gone? All of it? Beneatha's money too?

WALTER (*Lifting his head slowly*) Mama . . . I never . . . went to the bank at all . . .

MAMA (*Not wanting to believe him*) You mean . . . your sister's school money . . . you used that too . . . Walter? . . .

WALTER Yessss! . . . All of it . . . It's all gone . . . (*There is total silence.* RUTH *stands with her face covered with her hands;* BENEATHA *leans forlornly against a wall, fingering a piece of red ribbon from the mother's gift.* MAMA *stops and looks at her son without recognition and then, quite without thinking about it, starts to beat him senselessly in the face.* BENEATHA *goes to them and stops it*)

BENEATHA Mama!

(MAMA *stops and looks at both of her children and rises slowly and wanders vaguely, aimlessly away from them*)

MAMA I seen . . . him . . . night after night . . . come in . . . and look at that rug . . . and then look at me . . . the red showing in his eyes . . . the veins moving in his head . . . I seen him grow thin and old before he was forty . . . working and working and working like somebody's old horse . . . killing himself . . . and you —you give it all away in a day . . .

BENEATHA Mama—

MAMA Oh, God . . . (*She looks up to Him*) Look down here—and show me the strength.

BENEATHA Mama—

MAMA (*Folding over*) Strength . . .

BENEATHA (*Plaintively*) Mama . . .

MAMA Strength!

CURTAIN

ACT THREE

An hour later.

   At curtain, there is a sullen light of gloom in the living room, gray light not unlike that which began the first scene of Act One. At left we can see WALTER *within his room, alone with himself. He is stretched out on the bed, his shirt out and open, his arms under his head. He does not smoke, he does not cry out, he merely lies there, looking up at the ceiling, much as if he were alone in the world.*

   In the living room BENEATHA *sits at the table, still surrounded by the now almost ominous packing crates. She sits looking off. We feel that this is a mood struck perhaps an hour before, and it lingers now, full of the empty sound of profound disappointment. We see on a line from her brother's bedroom the sameness of their attitudes. Presently the bell rings and* BENEATHA *rises without ambition or interest in answering. It is* ASAGAI, *smiling broadly, striding into the room with energy and happy expectation and conversation.*

ASAGAI I came over . . . I had some free time. I thought I might help with the packing. Ah, I like the look of packing crates! A household in preparation for a journey! It depresses some people . . . but for me . . . it is another feeling. Something full of the flow of life, do you understand? Movement, progress . . . It makes me think of Africa.
BENEATHA Africa!

ASAGAI What kind of a mood is this? Have I told you how deeply you move me?

BENEATHA He gave away the money, Asagai . . .

ASAGAI Who gave away what money?

BENEATHA The insurance money. My brother gave it away.

ASAGAI Gave it away?

BENEATHA He made an investment! With a man even Travis wouldn't have trusted.

ASAGAI And it's gone?

BENEATHA Gone!

ASAGAI I'm very sorry . . . And you, now?

BENEATHA Me? . . . Me? . . . Me I'm nothing . . . Me. When I was very small . . . we used to take our sleds out in the wintertime and the only hills we had were the ice-covered stone steps of some houses down the street. And we used to fill them in with snow and make them smooth and slide down them all day . . . and it was very dangerous you know . . . far too steep . . . and sure enough one day a kid named Rufus came down too fast and hit the sidewalk . . . and we saw his face just split open right there in front of us . . . And I remember standing there looking at his bloody open face thinking that was the end of Rufus. But the ambulance came and they took him to the hospital and they fixed the broken bones and they sewed it all up . . . and the next time I saw Rufus he just had a little line down the middle of his face . . . I never got over that . . .

ASAGAI What?

BENEATHA That that was what one person could do for another, fix him up—sew up the problem, make him all right again. That was the most marvelous thing in the world . . . I wanted to do that. I always thought it was the one concrete thing in the world that a human being could do. Fix up the sick, you know—and make them whole again. This was truly being God . . .

ASAGAI   You wanted to be God?

BENEATHA   No—I wanted to cure. It used to be so important to me. I wanted to cure. It used to matter. I used to care. I mean about people and how their bodies hurt . . .

ASAGAI   And you've stopped caring?

BENEATHA   Yes—I think so.

ASAGAI   Why?

BENEATHA   Because it doesn't seem deep enough, close enough to the truth.

ASAGAI   Truth? Why is it that you despairing ones always think that only you have the truth? I never thought to see *you* like that. You! Your brother made a stupid, childish mistake—and you are grateful to him. So that now you can give up the ailing human race on account of it. You talk about what good is struggle; what good is anything? Where are we all going? And why are we bothering?

BENEATHA   *And you cannot answer it!* All your talk and dreams about Africa and Independence. Independence and then what? What about all the crooks and petty thieves and just plain idiots who will come into power to steal and plunder the same as before—only now they will be black and do it in the name of the new Independence— You cannot answer that.

ASAGAI   (*Shouting over her*)   *I live the answer!* (*Pause*) In my village at home it is the exceptional man who can even read a newspaper . . . or who ever *sees* a book at all. I will go home and much of what I will have to say will seem strange to the people of my village . . . But I will teach and work and things will happen, slowly and swiftly. At times it will seem that nothing changes at all . . . and then again . . . the sudden dramatic events which make history leap into the future. And then quiet again. Retrogression even. Guns, murder, revolution. And I even will have moments when I wonder if the quiet was not better than all that death and hatred. But I will look about my village at the illiteracy and disease and ignorance and I will not wonder long. And perhaps . . . perhaps I will be a great man . . . I mean perhaps I will hold on to the substance of truth and find my way always with the right course . . . and perhaps for it I will be butchered in my bed some night by the servants of empire . . .

BENEATHA   *The martyr!*

ASAGAI   . . . or perhaps I shall live to be a very old man respected and esteemed in my new nation . . . And perhaps I shall hold office and this is what I'm trying to tell you, Alaiyo; perhaps the things I believe now for my country will be wrong and outmoded, and I will not understand and do terrible things to have things my way or merely to keep my power. Don't you see that there will be young men and women, not British soldiers then, but my own black countrymen . . . to step out of the shadows some evening and slit my then useless throat? Don't you see they have always been there . . . that they always will be. And that such a thing as my own death will be an advance? They who might kill me even . . . actually replenish me!

BENEATHA   Oh, Asagai, I know all that.

ASAGAI   Good! Then stop moaning and groaning and tell me what you plan to do.

BENEATHA   Do?

ASAGAI   I have a bit of a suggestion.

BENEATHA   What?

ASAGAI   (*Rather quietly for him*)   That when it is all over —that you come home with me—

BENEATHA   (*Slapping herself on the forehead with exasperation born of misunderstanding*)   Oh—Asagai—at this moment you decide to be romantic!

ASAGAI   (*Quickly understanding the misunderstanding*)   My dear, young creature of the New World—I do not mean across the city—I mean across the ocean; home—to Africa.

192

BENEATHA (*Slowly understanding and turning to him with murmured amazement*)   To—to Nigeria?

ASAGAI   Yes! . . . (*Smiling and lifting his arms playfully*) Three hundred years later the African Prince rose up out of the seas and swept the maiden back across the middle passage over which her ancestors had come—

BENEATHA (*Unable to play*)   Nigeria?

ASAGAI   Nigeria. Home. (*Coming to her with genuine romantic flippancy*)   I will show you our mountains and our stars; and give you cool drinks from gourds and teach you the old songs and the ways of our people—and, in time, we will pretend that—   (*Very softly*)   —you have only been away for a day—

(*She turns her back to him, thinking. He swings her around and takes her full in his arms in a long embrace which proceeds to passion*)

BENEATHA (*Pulling away*)   You're getting me all mixed up—

ASAGAI   Why?

BENEATHA   Too many things—too many things have happened today. I must sit down and think. I don't know what I feel about anything right this minute.

(*She promptly sits down and props her chin on her fist*)

ASAGAI (*Charmed*)   All right, I shall leave you. No—don't get up. (*Touching her, gently, sweetly*)   Just sit awhile and think . . . Never be afraid to sit awhile and think. (*He goes to door and looks at her*)   How often I have looked at you and said, "Ah—so this is what the New World hath finally wrought . . ."

(*He exits.* BENEATHA *sits on alone. Presently* WALTER *enters from his room and starts to rummage through things, feverishly looking for something. She looks up and turns in her seat*)

BENEATHA (*Hissingly*)   Yes—just look at what the New World hath wrought! . . . Just look! (*She gestures with bitter disgust*)   There he is! *Monsieur le petit bourgeois noir*—himself! There he is—Symbol of a Rising Class! Entrepreneur! Titan of the system! (WALTER *ignores her completely and continues frantically and destructively looking for something and hurling things to floor and tearing things out of their place in his search.* BENEATHA *ignores the eccentricity of his actions and goes on with the monologue of insult*) Did you dream of yachts on Lake Michigan, Brother? Did you see yourself on that Great Day sitting down at the Conference Table, surrounded by all the mighty bald-headed men in America? All halted, waiting, breathless, waiting for your pronouncements on industry? Waiting for you—Chairman of the Board? (WALTER *finds what he is looking for—a small piece of white paper—and pushes it in his pocket and puts on his coat and rushes out without ever having looked at her. She shouts after him*) I look at you and I see the final triumph of stupidity in the world!

(*The door slams and she returns to just sitting again.* RUTH *comes quickly out of* MAMA'S *room*)

RUTH   Who was that?

BENEATHA   Your husband.

RUTH   Where did he go?

BENEATHA   Who knows—maybe he has an appointment at U. S. Steel.

RUTH (*Anxiously, with frightened eyes*)   You didn't say nothing bad to him, did you?

BENEATHA   Bad? Say anything bad to him? No—I told him he was a sweet boy and full of dreams and everything is strictly peachy keen, as the ofay kids say!

(MAMA *enters from her bedroom. She is lost, vague, trying to catch hold, to make some sense of her former command of the world, but it still eludes her. A sense of waste overwhelms her gait; a measure of apology rides on her shoulders. She goes to her plant, which has remained on the table, looks at it, picks it up and takes it to the window sill and sits it outside, and she stands and looks at it a long moment. Then she closes the window, straightens her body with effort and turns around to her children)*

MAMA Well—ain't it a mess in here, though? (*A false cheerfulness, a beginning of something*) I guess we all better stop moping around and get some work done. All this unpacking and everything we got to do. (RUTH *raises her head slowly in response to the sense of the line; and* BENEATHEA *in similar manner turns very slowly to look at her mother*) One of you all better call the moving people and tell 'em not to come.

RUTH Tell 'em not to come?

MAMA Of course, baby. Ain't no need in 'em coming all the way here and having to go back. They charges for that too. (*She sits down, fingers to her brow, thinking*) Lord, ever since I was a little girl, I always remembers people saying, "Lena—Lena Egglston, you aims too high all the time. You needs to slow down and see life a little more like it is. Just slow down some." That's what they always used to say down home—"Lord, that Lena Eggleston is a high-minded thing. She'll get her due one day!"

RUTH No, Lena . . .

MAMA Me and Big Walter just didn't never learn right.

RUTH Lena, no! We gotta go. Bennie—tell her . . . (*She rises and crosses to* BENEATHEA *with her arms outstretched.* BENEATHEA *doesn't respond*) Tell her we can still move . . . the notes ain't but a hundred and twenty five a month. We got four grown people in this house— we can work . . .

MAMA (*To herself*) Just aimed too high all the time—

RUTH (*Turning and going to* MAMA *fast—the words pouring out with urgency and desperation*) Lena—I'll work . . . I'll work twenty hours a day in all the kitchens in Chicago . . . I'll strap my baby on my back if I have to and scrub all the floors in America and wash all

the sheets in America if I have to—but we got to move
. . . We got to get out of here . . .

(MAMA *reaches out absently and pats* RUTH'S *hand*)

MAMA   No—I sees things differently now. Been thinking
'bout some of the things we could do to fix this place up
some. I seen a second-hand bureau over on Maxwell
Street just the other day that could fit right there. (*She
points to where the new furniture might go.* RUTH *wanders away from her*)   Would need some new handles on
it and then a little varnish and then it look like something
brand-new. And—we can put up them new curtains in
the kitchen . . . Why this place be looking fine. Cheer
us all up so that we forget trouble ever came . . . (*To*
RUTH)   And you could get some nice screens to put up
in your room round the baby's basinet . . . (*She looks
at both of them, pleadingly*)   Sometimes you just got to
know when to give up some things . . . and hold on to
what you got.

(WALTER *enters from the outside, looking spent and
leaning against the door, his coat hanging from him*)

MAMA   Where you been, son?

WALTER   (*Breathing hard*)   Made a call.

MAMA   To who, son?

WALTER   To the Man.

MAMA   What man, baby?

WALTER   The Man, Mama. Don't you know who The Man
is?

RUTH   Walter Lee?

WALTER   *The Man.* Like the guys in the street say—The
Man. Captain Boss—Mistuh Charley . . . Old Captain
Please Mr. Bossman . . .

BENEATHA   (*Suddenly*)   Lindner!

WALTER   That's right! That's good. I told him to come
right over.

BENEATHA   (*Fiercely, understanding*)   For what? What do
you want to see him for!

WALTER (*Looking at his sister*)   We going to do business
with him.

MAMA   What you talking 'bout, son?

WALTER   Talking 'bout life, Mama. You all always telling
me to see life like it is. Well—I laid in there on my back
today . . . and I figured it out. Life just like it is. Who
gets and who don't get. (*He sits down with his coat on
and laughs*)   Mama, you know it's all divided up. Life
is. Sure enough. Between the takers and the "tooken."
(*He laughs*)   I've figured it out finally. (*He looks
around at them*)   Yeah. Some of us always getting
"tooken." (*He laughs*)   People like Willy Harris, they
don't never get "tooken." And you know why the rest
of us do? 'Cause we all mixed up. Mixed up bad. We
get to looking 'round for the right and the wrong; and
we worry about it and cry about it and stay up nights
trying to figure out 'bout the wrong and the right of
things all the time . . . And all the time, man, them
takers is out there operating, just taking and taking.
Willy Harris? Shoot—Willy Harris don't even count. He
don't even count in the big scheme of things. But I'll say
one thing for old Willy Harris . . . he's taught me
something. He's taught me to keep my eyes on what
counts in this world. Yeah— (*Shouting out a little*)
Thanks, Willy!

RUTH   What did you call that man for, Walter Lee?

WALTER   Called him to tell him to come on over to the
show. Gonna put on a show for the man. Just what he
wants to see. You see, Mama, the man came here today
and he told us that them people out there where you
want us to move—well they so upset they willing to pay
us not to move out there. (*He laughs again*)   And—and
oh, Mama—you would of been proud of the way me
and Ruth and Bennie acted. We told him to get out . . .
Lord have mercy! We told the man to get out. Oh, we
was some proud folks this afternoon, yeah. (*He lights a*

cigarette) We were still full of that old-time stuff . . .

RUTH *(Coming toward him slowly)* You talking 'bout taking them people's money to keep us from moving in that house?

WALTER I ain't just talking 'bout it, baby—I'm telling you that's what's going to happen.

BENEATHA Oh, God! Where is the bottom! Where is the real honest-to-God bottom so he can't go any farther!

WALTER See—that's the old stuff. You and that boy that was here today. You all want everybody to carry a flag and a spear and sing some marching songs, huh? You wanna spend your life looking into things and trying to find the right and the wrong part, huh? Yeah. You know what's going to happen to that boy someday—he'll find himself sitting in a dungeon, locked in forever—and the takers will have the key! Forget it, baby! There ain't no causes—there ain't nothing but taking in this world, and he who takes most is smartest—and it don't make a damn bit of difference *how*.

MAMA You making something inside me cry, son. Some awful pain inside me.

WALTER Don't cry, Mama. Understand. That white man is going to walk in that door able to write checks for more money than we ever had. It's important to him and I'm going to help him . . . I'm going to put on the show, Mama.

MAMA Son—I come from five generations of people who was slaves and sharecroppers—but it ain't nobody in my family never let nobody pay 'em no money that was a way of telling us we wasn't fit to walk the earth. We ain't never been that poor. *(Raising her eyes and looking at him)* We ain't never been that dead inside.

BENEATHA Well—we are dead now. All the talk about dreams and sunlight that goes on in this house. All dead.

WALTER What's the matter with you all! I didn't make this world! It was give to me this way! Hell, yes, I want

me some yachts someday! Yes, I want to hang some real
pearls 'round my wife's neck. Ain't she supposed to wear
no pearls? Somebody tell me—tell me, who decides
which women is suppose to wear pearls in this world. I
tell you I am a *man*—and I think my wife should wear
some pearls in this world!

(*This last line hangs a good while and* WALTER *begins
to move about the room. The word "Man" has pene-
trated his consciousness; he mumbles it to himself re-
peatedly between strange agitated pauses as he moves
about*)

MAMA   Baby, how you going to feel on the inside?

WALTER   Fine! . . . Going to feel fine . . . a man . . .

MAMA   You won't have nothing left then, Walter Lee.

WALTER   (*Coming to her*)   I'm going to feel fine, Mama.
I'm going to look that son-of-a-bitch in the eyes and say
— (*He falters*)   —and say, "All right, Mr. Lindner—
(*He falters even more*)   —that's your neighborhood out
there. You got the right to keep it like you want. You
got the right to have it like you want. Just write the
check and—the house is yours." And, and I am going
to say— (*His voice almost breaks*)   And you—you
people just put the money in my hand and you won't
have to live next to this bunch of stinking niggers! . . .
(*He straightens up and moves away from his mother,
walking around the room*)   Maybe—maybe I'll just get
down on my black knees . . . (*He does so;* RUTH *and*
BENNIE *and* MAMA *watch him in frozen horror*)   Captain, Mistuh, Bossman. (*He starts crying*)   A-hee-hee-
hee! (*Wringing his hands in profoundly anguished imitation*)   Yasssssuh! Great White Father, just gi' ussen de
money, fo' God's sake, and we's ain't gwine come out
deh and dirty up yo' white folks neighborhood . . .
(*He breaks down completely, then gets up and goes into
the bedroom*)

BENEATHA   That is not a man. That is nothing but a tooth-less rat.

MAMA   Yes—death done come in this here house. (*She is nodding slowly, reflectively*)   Done come walking in my house. On the lips of my children. You what sup-posed to be my beginning again. You—what supposed to be my harvest. (*To* BENEATHA)   You—you mourning your brother?

BENEATHA   He's no brother of mine.

MAMA   What you say?

BENEATHA   I said that that individual in that room is no brother of mine.

MAMA   That's what I thought you said. You feeling like you better than he is today? (BENEATHA *does not an-swer*)   Yes? What you tell him a minute ago? That he wasn't a man? Yes? You give him up for me? You done wrote his epitaph too—like the rest of the world? Well, who give you the privilege?

BENEATHA   Be on my side for once! You saw what he just did, Mama! You saw him—down on his knees. Wasn't it you who taught me—to despise any man who would do that. Do what he's going to do.

MAMA   Yes—I taught you that. Me and your daddy. But I thought I taught you something else too . . . I thought I taught you to love him.

BENEATHA   Love him? There is nothing left to love.

MAMA   There is always something left to love. And if you ain't learned that, you ain't learned nothing. (*Looking at her*)   Have you cried for that boy today? I don't mean for yourself and for the family 'cause we lost the money. I mean for him; what he been through and what it done to him. Child, when do you think is the time to love somebody the most; when they done good and made things easy for everybody? Well then, you ain't learning —because that ain't the time at all. It's when he's at his lowest and can't believe in hisself 'cause the world done whipped him so. When you starts measuring somebody, measure him right, child, measure him right. Make sure you done taken into account what hills and valleys he come through before he got to wherever he is.

(TRAVIS *bursts into the room at the end of the speech, leaving the door open*)

TRAVIS Grandmama—the moving men are downstairs! The truck just pulled up.

MAMA (*Turning and looking at him*) Are they baby? They downstairs?

(*She sighs and sits. Lindner appears in the doorway. He peers in and knocks lightly, to gain attention, and comes in. All turn to look at him*)

LINDNER (*Hat and briefcase in hand*) Uh—hello . . .

(RUTH *crosses mechanically to the bedroom door and opens it and lets it swing open freely and slowly as the lights come up on* WALTER *within, still in his coat, sitting at the far corner of the room. He looks up and out through the room to* LINDNER)

RUTH He's here.

(*A long minute passes and* WALTER *slowly gets up*)

LINDNER (*Coming to the table with efficiency, putting his briefcase on the table and starting to unfold the papers and unscrew fountain pens*) Well, I certainly was glad to hear from you people. (WALTER *has begun the trek out of the room, slowly and awkwardly, rather like a small boy, passing the back of his sleeve across the back of his mouth from time to time*) Life can really be so much simpler than people let it be most of the time. Well—with whom do I negotiate? You, Mrs. Younger, or your son here? (MAMA *sits with her hands folded on her lap and her eyes closed as* WALTER *advances.* TRAVIS *goes close to* LINDNER *and looks at the papers curiously*) Just some official papers, sonny.

RUTH Travis, you go downstairs.

MAMA (*Opening her eyes and looking into* WALTER'S)

201

No. Travis, you stay right here. And you make him understand what you doing, Walter Lee. You teach him good. Like Willy Harris taught you. You show where our five generations done come to. Go ahead, son—

WALTER (*Looks down into his boy's eyes.* TRAVIS *grins at him merrily and* WALTER *draws him beside him with his arm lightly around his shoulder*) Well, Mr. Lindner. (BENEATHA *turns away*) We called you— (*There is a profound, simple groping quality in his speech*) —because, well, me and my family (*He looks around and shifts from one foot to the other*) Well—we are very plain people . . .

LINDNER Yes—

WALTER I mean—I have worked as a chauffeur most of my life—and my wife here, she does domestic work in people's kitchens. So does my mother. I mean—we are plain people . . .

LINDNER Yes, Mr. Younger—

WALTER (*Really like a small boy, looking down at his shoes and then up at the man*) And—uh—well, my father, well, he was a laborer most of his life.

LINDNER (*Absolutely confused*) Uh, yes—

WALTER (*Looking down at his toes once again*) My famer almost beat a man to death once because this man called him a bad name or something, you know what I mean?

LINDNER No, I'm afraid I don't.

WALTER (*Finally straightening up*) Well, what I mean is that we come from people who had a lot of pride. I mean—we are very proud people. And that's my sister over there and she's going to be a doctor—and we are very proud—

LINDNER Well—I am sure that is very nice, but—

WALTER (*Starting to cry and facing the man eye to eye*) What I am telling you is that we called you over here to tell you that we are very proud and that this is—this is my son, who makes the sixth generation of our family in this country, and that we have all thought about your offer and we have decided to move into our house because my father—my father—he earned it. (MAMA *has her eyes closed and is rocking back and forth as though she were in church, with her head nodding the amen yes*) We don't want to make no trouble for nobody or fight no causes—but we will try to be good neighbors. That's all we got to say. (*He looks the man absolutely in the eyes*) We don't want your money.

(*He turns and walks away from the man*)

LINDNER (*Looking around at all of them*) I take it then that you have decided to occupy.

BENEATHA That's what the man said.

LINDNER (*To* MAMA *in her reverie*) Then I would like to appeal to you, Mrs. Younger. You are older and wiser and understand things better I am sure . . .

MAMA (*Rising*) I am afraid you don't understand. My son said we was going to move and there ain't nothing left for me to say. (*Shaking her head with double meaning*) You know how these young folks is nowadays, mister. Can't do a thing with 'em. Good-bye.

LINDNER (*Folding up his materials*) Well—if you are that final about it . . . There is nothing left for me to say. (*He finishes. He is almost ignored by the family, who are concentrating on* WALTER LEE. *At the door* LINDNER *halts and looks around*) I sure hope you people know what you're doing.

(*He shakes his head and exits*)

RUTH (*Looking around and coming to life*) Well, for God's sake—if the moving men are here—LET'S GET THE HELL OUT OF HERE!

MAMA (*Into action*) Ain't it the truth! Look at all this here mess. Ruth put Travis' good jacket on him . . . Walter Lee, fix your tie and tuck your shirt in, you look just like somebody's hoodlum. Lord have mercy, where is my plant? (*She flies to get it amid the general bustling of the family, who are deliberately trying to ignore the nobility of the past moment*) You all start on down . . . Travis child, don't go empty-handed . . . Ruth, where did I put that box with my skillets in it? I want to be in charge of it myself . . . I'm going to make us the biggest dinner we ever ate tonight . . . Beneatha, what's the matter with them stockings? Pull them things up, girl . . .

(*The family starts to file out as two moving men appear and begin to carry out the heavier pieces of furniture, bumping into the family as they move about*)

BENEATHA Mama, Asagai—asked me to marry him today and go to Africa—

MAMA (*In the middle of her getting-ready activity*) He did? You ain't old enough to marry nobody— (*Seeing the moving men lifting one of her chairs precariously*) Darling, that ain't no bale of cotton, please handle it so we can sit in it again. I had that chair twenty-five years . . .

(*The movers sigh with exasperation and go on with their work*)

BENEATHA (*Girlishly and unreasonably trying to pursue the conversation*) To go to Africa, Mama—be a doctor in Africa . . .

MAMA (*Distracted*) Yes, baby—

WALTER Africa! What he want you to go to Africa for?

BENEATHA To practice there . . .

WALTER Girl, if you don't get all them silly ideas out your head! You better marry yourself a man with some loot . . .

BENEATHA (*Angrily, precisely as in the first scene of the play*) What have you got to do with who I marry!

WALTER Plenty. Now I think George Murchison—

(*He and* BENEATHA *go out yelling at each other vigorously;* BENEATHA *is heard saying that she would not marry* GEORGE MURCHISON *if he were Adam and she were Eve, etc. The anger is loud and real till their voices diminish.* RUTH *stands at the door and turns to* MAMA *and smiles knowingly*)

MAMA (*Fixing her hat at last*) Yeah—they something all right, my children . . .

RUTH Yeah—they're something. Let's go, Lena.

MAMA (*Stalling, starting to look around at the house*) Yes—I'm coming. Ruth—

RUTH Yes?

MAMA (*Quietly, woman to woman*) He finally come into his manhood today, didn't he? Kind of like a rainbow after the rain . . .

RUTH (*Biting her lip lest her own pride explode in front of* MAMA) Yes, Lena.

(WALTER'S *voice calls for them raucously*)

MAMA (*Waving* RUTH *out vaguely*) All right honey—go on down. I be down directly.

(RUTH *hesitates, then exits.* MAMA *stands, at last alone in the living room, her plant on the table before her as the lights start to come down. She looks around at all the walls and ceilings and suddenly, despite herself, while the children call below, a great heaving thing rises in her and she puts her fist to her mouth, takes a final desperate look, pulls her coat about her, pats her hat and goes out. The lights dim down. The door opens and she comes back in, grabs her plant, and goes out for the last time*)

CURTAIN

Lillian Hellman

Toys in the Attic

FOR RICHARD WILBUR

Toys in the Attic was first presented by Kermit Bloomgarden at the Hudson Theatre, New York City, on February 25, 1960, with the following cast:

(IN ORDER OF APPEARANCE)

CARRIE BERNIERS	Maureen Stapleton
ANNA BERNIERS	Anne Revere
GUS	Charles McRae
ALBERTINE PRINE	Irene Worth
HENRY SIMPSON	Percy Rodriguez
JULIAN BERNIERS	Jason Robards, Jr.
LILY BERNIERS	Rochelle Oliver
TAXI DRIVER	William Hawley
THREE MOVING MEN	Clifford Cothren, Tom Manley, Maurice Ellis

DIRECTED BY Arthur Penn
SETTING AND LIGHTING BY Howard Bay
COSTUMES BY Ruth Morley

Place: The Berniers house in New Orleans.

ACT ONE

SIX P.M. on a summer day.

ACT TWO

EIGHT A.M. the following morning.

ACT THREE

Shortly after.

ACT ONE

Place: The BERNIERS' *living room, the entrance porch to the house, and a small city garden off the porch. The house is solid middle-class of another generation. The furniture is heavy and old. Everything inside and outside is neat, but in need of repairs. The porch has two rocking chairs and is crowded with plants. The garden has a table and chairs that have been painted too often and don't stay together very well. It is a house lived in by poor, clean, orderly people who don't like where they live.*

At rise: ANNA BERNIERS, *carrying her gloves and purse and still wearing her hat, pushes open the blinds of the windows that give on the garden. She lifts a large camellia pot and puts it outside. She pours a glass of water on the plant and moves back into the room to take off her hat.* ANNA *is a nice-looking woman, calm and quiet. She is about forty-two.* CARRIE BERNIERS *appears from the street, climbs the porch steps, and sits down in a porch chair. She is about thirty-eight, still pretty, but the prettiness is wearing thin and tired. She fans herself, rocks back and forth, the chair creaks and sways, and, wearily, she rises and moves to the other chair.*

CARRIE (*As she hears* ANNA *moving about in the kitchen*)
   That you, Anna?
ANNA (*Her voice*)   Just got home.
CARRIE   Hot.
ANNA   Paper says a storm.
CARRIE   I know. I'll take the plants in.

ANNA   I just put them out. Let them have a little storm air.

CARRIE   I don't like them out in a storm. Worries me. I don't like storms. I don't believe plants do, either.

ANNA   (*Appears in the living room with a broom and a dust rag; speaks out toward the porch*)   Did you have a hard day?

CARRIE   He let me leave the office after lunch. "You're looking a little peaked, Miss Berniers, from the heat." I said I've been looking a little peaked for years in heat, in cold, in rain, when I was young, and now. You mean *you're* hot and want to go home, you faker, I said. Only I said it to myself.

ANNA   We had a private sale at the store. Coats. Coats on a day like this. There was a very good bargain, red with black braid. I had my eye on it for you all last winter. But—

CARRIE   Oh, I don't need a coat.

ANNA   Yes, you do. Did you go to the park? I wanted to, but the sale went so late. Old lady Senlis and old lady Condelet just sat there, looking at everything, even small coats. How can rich people go to a sale on a day like this?

CARRIE   I feel sorry for them. For all old ladies. Even rich ones. Money makes them lonely.

ANNA   (*Laughs*)   Why would that be?

CARRIE   Don't you feel sorry for old ladies? You used to.

ANNA   When my feet don't hurt and I don't have to sell them coats at a sale. Was it nice in the park?

CARRIE   I didn't go to the park. I went to the cemetery.

ANNA   (*Stops dusting, sighs*)   Everybody still there?

CARRIE   I took flowers. It's cool there. Cooler. I was the only person there. Nobody goes to see anybody in summer. Yet those who have passed away must be just as lonely in summer as they are in winter. Sometimes I think we shouldn't have put Mama and Papa at Mount Olive cemetery. Maybe it would have been nicer for

212

them at Mount Great Hope with the new, rich people.
What would you think, if we don't get buried at Mount
Olive with Mama and Papa?

ANNA   Any place that's cool.

CARRIE   I bought you a small bottle of Eau d'haut Alpine.
Cologne water of the high Alps, I guess. (*Holds up a
package*)   Your weekly present. What did you buy me,
may I ask, who shouldn't?

ANNA   Jar of candied oranges.

CARRIE   Oh, how nice. We'll have them for a savory. Do
you know I read in our travel book on England that *they*
think a proper savory is an anchovy. Anchovy after
dinner. They won't make me eat it. What are you doing?

ANNA   Nothing. I'm going to clean.

CARRIE   Oh, don't. Sunday's cleaning day. Was this house
always so big?

ANNA   It grew as people left it.

CARRIE   I want to tell you something I've never told you
before. I never, ever, liked this house. Not even when
we were children. I know *you* did, but I didn't.

ANNA   You know I liked it?

CARRIE   I don't think Julian ever liked it, either. That's
why we used to have our supper out here on the steps.
Did you ever know that's why I used to bring Julian out
here, even when he was a baby, and we'd have our supper on the steps? I didn't want him to find out about
the house. Julian and I. Nice of Mama and Papa to let
us, wasn't it? Must have been a great deal of trouble
carrying the dishes out here. Mama had an agreeable
nature.

ANNA   I carried the dishes out.

CARRIE   Did you? Yes, so you did. Thank you, Anna.
Thank you very much. Did you mind eating with Mama
and Papa— (*Points off*)   —in that awful oak tomb?

ANNA   Yes, I minded.

CARRIE   Well, it sure was a nice thing to do. I never knew

213

you minded. Funny how you can live so close and long and not know things, isn't it?

ANNA Yes, indeed. I called Mr. Shine today. He said he hadn't had an inquiry in months. He said we should reduce the price of the house. I said we would, but there wasn't anything to reduce it to.

CARRIE (*Gets up, goes into the living room*) Oh, somebody'll come along will like it, you'll see.

ANNA Nobody's ever liked this house, nobody's ever going to.

CARRIE You always get mean to the house when something worries you. What's the matter?

ANNA And you always go to the cemetery.

CARRIE (*Opens the waist of her dress*) Just cooler. I so much like the French on the graves. *Un homme brave, mort pour la cité pendant la guerre*— Sounds better in French. A man gallant is so much more than just a gallant man. Nobody in our family's ever been killed in a war. Not Grandpapa, not Papa— Why, don't you think?

ANNA Some people get killed, some people don't.

CARRIE (*Laughs*) Papa always said he was scared to death and ran whenever he could. But Papa said just anything. Julian didn't like it when he said things like that. No little boy would. Papa shouldn't have talked that way.

ANNA Papa's been dead twenty-two years, Carrie. You should have taken it up with him before this.

CARRIE No letter for two weeks. I went to the main post office today, and said I was sure there'd been some confusion. Would they please call the other Berniers and see if a letter was there. And Alfie said, "Carrie, there are no other Berniers in New Orleans. There are some live in Biloxi, Mississippi, with a hardware store, but the central government of the United States does not give money to Louisiana to make calls to Mississippi, although maybe you could change that if you said it was Julian who had written the letter he didn't write." I was angry, but I didn't show it. How do you know it's Julian I am talking about, I said. We're expecting letters from Paris and Rome in reply to inquiries about our forthcoming tour.

(*She stops suddenly, run down*)

ANNA   Julian's busy. That's all.

(GUS, *a colored man of about thirty-five, carrying a block of ice, comes up the porch steps*)

GUS   You home?

ANNA   We're home.

(GUS *goes off toward the kitchen*)

CARRIE   (*Goes toward the piano*)   I bought a book called *French Lessons in Songs*. I don't believe it. Never been two weeks before in his whole life. (*Softly, slowly*)   I telephoned to Chicago and the hotel manager said Julian and Lily had moved months ago. Why didn't Julian tell us that?

ANNA   (*Quietly*)   I knew. I knew last week. Two letters came back here with address unknown. Carrie, Julian's married, he's moved away, he's got a business to take care of, he's busy. That's all.

CARRIE   He's never been too busy to write or phone to us. You know that.

ANNA   I know things have changed. That's as it should be.

CARRIE   Yes, of course. Yes.

GUS   (*Puts his head into the room*)   Icebox all on one side. Miss Anna, you all sure need a new icebox. You all ought to treat yourselves.

ANNA   You know, Gus, colored people are getting to talk just like white people. Kind of a shame.

GUS   Ought to treat yourselves. Get a new little house, new little icebox. No more Julian to worry about. Just yourselves now to treat good.

CARRIE   It's true. You getting to talk just like that white trash in my office. Just yourselves now and all that. (*With force*)   Well, what do you think? We *are* going

to treat ourselves good. We're going to sell this house
and never come back. We're going on a great, big, long
trip. For a *year,* or five. What do you think of that?

GUS (*To* ANNA) Ought to get yourselves a nice cat. I'll
water the yard for you. Where are you going this time?

CARRIE Where we were always going. To Europe.

GUS You told me that last year. And I stopped the ice.
And you told me around seven years back when Julian
went on his other business trip, and I stopped the ice
then— (*He laughs*) When I stop it now?

CARRIE (*Angry, too upset*) Very soon. *Very* soon. You
hear me, Gus? *Very* soon. And if you just don't believe
me you come around to church Sunday and hear us take
a solemn oath right in church. We don't break a solemn
oath in church.

GUS That's good. Lot of people do.

CARRIE How dare you, Gus? When I say a solemn oath
in church?

ANNA (*To* GUS) There's food in the icebox. Help yourself.

CARRIE Remember, Gus, when Julian and I used to eat
out there and you and your sister and brother'd walk
past and stare at us, and Julian would go tell Mama we
wanted more food, and he'd bring it to you himself?

GUS Yes'm. Came in handy. Just like now.
(*He exits from the porch. He picks up a garden hose and
disappears to the rear of the house*)

CARRIE (*Looks at* ANNA) Why did I tell him that about
Europe?

ANNA I don't know.

CARRIE Let's get out our travel books this evening and
write out all our plans.

ANNA No. Don't let's ever speak about it, until we're
ready to go, or think about it, or listen to each other, or
tell Gus—I don't want to write things down again.

216

CARRIE   It was you who wanted to wait last time. After the wedding.

ANNA   It was you, Carrie.

CARRIE   For a very good reason. Could we give them a smaller wedding present? Lily is a very rich girl and the one thing a very rich girl knows about is sterling silver. Her mother gave them ten thousand dollars. What would Lily have thought of us?

ANNA   I don't know. I don't think she cares about things like that. Lily was so in love with Julian—

CARRIE   Oh, I imagine even in love you take time off to count your silver.

CARRIE   (*Softly*)   We could still go to Europe this year. Do you want to? How much money have we got? Did you make the deposit this week?

ANNA   Twenty-eight hundred and forty-three dollars. No, I didn't have time.

CARRIE   (*Quickly*)   Oh, it's too hot tonight. Should we treat ourselves and go out for supper? It's been so long since we ate in a restaurant. Let's start doing our French lessons again because we'll need them now for the trip— (*She moves to the piano and plays and sings the next speech*)   "*Une chambre pour deux dames.*" Have you one room for two ladies? "*Ah non! Trop chère!*" Oh no! Too expensive! "*Merci, M'sieur. Trop chère.*" We'll stay in Paris, of course, for just as long as we want. Then we'll go to Strasbourg, have the famous pâté, and put flowers on the graves of Mama's relatives.

ANNA   I'll have the pâté. You put flowers on the graves of Mama's relatives.

CARRIE   Remember the night Julian told us about the marriage? He said that night we would all go to Europe together, the way we always planned. Mama would want us to put flowers on the graves in Strasbourg. She would, Anna, and so we must.

217

ANNA I don't know what the dead would like. Maybe Mama's changed.

CARRIE As soon as we do set a date for departure, I'll have my evening dress fixed. No, I won't. Pink's no good for me now. I've kind of changed color as I got older. You, too. Funny. To change color. *"C'est trop chère, M'sieur."* I don't want to go if we have to say that all the time.

ANNA We've always said it, we always will say it. And why not?

CARRIE I just think it would be better not to go to Europe right now.

ANNA (*Laughs*) We weren't going.

CARRIE Save enough until we can go real right. That won't take long. Maybe just another year.

ANNA A year is a long time—now.

CARRIE If you want to go, just let's get up and go. (*In sudden, false excitement*) Come on. Let's do. I can't tell you how much I want to go— (*Points to the piano*) That and a good piano. Every time there's a wishbone I say I want a good life for Julian, a piano, a trip to Europe. That's all. You know, even if we can't go to Europe we could afford a little trip to Chicago. The coach fares are very cheap—

ANNA I don't think we should run after Julian and Lily and intrude on their lives.

CARRIE Who's doing that? What an unpleasant idea. (*As ANNA starts toward the kitchen*) We haven't got twenty-eight hundred and forty-three dollars. I took out a thousand dollars yesterday and sent it to Chicago. I didn't know then that Julian had moved from the hotel. But I am sure they'll forward the money—I signed the wire with love from Anna and Carrie, so he knows it comes from you, too.

ANNA (*Slowly*) I don't think you should have done that.

CARRIE But I knew you would want to send it—

ANNA How do you know what I would want?

CARRIE (*Slowly, hurt*) Shouldn't I know what you want
  for Julian? (*When* ANNA *does not answer*) I'm sorry
  our trip will have to wait a little longer, but—

ANNA I'm sorry, too. But it's not the trip. Nor the money.
  We are interfering, and we told ourselves we wouldn't.

CARRIE But if he needs money—

ANNA Needs it? Julian has a good business. Why do you
  think he needs it?

CARRIE He's always needed it. (*Quickly*) I mean I don't
  mean that. I mean it's because the letter didn't come.
  Anyway, even people with a good business can use a little
  money— You think I did wrong?

ANNA Yes, I do.
  (*She exits*)

CARRIE (*Calling after* ANNA) Julian won't be angry with
  me. He never has been. I'll just telephone to him and
  say— (*She makes a half move to the phone*) But
  there's no place to phone to. Anna, what do you think?
  (*There is no answer. After a second she moves back to
  the piano and begins to play. During her speech* ALBER-
  TINE PRINE *and* HENRY SIMPSON *appear in the garden.*
  ALBERTINE PRINE *is a handsome woman of about forty-
  five, dressed with elegance, but in no current fashion. She
  speaks carefully, as if she were not used to talking very
  much. Her movements are graceful and quiet.* HENRY *is
  a colored man of about forty-five. He is dressed in a
  summer suit, but he carries a chauffeur's cap.* MRS. PRINE
  stops as she hears the piano)

ALBERTINE Is the older one Miss Caroline?

HENRY (*Laughs*) They call her Carrie. No. Miss Anna
  is the older one.

ALBERTINE (*Smiles*) You laugh at me. But I only met
  them twice before the marriage. Two long dinners. Many
  savage tribes have a law that people must eat alone, in
  silence. Sensible, isn't it? (*She moves toward the porch
  steps, then stops*) Perhaps it would be best if you went

in. I'm not good at seeing people any more, and there will be much chatter. (*He doesn't answer her. She laughs*) Very well. But I am sure it's hot in there. Would you tell them I'm out here?

HENRY (*Gently*)   *You* have come to call on *them.*

ALBERTINE   Nice to live this close to the river. I still like it down here. Soggy and steaming. The flowers aren't strong enough to cover the river smells. That's the way it should be. Very vain of flowers to compete with the Mississippi. My grandmother lived on this street when I was a little girl, and I liked it then. I used to pretend I slept under the river, and had a secret morning door up into this street. What are you holding?

HENRY   A chauffeur's cap.

ALBERTINE   You win many small battles. Never mind. Wear it if you must. Put it on now and say I am here.

HENRY   No. Just go and ring the bell.

(*She smiles and moves up the porch steps.* ANNA *comes back into the room, dressed in an apron and carrying a tray*)

ANNA (*To* CARRIE)   I'm making jambalaya for you.

CARRIE   Isn't that nice?

(*The bell rings.* CARRIE *jumps and runs to the door*)

ALBERTINE (*To* CARRIE)   Hello, Miss Anna.

CARRIE (*Amazed*)   Mrs. Prine. Mrs. Prine. Do come in. (*She moves ahead of* ALBERTINE, *calling*)   Mrs. Prine is here. Isn't that nice?

ANNA (*Moves forward*)   Mrs. Prine, it's gracious of you to come. We should have come to call on you.

CARRIE (*Flustered*)   We're relatives now, after all. We did phone, three times. But, of course, you never got the messages.

ALBERTINE (*To* CARRIE)   Yes, I did get them, Miss Anna.

ANNA   *I* am Anna.

ALBERTINE   Forgive me.

ANNA (*Turns to* CARRIE)   And this is Carrie. Close your dress.

CARRIE   Oh, my goodness. (*She turns away and nervously buttons her dress*)   You must forgive me—

ANNA   How are you, Mrs. Prine? Are you spending the summer across the lake?

ALBERTINE   No. I've closed the lake house. Now that Lily is married, I stay right here in summer. I don't like the country.

CARRIE   Not like the country. My. I never heard anybody say a thing like that before. It takes courage to just up and say you don't like the country. Everybody likes the country.

ALBERTINE   Do they? I see so few people.

ANNA (*Quickly*)   You must be lonely without Lily.

ALBERTINE   No.

CARRIE   Oh. Goodness.

ALBERTINE   I've come at your supper time—

ANNA   And we'd like to share it with you.

CARRIE   Oh, please do stay. I'll just go and primp myself—

ALBERTINE   No, thank you. I eat at midnight. It's my bad habit to live at night and sleep the days away.

CARRIE   Lily said that— Well, she just said that.

ALBERTINE   I suppose it was hard on a child, a young girl, not to have her mother available during the day. But perhaps it was just as well. What time do you expect Lily and Julian?

CARRIE   Expect them? Expect them? We haven't heard for seventeen days—

ALBERTINE   Lily left a message that they'd be here tonight. I came to say—

ANNA (*As* CARRIE *turns to her*)   They'd be *here* tonight? We've had no word, Mrs. Prine.

CARRIE (*In great excitement*)   The Chicago train comes in at seven. Have we time to get to the station? I'll phone. It's never on time. I'll get dressed right away. Are there

221

enough shrimps? Is there crayfish bisque left? We can
still buy some wine—Get dressed, Anna—

ALBERTINE   Miss Carrie, they are not on the Chicago train.

CARRIE   You said you had a message—

ALBERTINE   Yes, Lily spoke with Henry on the phone. She
said they would be coming here tonight.

CARRIE   Then they *must* be on that train—

ALBERTINE   No. The call was not from Chicago. The call
came from here.

CARRIE   (*Carefully*)   It could not have come from here.

ALBERTINE   I am sure of it, Miss Carrie, because I saw
Lily two nights ago.

CARRIE   Saw her? Here? Here? (*After a second*)   What
did Lily say?

ALBERTINE   I didn't speak to her. She was moving back
and forth in front of the house as if she wished to come
in and didn't wish to come in.

CARRIE   (*After a pause*)   You saw your daughter, after a
whole year, walking in front of your house and you didn't
speak to her? I don't understand, Mrs. Prine.

ALBERTINE   That's quite all right.

ANNA   (*Softly*)   But we need to understand.

ALBERTINE   (*Turns her head, looks at* CARRIE *and then at*
ANNA)   Strange. Sometimes I can't tell which of you
is speaking. (*To* CARRIE)   Your manner, Miss Carrie,
is so, well, so Southern. And then, suddenly, you are
saying what I had thought Miss Anna might say. It is as
if you had exchanged faces, back and forth, forth and
back.

CARRIE   (*Sharply*)   Did you see Julian?

ALBERTINE   There. That's what I mean. No. Julian was
not with Lily. I have simply had a mesage saying they
would be here this evening. I have told you all I know.

CARRIE   (*To* ANNA)   What should we do? (*To* ALBERTINE)
What are you going to do?

ALBERTINE   I will go home now and ask you to tell Lily

222

that I will come again in the morning. Please tell them that the house is mostly closed up, but by tomorrow I can make them comfortable.

CARRIE   Oh, no. Julian will want to be here.

ALBERTINE   Ah, I am sure they prefer to stay here, but—

ANNA   There must be a good reason why Julian hasn't told us he is in town. If we seem upset, Mrs. Prine, it is because we are not accustomed to—

ALBERTINE   —daughters who walk in the night and mothers who do not speak to daughters who walk in the night. I really don't know why Lily didn't come in to me, nor why I didn't ask her. Good night. Thank you. (*She moves out, followed by* ANNA, *followed by a dazed* CARRIE. HENRY *is waiting in the garden.* ALBERTINE *moves toward him, then turns toward the porch*)   I think you have met Henry Simpson. Miss Anna and Miss Carrie Berniers, Henry.

HENRY   Good evening.

(ALBERTINE *takes his arm and they exit*)

CARRIE   (*Softly*)   Is *that* the man Lily calls Henry? *That* man was there in a white coat when we went for dinner, but I didn't know that was the Henry. You mean he's a nigger? I never heard anybody introduce a nigger before. I'm sorry I didn't say something. I never think of things in time. (*She turns, sees* ANNA *has gone back to the living room, and moves to join her*)   That man Lily called Henry is a nigger. Is he a chauffeur? What is he? Last time, he was a butler. Introduces us to a nigger— (*Sits down, desperate*)   Do you believe that strange woman? Do you believe they're in town?

ANNA   Maybe Lily's pregnant. They arrived and wanted to go to a doctor first so they could tell us the good news. I'm sure something like that—

CARRIE   She's not pregnant.

ANNA   How do you know?

CARRIE   Girls like Lily don't have babies right away. Too

full of good times the first year of marriage, I can tell
you that.

ANNA What do you know about the first year of marriage?

CARRIE I just know.

ANNA How? From books you don't read any more?

CARRIE You're saying that again. Teasing me again. No,
I don't read much any more, and I don't play the piano,
or put ice on my face, or walk for wild flowers— (*Very
loudly, as if she were going to cry*) I get tired now after
work and that terrible man. All I want to do is have a
little something to eat and play casino, and— Don't you
like to play casino with me, is that what you're saying?

ANNA Not every night. I like to read—

CARRIE You don't ever have to play casino again. Read
whenever you like, but don't nag me about it. You used
to do it with Julian, too. Some people read and some
people learn other ways— I think she's crazy, that Mrs.
Prine. And you know what? I don't believe they're in
New Orleans without coming here. (*Lamely*) Do you?
What do you think?

ANNA I think it's happened again. And he feels bad and
doesn't want to tell us.

CARRIE Well, that's natural enough. Who wants to come
home and say they've failed? What do you mean? *What's*
happened again?

ANNA (*Gently*) You understand me.

  (*She rises and exits toward the kitchen*)

CARRIE I don't think it's nice of us to guess this way. We
don't know anything, and yet here we are— (*But* ANNA
has left the room) A great many men take a long time
to find themselves. And a lot of *good* business men just
aren't worth bowing to. Goodness. Look at the people
in my office. Dull, stupid—ugly, too. I don't like ugly
people. I just can't help it, and I'm not ashamed any more
to say it. (ANNA *comes back carrying a tray of food*)
Are you going to *eat*?

ANNA   I always have. I think it's best to continue.

CARRIE   You're just as worried and nervous as I am. You always talk cold when you get nervous. Anna. Please. When he comes, don't be cold. Please. It will hurt him—

ANNA   Why do you so often make it seem as if I had always been severe and unloving? I don't think it's true.

CARRIE   I don't believe I do that. It's you who gave him everything, long before I was old enough to help. But sometimes you go away from us both, and, well, it worries Julian when you do that.

ANNA   (*Takes a bankbook from her pocket*)   Here is the savings bankbook. Give it to him.

CARRIE   (*Deeply pleased*)   Oh, thank you. I'll give it to him when we're alone and Lily doesn't see. (ANNA *sits at the table, and puts food on* CARRIE'S *plate.* CARRIE *moves about*)   It's only for a short time. We'll have it back. After all, in a sense, this money is his. We lent it to him and he paid us back. This is the very money he paid us back, Anna. So, in a sense, its his.

ANNA   Do come and eat.

CARRIE   You're thinking that what I just said is foolish. You're thinking that you never understood where he got the money to pay for your operation—

ANNA   You know very well where he got it: He played in a dangerous poker game.

CARRIE   I'm not so sure. I often wondered—

ANNA   The shrimps are getting cold.

   (*She begins to eat*)

CARRIE   I can't eat. I don't know how you can. (*Sighs, then brightens*)   You know, it sounds strange, but I am positive he will make a fortune someday.

ANNA   A fortune isn't necessary. A job is.

CARRIE   All those self-made men at the office. Like Mr. Barrett. No interest in anything. Making fun of opera and poetry and women. Mean, too, ever since he tried to put his hands on me years ago. Pig. Things can go

225

wrong for a long time and then suddenly everything in a man's life clears up— Have you a headache, Anna? Do your eyes worry you tonight? Can I get you something?

ANNA   I haven't a headache. And if I had I wouldn't know the remedy. A prescription put up fresh each time Julian fails.

CARRIE   Oh, don't be sad. I'm not. I feel cheerful. Place and people and time make things go wrong, and then all of a sudden— (*There is the offstage noise of a car. She jumps up, runs to the window, stares out, nods at what she sees. Slowly, suddenly cool and calm, she turns back to* ANNA)   I am going to wait on the porch. Please don't show what you feel. Welcome him as he should always be welcomed in this, his house.

(*She moves to the porch.* JULIAN's *voice is heard offstage*)

JULIAN   Is that my Carrie on the porch?

CARRIE   (*Laughs with enormous pleasure*)   Yes, that's your Carrie on the porch. I can still jump. Shall I jump and you will catch me? (*In the middle of her speech, as she begins a jump movement, a* TAXI DRIVER *appears carrying a very large number of packages and valises*)   Oh. (JULIAN *and* LILY BERNIERS *appear. He is a handsome, tall man of about thirty-four.* LILY *is a frail, pretty girl of about twenty-one. She moves behind him.* JULIAN's *arms and hands are filled with valises and packages*)

JULIAN   Don't jump. I have no hands to catch you. (*Grinning, he moves up the steps as* CARRIE *waits for him. He puts the valises down and takes her in his arms, lifting her from the ground*)   Darling Carrie-Pie.

CARRIE   Julian.

(*He kisses her, puts her down. She clings to him a minute and follows him as he moves quickly into the house and toward* ANNA. LILLY *follows* CARRIE. ANNA *stands waiting for him, smiling warmly. When he kisses* ANNA

226

*it is quite different—no less warm, but different—from
his greeting to* CARRIE. ANNA *moves away from him and
toward* LILY)

ANNA   My dear Lily, how good to see you.

CARRIE (*To* JULIAN)   One year and six days. (*As she
hears* ANNA'S *greeting to* LILY)   Lily! I didn't see you.
(*Kisses* LILY. LILY *smiles and kisses her*)   Forgive me.
One year and six days. I was so excited that I didn't see
you—

JULIAN (*To the* TAXI DRIVER, *who comes in carrying the
valises and packages*)   Bring them in. Bring them in. I'm
hungry, Anna. Hungry for your cooking. Not a good
restaurant in Chicago. Would *not* know a red pepper if
they saw one.

CARRIE   There's crayfish in the icebox, thank God, and
jambalaya on the table—

JULIAN   Then go and get them. I'm weak. *Very,* very
weak.

ANNA (*Laughs*)   You don't look it.

CARRIE   Sit down, dear—

(*She starts to run off to the kitchen. Before she does,*
JULIAN *hands the* TAXI DRIVER *several bills. She peers at
them.* JULIAN *laughs*)

JULIAN   Don't be nosey. He deserves them. No porters at
the station because the train came in early.

TAXI DRIVER (*Stares at the bills*)   Thank you, sir. Thank
you— (*Puzzled*)   The train came in—

JULIAN (*Quickly*)   All right. Good-bye. (*Gives him another bill*)   Buy your baby something from me.

TAXI DRIVER   Thank you, sir. But I have to say in frank and
complete honesty that I haven't got a baby.

JULIAN (*Gives him another bill*)   Then take this and get
one and name it Julian.

(*The* TAXI DRIVER *laughs and exits*)

ANNA   You still say that to waiters and taxi drivers? That

means you've been in a poker game. And what train came in early?

CARRIE (*Very quickly*) Anna, go get the crayfish. And make fresh, hot coffee. Lily, shall I take you to your room? Oh, my no, it needs cleaning. Well, just sit down. Anna, get the crayfish for Julian.

ANNA There are no crayfish.

JULIAN (*Is eating the dinner on the table with great pleasure*) We'll go out later and have them with champagne. (*To* ANNA) The same dress?

ANNA The same dress. You look tired, Lily. Can I get you something?

LILY I am tired. Julian doesn't like me to be tired.

JULIAN I don't like anybody to be tired. But it was a long trip, darling— (*As if he is prompting her*) Wasn't it a long trip, Lily?

LILY Yes. When it happened. It was long when it happened.

JULIAN Lily.

LILY (*Quickly, to* CARRIE *and* ANNA) It was a very long trip. Longer than going.

ANNA The wedding day. My how it rained. And Julian put his new coat round your pretty dress and the drawing room was full of flowers. Remember?

LILY (*Smiling, suddenly uplifted, happy*) Did it rain? I don't remember. It was all days to me: Cold and hot days, fog and light, and I was on a high hill running down with the top of me, and flying with the left of me, and singing with the right of me— (*Softly, as if she is worn out*) I was doing everything nice anybody had ever done nice.

ANNA (*Touched*) Nice.

LILY What were you doing when I was doing all that, Julian?

JULIAN (*His mouth very full*) Being my kind of happy.

LILY You're always happy.

JULIAN   I am glad you think that, darling.

ANNA   You've given us no news. How is the shoe factory?

JULIAN   What shoe factory?

(*There is a long silence. He is grinning and eating.* ANNA *moves toward the window, and takes in a plant.* CARRIE, *standing behind* JULIAN, *holds up her hand in an attempt to stop* ANNA'S *questions.* ANNA *sees it and ignores it*)

ANNA   (*Carefully*)   The shoe factory that you bought in Chicago.

JULIAN   Oh, *that* shoe factory. It's gone.

ANNA   Don't be flip with me, Julian.

CARRIE   (*Gesturing wildly*)   He's not. He's just trying to explain—

JULIAN   (*Turns, sees* CARRIE, *laughs, catches the gesturing hand*)   No, I'm not. I'm not trying to explain anything. (*To* ANNA)   I was being flip. I forget that you worry about the money I lose.

ANNA   It's not the money— It's that you don't seem to care. And the money was—

JULIAN   Lily's money.

LILY   My money? Doesn't matter about my money. I don't want money.

CARRIE   (*To* LILY)   You mustn't worry about it. Not worth it.

LILY   I'm not worried about money, Miss Carrie.

CARRIE   I suppose rich people always worry about money. People like us have to learn there are more important things.

LILY   I said I wasn't worried about money, Miss Carrie.

CARRIE   Well, you mustn't.

JULIAN   (*To* ANNA)   The factory was a crooked sell. The machinery wasn't any good. I didn't know anything about shoe machinery and I never should have thought I did. Man who sold it to me faked the books. That's all.

CARRIE   (*Softly*)   That could happen to anybody.

JULIAN   (*Laughs*)   No. Not to anybody. Just me.

CARRIE That's not·true. And you mustn't ever believe it.

JULIAN Darling Carrie. Hiding her hopes that I would come home with Chicago over my shoulder, dressed in pure gold, bringing candied oranges to hang in your hair. Well, that's just what I've done. Your hair don't look nice, Carrie-Pie.

ANNA (*Rises, crosses to the pile of dishes to carry them out*) We can help you.

CARRIE Yes, indeed we can. Julian, come in the kitchen and help me wash the dishes.

JULIAN No, ma'am. And you're never going to wash dishes again.

ANNA I don't wish to ask questions that you might not like, Julian. But it's uncomfortable this way. Your mother was here, Lily. She said she had seen you, had a message from you. She said she would come back tomorrow. (*To* JULIAN, *who has turned to stare at* LILY) So this is not your first night in town. You need not explain, but I thought we should.

JULIAN We've been in New Orleans for a week, at the hotel. I had a good reason for that. It was no neglect of you. I even came by and stared in at you— (*Points outside*) —the first hour back. You were playing casino and Anna was yawning. You look tired, both of you. You need a long, long good time. (*To* ANNA) This time, no need to be sad. I used to tell you: never was any good; never came out anywhere.

ANNA I am sad that you think it all so easy, so unimportant, so—"Never came out anywhere." I guess not, although I don't think those words mean very much.

CARRIE (*To* ANNA, *in a voice used once before*) I won't have that kind of talk. This is a happy, joyous night. Julian is home and that's all we need to know. It's a happy, joyous night.

(ANNA *exits*)

LILY (*To* JULIAN) I didn't see my mother, I didn't go

in. And I only sent the message today. I knew we'd arrive here, anyway, so— (*Softly, when there is no answer*) —I disobeyed you. But not much. Have I done harm?

JULIAN   No.

(CARRIE, *listening, pretending she isn't, is idly playing on the piano with one hand*)

LILY   I know you told me not to see anybody. But you didn't tell me why or anything. You just kept leaving the hotel. I want to see my mother. I want to talk with my mother.

JULIAN (*Smiles*)   I'm glad to hear that. I've never heard you want that before.

LILY   Are you angry with me?

JULIAN (*Smiles at her, shakes his head, moves away*) Carrie, stop that awful sound, darling. Just wait for the good piano—

CARRIE (*Laughs*)   No, I'd only find out I couldn't really play.

(JULIAN *has moved out to porch and is hauling in valises.* LILY *rises and follows him*)

JULIAN (*Calling to* CARRIE)   You all been to the opera?

CARRIE   No. We'll wait until Europe.

JULIAN (*Laughs*)   Still talking about Europe?

CARRIE   Oh, we'll go someday. You'll see.

JULIAN (*Bringing in valises*)   Someday soon?
(*He goes out again for more*)

CARRIE   In a few years. Plenty of time. We're not that old.
(*She moves quickly out of the room*)

JULIAN   Yes, you are. Old enough to have fun. Have to crowd it in now, Carrie, both of you. Crowd it in fast. (*Smiling at* LILY)   You, too. Twenty-one is very, very old.

LILY (*She has followed him to the porch*)   Tell me you're not angry with me.

JULIAN (*His arms heavy with valises*)   I am not angry

231

with you. Have I ever been angry with you? Why do you ask me that so often?

LILY (*As she steps aside*)   Julian, who is the lady you talked to on the train?

JULIAN (*Too lightly*)   Which lady?—I talk to everybody.

LILY   The not such a young lady with the sad face.

JULIAN   Most ladies on trains are not so young and have sad faces. I often wondered why. (*He tries to pass her*) Move, darling.

LILY   The one you were with today and yesterday and—

JULIAN (*Turns, stares at her*)   Where did you see me?

LILY   I don't know. Just on the street. In front of the hotel—

JULIAN   No, you didn't.

LILY   No, I didn't. That's the first lie I ever told you, Julian.

JULIAN   Then it's one more than I ever told you.
(*Carrying the valises, he moves into the living room. LILY follows him*)

LILY   I saw you in Audubon Park. On a bench. By the ducks.

JULIAN   Have you told anybody?

LILY   No.

JULIAN   Don't. The lady would be in trouble. And so would we.

LILY   And in that little restaurant. At a table—

JULIAN   Oh, Lily.

LILY   I didn't mean to walk after you, to follow you. But I was so lonely in the hotel room, locked up the way you asked me to be.

JULIAN   All right, darling, all right. Don't follow me, Lily, ever again. That's not the way to be married. (LILY *hesitates, as if to say something, then exits*) Hey, everybody. Come and get your presents. Hey, where is everybody?

CARRIE (*Appears in the garden, runs up the porch, speaks*

232

in a whisper) Julian. I want to speak to you. Come here.

JULIAN Can't. You come here.

CARRIE Sssssh. (*He comes to the porch. She sits down on the porch steps*) Come here. I've got a nice secret. And this is where we always told nice secrets.

JULIAN You come here. *I* got nice secrets. Where's Anna? Anna!

CARRIE Ssh. Ssh.

JULIAN (*Sits beside her*) What's the matter with you?

CARRIE (*Gives him the savings bankbook*) No need for Lily to see. You'll just tell her it's yours. More than twenty-eight hundred dollars. And we don't need any of it, not any of it, so don't say anything— (*He takes her hands, kisses them. She is very moved. Softly, embarrassed*) Don't say anything, please. And if that isn't enough, we can manage other things, too.

JULIAN (*Stares at the book, then rises and calls out*) Anna!

CARRIE Anna doesn't want any thanks—

(ANNA *comes into the room*)

JULIAN (*Enters the room, holds out the bankbook*) God bless you. All my life it's been this way.

ANNA (*Smiles*) You are our life. It is we who should thank you.

(*He takes her in his arms*)

JULIAN How many, many times?

CARRIE (*Comes into the room*) You paid it back, always.

JULIAN You know I didn't. But this time I will.

CARRIE Of course you will. But Lily doesn't have to know about all this— So ssh.

JULIAN Stop ssshing me and come here and sit down and stop talking. (*He puts* CARRIE *in a chair and motions to* ANNA *to be seated. Then he leans down to unwrap the boxes and open the valises. The boxes are dressmaker boxes, and he pulls from them two fancy evening dresses.*

They are too grand for anything less than a ball. CARRIE
leans forward, stares at them) For a ball. Wear them
the second time at the opera, if you like. But I don't
think dresses like these should be worn twice in the same
city, do you? Everybody in Paris will talk, and we can't
have that. (*He opens another box*) Maybe you can
wear them again when you get to Strasbourg. (*Points his
finger at* CARRIE) Not to the cemetery. I bet the opera
house there is drafty— (*He has taken out two fur pieces
and arranged them over the dresses*) No, No. I've got
things mixed up. (*He begins to fumble in another box*)
Or so the lady said. The furs are for breakfast or something. (*He is now holding up two fur-trimmed opera
coats. They are royal in feeling*) These are for the
dresses. And maybe they can be worn the second time.
(*He moves to arrange them over* ANNA *and* CARRIE.
CARRIE'S *is much too large and she looks drowned. He
points to the other boxes and valises*) Suits for traveling. Dresses for informal evenings, whatever that is.
(*Pulls out frothy, very youthful negligees*) For flirta-
tions on Italian terraces. (*Drapes them over* ANNA *and*
CARRIE. *He goes to* CARRIE *with a large rather flashy
necklace*) Garnets. Your birthstone. Next time, pearls.
(*He drapes over* ANNA'S *arm a large gold mesh bag*)
Remember when old lady Senlis used to come along
swinging her gold mesh bag, and your eyes would pop
out wondering what was in it? Look and see what's in
this one.

ANNA (*Softly*) What is all this, Julian?

JULIAN It is that we're rich. Just open your gold mesh
bag with diamond initials—Anna, *diamond* initials—and
see what's inside.

CARRIE (*Loud, nervous giggle*) The only thing could be,
is a certificate to an insane asylum.

JULIAN (*Takes an envelope from the purse*) You're
wrong. A certificate to a boat called the *Ottavia*, sailing

234

day after tomorrow. Two rooms, one of them a parlor. Think of that, a parlor on a boat. (*He takes the envelope to* CARRIE) Look at it, look at it. Of course, we had always planned to go together. But I won't be able to go with you, darling, not this time, big business here, and all that. But we'll join you in a few months—

CARRIE (*Dully*) We'll wait for you.

JULIAN No, you won't. No more waiting for anything.

ANNA (*Softly*) Where does all this come from, Julian?

JULIAN All over town. I just went in places and said bring out the best for two pretty ladies who are on their way. On their way.

ANNA You know what I mean.

JULIAN I know what you mean. They were bought with my money. Mine. Yours. Ours. We're rich. How do you like that, how do you like it?

CARRIE We'll like it fine—when it happens. (*Giggles*) Rich. Us!

JULIAN What are you doing?

CARRIE Trying to make a neat package.

JULIAN Stop it. (*When she doesn't*) I said to stop it. Nothing's going back this time. Listen to me. Now listen to me. We're rich. (LILY *comes into the room. She is in her slip and is carrying a hairbrush. He smiles at her*) Aren't we rich?

LILY Mama's rich, I guess.

JULIAN No, us, us. I've been telling you for a week.

LILY There are three men at the back door. From a trucking company—

JULIAN Tell them to bring them in, darling. (*She exits*) Right in here. Now you're going to see something.

CARRIE (*Stares at the boat tickets*) Are these real boat tickets? I mean, stamped and bought?

JULIAN Bought and stamped. Look. It's going to be this way. The first money is for us to have things. Have fun. After that, I promise you, we'll invest. And like all people with money, we'll make more and more and more until we get sick from it. Rich people get sick more than we do. Maybe from worry.

ANNA Poor people, too. Like me, right now. (*Very sharply*) Where did you get this money, Julian?

CARRIE Oh, now don't start that tone. You know very well he's been in a poker game.

JULIAN No, she doesn't know that, and you don't either. (*Two* MOVING MEN *appear, carrying a fancy, highly carved spinet. There is a big sign on the spinet lettered* CARRIE) Come in. Just put it down. (*Motions to* CARRIE) By that lady.

(*The* MEN *carry the spinet to* CARRIE *and place it near her*)

CARRIE My God.

(*Another* MOVING MAN *comes in wheeling a large refrigerator on a dolly. The first two* MEN *move to help him*)

JULIAN And put that by this lady (*He motions toward* ANNA. *They wheel the refrigerator and place it almost in front of* ANNA. LILY *comes back into the room*) Good. (*He pulls out several large bills*) Thank you. Buy the babies something from me. (*To the head* MOVING MAN) Name the next one Julian.

MOVING MAN There ain't going to be no next one. Thank you.

(*They exit*)

LILY Why do you always say that? We'll name our son Julian. Don't you believe—

JULIAN (*Laughs*) Insurance. That's all.

CARRIE (*To* LILY) You're in your slip. In front of men.

JULIAN Can't harm them.

CARRIE I never heard of such a thing. Answering the door in your underwear. Don't you mind?

JULIAN I mind that you haven't looked at your piano. Think, Carrie, a fine new piano, what you always

wanted, right in front of you— Play it. Play it for me,
Carrie, the way we used to always say.

(*She puts out her hand, touches a note, takes her hand
away and puts it over her face*)

JULIAN (*Softly, smiling*)   I know. Take your time.

ANNA   What is all this? Answer me, please, Julian.

JULIAN   I'm going to tell you all about it someday soon. I
can't now. But I'll tell you this much, I didn't play poker.
All I did was sell some real estate.

ANNA   You never owned any real estate.

JULIAN   No. But I do now, see?

ANNA   No, I don't see. I don't see at all.

JULIAN   Once I liked somebody and they liked me, and
she thought I was kind to her. So years go by and she
hears about a good thing, and gives me the tip on it.
And the tip works. Boy, how it worked. Now let it go.
I'll tell you soon, but in the meantime I give my word
because she could be in bad trouble. Now stop worrying, and sit back— (*He guides* ANNA's *hand to refrigerator door, opens it, pulls an envelope from it*)   I finished
the deal and collected the money at two o'clock today.
At two-eighteen, I rang the bells of Mr. Maxwell Shine.
And so here's the mortgage to the house. (*Kneels; softly*)
Look, Anna, first time in our lives, first time in our
father's life. You have a house, without worry or asking
him to wait. Remember when I was a kid and the time
you took me with you and you made me tell Mr. Shine
how I wouldn't have anyplace to live unless— Christ
God, how I hated— Do you remember?

ANNA   I remember.

JULIAN   Well, there'll never be such things to say again.
Not for any of us. (*He rises and shouts*)   Not ever,
ever. (*To* CARRIE)   I wrote your Mr. Barrett a letter
last night. I wrote it three times. "Your petty angers, the
silk stockings at Christmas that were always cheaper

than a decent salary. Miss Caroline Berniers will not return to work." (CARRIE *rises, makes a sound in her throat, stands staring at him. He turns to* ANNA) For you I just wrote that Miss Anna Berniers was resigning from the coat department because she was leaving for an extended European tour. (*He sits down.* ANNA *lifts her head and stares at him. There is a long silence*) Well. Say something.

ANNA   I can't say something.

JULIAN   I know, I know. All came so fast. Well, we don't have to say things to each other, never did. Just sit back and have fun. That's all I want. (*To* LILY) And for you— Give me the wedding ring. (*Sharply she pulls back from him*) Give it to me. (*He takes the ring from her finger*) Twenty dollars in a pawnshop, and I polished it, and prayed you wouldn't mind, or say anything. (*He takes from his pocket, and puts on her finger, a very large diamond ring*) With this, I you wed again, and forever.

LILY   Please give me my ring.

JULIAN   (*Now he holds up her hand so that she can see her new diamond ring*) Look, darling, look at it. Superstitious? (*He looks at* LILY, *then at* CARRIE, *then at* ANNA) Please don't cry or look it, all of you. (*He takes an envelope from his pocket, goes to each of them as he speaks, lets them look into the envelope*) One hundred and fifty thousand dollars, less peanuts— (*Motions to the packages*) —for this. Seventy-five thousand for my partner, seventy-five thousand for me. My lawyer said I shouldn't carry all that cash around, rich people don't carry cash, not more than ten or twenty dollars, so other people pay the bills. But I said I'll carry this, I like it— Hey, did you hear—my lawyer. *I've* got a *lawyer*. What do you think of that? (CARRIE *has paid little attention to the money in the envelope, but* ANNA *is staring at it*) Ain't counterfeit. Twenty, five thousand

dollar bills; fifty, one thousand dollar bills— You'll be‑
lieve it all by tomorrow. Big, successful Julian, the way
you wanted me. The man who was never good at any‑
thing except living on his sisters, and losing his wife's
money. I never minded failure much, you minded. But
you know what? I like things this way: Making bargains,
talking big— I don't take my hat off in elevators any
more— (*Laughs with great pleasure and picks up a
large package*) Now to *important* business. Last night
I drew up a budget list, you know, the way we used to.
Only where we put carfare for the week, I put cham‑
pagne, and where we put lunch money, sixty cents each,
I put caviar. You'll like caviar.

CARRIE I hate caviar. The one time I ever ate it, I hated
it. Just hated it.

JULIAN (*Holds up the package*) Champagne. *And* caviar,
Carrie-Pie. You'll learn to like it. (*He starts toward the
kitchen*) We're going to have a champagne-caviar party
just for us. Sit down and play the piano.
(*He exits*)

CARRIE (*Softly*) Since when do you give me orders?
(*Very loudly*) I said since when do you give me or‑
ders? (ANNA *puts up a hand, as if to quiet her*) I don't
believe it all. I don't believe it. (*When* ANNA *doesn't an‑
swer her*) We have no jobs. (*To* LILY) What is this
all about?

LILY I want my ring. I was married in my ring.

CARRIE I asked you a question, Lily.

LILY I didn't hear you.

CARRIE What is this all about? Where did Julian get this
money?

LILY I don't know, ma'am. A lady came to Chicago and
phoned him, and he went to see her, and everything
changed and he said we were coming here, and she was
on the train, and he didn't want me to know. She calls
him every night at six o'clock.

CARRIE I'm not talking about women. That's not my business. I'm talking about this— (*She motions around*) Europe day after tomorrow! Has he gone crazy? What does he think we are, fine ladies with maids and secretaries who can move whenever they like? Whore's clothes. I wouldn't be seen in this. Not seen in them. (*Turns on* ANNA) For God's sake take off that stuff. What are you doing?

ANNA (*Who is reading the mortgage document*) Trying to understand.

CARRIE (*In a whisper*) Does it really say—

ANNA Yes. It really says we own this house.

CARRIE This house. This awful house. He's changed. He even talks different. Didn't he know we hated this house, always, always, always.

ANNA You used to tell him how much we liked it, and the garden, and the street, and the memories of Mama and Papa.

CARRIE You know very well I said all that to keep him from being ashamed of the house and what we didn't have—

ANNA (*Hands her the paper*) Well. We've been rewarded.

LILY I want my ring. I was married in my ring. (*She holds up her hand*) This is a vulgar ring.

CARRIE (*Points to a tiny pin she is wearing*) Topaz is my birthstone. How could he forget when he gave me this pin with the first job he ever lost. I even wear it at night—

LILY I want my married ring.

CARRIE You said that before.

(LILY *runs toward the table, picks up the ring. As she does, the phone rings, and she continues the run that will bring her to the phone*)

LILY Hello. (*A slight pause*) No, ma'am. No, he isn't. This is his wife. What is *your* name?

240

(She stares at the phone and then hangs up. After a second, she puts on the old ring and, with a violent movement, throws the diamond toward the window. It hits the window and drops. JULIAN *comes into the room carrying an ice bucket, two bottles of champagne, glasses and two very large jars of caviar)*

JULIAN I heard the phone. Didn't the phone ring?

ANNA *(After a second)* No.

JULIAN *(Pouring)* Now. *(To* CARRIE, *points to the piano)* Why aren't you playing? And you took off— Put the pretty clothes on so I can be proud.

CARRIE *(Sharply)* All of them?

LILY The phone did ring. It was that lady who calls every evening. I told her you weren't here. I don't know why I said it, but I did.

JULIAN I have business with that lady. I've told you that before. I was to meet her this evening. It's not easy for her to call me and I can't call her. Did she say she'd call back tonight? *(*LILY *shakes her head)* Why did you tell her I wasn't here?

LILY I didn't know I was going to do it. Please forgive me. It wasn't nice.

JULIAN Not nice, wasn't it? You know what I think it wasn't? Respectful. *(He moves toward* CARRIE*)* Respect-ful— Respectful. I don't think I can spell that word. I never used it before. But I like it. *(He hits his chest)* A man. Respect. That's what you always said, success isn't everything but it makes a man stand straight, and you were right. *(He hands a glass of champagne to* ANNA *and offers caviar. He speaks to* CARRIE*)* You want to know something? I bring you a piano, I ask you to play it for me, you don't. I don't think that's respectful. *(He laughs)* I like that word. *(*CARRIE *sits down at the piano and begins to play. She fumbles, as if she is thinking of something else, then plays a waltz.* JULIAN *moves*

241

to LILY, *gives her a glass, whirls her around, kisses her hair*) I forgive you, my infant bride. (*He looks at her hand*) Where's your ring?

(ANNA *rises, crosses, and picks up the ring*)

LILY I don't know.

JULIAN You don't know?

ANNA I have it. I was looking at it.

(JULIAN *smiles, kisses* LILY'S *hair. The music stops sharply and he turns to* CARRIE)

JULIAN More, more. It's a party. We're having a party. (*To* ANNA) Dance?

(*He pulls her to her feet, whirls her around, the long evening coat tangled in her legs*)

CARRIE Anna. You look like a fool. Like a real fool.

JULIAN What's the matter? (*Moving to* CARRIE. *He hands her a glass of champagne. Staring at him, she sips it*) Good? (*He spoons out a large amount of caviar, sings*) *Avez-vous les chambres, Monsieur Hotel-keeper? Non, ils ne sont pas trop chères.* Nothing is too expensive now. Send up two pounds *de* caviar *pour* breakfast *pour ma soeur et moi.* (*He leans over her with the caviar*) Now.

(*He forces her mouth open.* JULIAN *laughs*)

CARRIE You're laughing at me. You've never laughed at me before. (*She rises, shrilly*) You're laughing at me.

JULIAN No, I wasn't. I'm just happy. I'm giving a party—(*He looks at* ANNA, *who has her head hung; at* LILY, *who looks sad and tearful*) What's the matter with everybody? (*He drinks his champagne. He pours himself another drink, bolts it, stares at them*) We're not having a very nice party. What's the matter?

CURTAIN

ACT TWO

*Early Thursday morning. The spinet and the refrigerator
are as they were the night before.* ANNA, *in a housedress, is
lowering the plants from the window into the garden. On a
chair is a large, old-fashioned trunk-type suitcase; near the
suitcase are two pairs of shoes.* ANNA *sits down, and begins
to polish the shoes with rag and paste.* CARRIE *enters carrying a coffee pot. She is dressed and has on her hat. She sits
down and pours herself a cup of coffee.*

CARRIE   Is your headache better?

ANNA   I didn't have a headache.

CARRIE   You said you did.

ANNA   No, I didn't.

CARRIE   Last night, before you went to bed, you said your
eyes were bothering you, you had a headache.

ANNA   No.

CARRIE   I think everybody's going crazy. I really do. No
wonder you can't remember what you said. I don't think
I slept an hour. I'd close my eyes, and say I don't believe
it, when I get up— (*Points to the spinet, the boxes, etc.*)
—that thing, and that, won't be there, and it will be
years ago. He stayed out in the garden drinking by himself till late last night. (*Points inside*)   Still asleep?

ANNA   I suppose so.

CARRIE   How could *you* have slept last night? Mama used
to say you could sleep through anything.

ANNA   Mama believed that lack of sleep was a sign of
good breeding. Do you remember the time she said she

243

hadn't slept for two years? (*Points inside*) Yes, I heard Lily, if that's what you mean.

CARRIE She rattled around half the night. She went out, she came back, she went out. She's a very strange girl. I remember thinking that the first time I ever met her. (*Points around the room*) And she doesn't know any more about all this than we do. That's not natural in a good marriage. In a good marriage a man doesn't have secrets from his wife.

ANNA How do you know?

CARRIE It's not natural in a good marriage, I can tell you that.

ANNA We don't know anything about a good marriage or a bad one. I read somewhere that old maids are the true detectives of the human heart. But I don't want to be a detective of other people's hearts. I'm having enough trouble with my own.

CARRIE I know you are. I know you're just as worried as I am. I know that's why you're having headaches again.

ANNA I said I didn't have a headache.

CARRIE I'll get you something for it. Julian pampers Lily as if she were a child. He never treated us that way, always boasted of our good sense.

ANNA He didn't marry us.

CARRIE Nobody wants a child for a wife.

ANNA There's no sense telling your opinions about marriage to me. I don't know anything about it.
(*She gets up, carries a pair of shoes to the valise, wraps them in paper, and packs them*)

CARRIE What are you doing?

ANNA Put your clothes out. I'm going to wash and iron today.

CARRIE What for?

ANNA (*Turns to stare at her*) Europe.

CARRIE We'll miss the eight-thirty streetcar. (*When there is no answer*) We'll miss the eight-thirty streetcar.

(*When there is no answer*) I know what Julian said. But I get the mail before Mr. Barrett, and if Julian did write such a letter I'll just throw it out. You better go down to the store and get somebody to do the same for you. (*Very sharply, when* ANNA *does not answer*) *We have no jobs.* They're not easy to get and we're not young. You told me all my life what that would mean to us. You said that as long as we could work and save a little then we could get sick when we were old, and take care of Julian, and not end as Mama and Papa did.

ANNA Julian has come home rich. We can get sick now.

CARRIE Rich! Do you really believe this foolishness? Julian rich! God knows what he's been up to. God knows when and how it will blow up. Doesn't it worry you?

ANNA Yes. It worries me. But I think we should go to Europe. He wants us to go.

CARRIE What do you mean, he wants us to go? You make it sound as if we're in his way.

ANNA I don't know what I mean.

CARRIE Go to Europe. What are you talking about? What's going to happen when trouble comes if we're not here to take care of it?

ANNA Why do you think trouble will come?

CARRIE Because it always has. You know very well what I mean. Well, you go to Europe and I'll go to work.

ANNA (*Laughs*) All right.

CARRIE If Mr. Samuel Barrett has seen the letter, I'll apologize. Mr. Barrett likes people to apologize. Nineteen years of faithful work matter for something. (*Giggles*) Ho, ho. I'd like to see you in Europe alone.

(LILY *appears from the bedroom. She has on a dress and over the dress she has on a nightgown. She stares at* CARRIE *and* ANNA *as if she didn't know who they were*)

ANNA Morning. (*She rises to pour* LILY *a cup of coffee*) Julian want his breakfast?

LILY   I don't know. (*She points to the left side of the room*)   He slept in there.

CARRIE   Mama and Papa's room.

LILY   He thought I was asleep when he went in there, but I wasn't.

CARRIE   No, you certainly weren't. You moved around most of the night. Are you dressed or undressed? Well, I'm off to work.

LILY   My. It's awfully hot to go to work.

CARRIE   Yes. And sometimes it's awfully cold.

(*She exits toward the porch. As she moves out,* MRS. PRINE *appears in the garden.* HENRY *stands outside the garden fence. During the scene between* LILY *and* ALBERTINE, *he will occasionally be seen moving back and forth*)

ALBERTINE   Good morning.

CARRIE   Good morning.

(CARRIE *hurries off. At the sound of her mother's voice,* LILY *runs to the porch, stares at her mother and runs back into the room*)

LILY   Oh. Where are my shoes? (*Stares down at herself, sees that she is barefoot, hestitates*)   Oh. (*Runs out again to the porch and down to the garden*)   Mama. I don't know why I did that.

(ALBERTINE *moves toward her and they kiss*)

ALBERTINE   I come calling much too early. I forget that other people sleep at night.

LILY   I didn't.

ALBERTINE   I know.

LILY   What did Henry tell you?

ALBERTINE   That you were out, er, visiting, and wanted to speak with me.

LILY   Yes. I didn't want Henry to come and get me. I didn't need his help.

ALBERTINE   He said the neighborhood worried him at two o'clock in the morning.

246

LILY   How did he know where I was?

ALBERTINE   You told him on the phone.

LILY   Did I? I don't remember—I was mean to Henry. Did he tell you that?

ALBERTINE   No.

LILY   (*After a second*)   I'm sorry I spoke that way.

ALBERTINE   How are you, Lily? I haven't seen you in a whole year. The garden wing of the house is being cleaned for you. You are very welcome, and I've come to say that to Julian.

LILY   Thank you. It's nice that you want us. Do you?

ALBERTINE   You are thinner, Lily. Have you been well?

LILY   Do you?

ALBERTINE   Do I what?

LILY   Do you really want me to come home again?

ALBERTINE   I'll come later. You must be tired from your —night's exercise.

LILY   (*Quickly*)   Mama, don't go. Please. I need help. Your help. I'll start at the start and try not to take long and say things nice and clear—

ALBERTINE   There's no need. Don't distress yourself. I've guessed your trouble and I've brought you a check. (*She takes a check from her bag and puts it on the garden table*)   Will you and Julian come and dine at eight? Then you'll decide if you wish to move in, or, if in this heat, you prefer the lake house. I've always meant to give you the lake house, Lily, and tomorrow we'll go around and have Warkins do the papers. (*When there is no answer*)   At eight?

LILY   What does Mrs. Warkins look like? Does she speak in a low voice?

ALBERTINE   I don't know. I haven't seen her in years, and then only once or twice.

LILY   You haven't seen anybody in years, except Henry, of course. How old is Mrs. Warkins?

ALBERTINE   I know little about her, Lily. It's bad enough

to know Warkins. I remember her as a tall woman with a sad face. Possibly from being married to a lawyer.

LILY Is she in love with Mr. Warkins?

ALBERTINE (*Smiles, shrugs*) That is a remarkable idea. Thank God I've never been in a position to find out. Let's waste our time saying things like each to his own taste, and shaking our heads in gossip, but let's do it another time.

LILY Please don't smile and shrug, Mama. It always makes me nervous. You are angry because I was mean to Henry last night, and he told you.

ALBERTINE He told me nothing.

LILY *I was mean to Henry*. That was bad of me, wasn't it?

ALBERTINE (*Wearily, softly*) I don't know.

LILY Well, tell him I'm sorry.

ALBERTINE You have been saying you are sorry, in space, for many years.

LILY You *are* angry now.

ALBERTINE Oh, Lily.

LILY I don't know what makes me speak so wrong. All I want is to tell you, and have you help me. But I get things out of order—Mama, I'm in trouble.

ALBERTINE I know Julian lost the factory. Well, perhaps he doesn't belong in a large city. He'll find something here. In the meantime—

(*She picks up the check and hands it to* LILY)

LILY What is it, Mama?

ALBERTINE (*Slowly, too patiently*) I told you. It's a check. A check is for money. Money. It's five thousand dollars. It's yours. Oblige me by not speaking of it again.

LILY Don't be angry with me.

ALBERTINE (*After a second*) Oh, Lily. Something always happens between us.

LILY If I could only speak in order, then I wouldn't—

ALBERTINE Don't fret. Everybody talks too much, too many words, and gets them out of order.

LILY   I know you think that. I know you do. That's what makes it so hard. It's that you never talk much, and you look down on people who don't do it very well.

ALBERTINE   You said you were in trouble. Do you wish to tell me about it?

LILY   You speak so severely, Mama.

ALBERTINE   Please, Lily, let us cease this talking about talking. Tell me or do not tell me.

LILY   (*Quickly, loudly*)   Mama, we're rich.

ALBERTINE   Who?

LILY   Julian.

ALBERTINE   When you say rich, do you mean *money* rich or spiritual rich, or moral rich or—

LILY   You're teasing me. Money rich.

ALBERTINE   Well, isn't that nice. Julian didn't lose the factory?

LILY   Yes, he lost it. We got rich some other way. There were phone calls from a lady and Julian would talk so I couldn't understand, and then we came here, and it all has to do with the lady, I think, and something else—

ALBERTINE   (*Very quickly*)   Never mind. Never mind. He'll probably tell me. What good news, Lily. I must say I hadn't expected it. Forgive my bringing the check. How impertinent of me to take for granted that Julian needed it. Don't tell him, just tear it up. Tonight we'll have a celebration—if I still know how. Shall we dine at Galatoire's? (*When there is no answer, she stares at* LILY)   What trouble are you in?

LILY   First we lived in a big hotel in Chicago, and I didn't like it, and didn't have anything to do. Then we moved to a little, poor hotel and I learned to cook in the bathroom, and Julian and I were close together, and he didn't have his friends any more, and he was sad and sweet and often he stayed with me all day, in bed, and we'd read or sleep, and he'd tell me about things. We were never really hungry, but I'd have to watch the meat and give him my share when he wasn't looking because he likes meat, and I was very happy.

ALBERTINE How often the rich like to play at being poor. A rather nasty game, I've always thought. You had only to write me.

LILY It wasn't a game, it wasn't. It was just after he lost all his money in the factory—

ALBERTINE *Your* money in the factory. You like being poor and you're not going to be. Is that the trouble you are in? I can't be sorry for you, Lily. I don't think Julian would have liked the meat game for very long; and neither would you if the shortage had lasted much longer. (*Laughs*) Cheer up. Good fortune isn't as bad as it seems.

LILY You're laughing at me, and you shouldn't. Julian will leave me now.

ALBERTINE Why?

LILY He is different. Things have changed.

ALBERTINE Marriages change from day to day and year to year. All relations between people. Women, of course, have regrets for certain delicate early minutes, but— There is no answer to that.

LILY Did you, Mama? Did you have those regrets?

ALBERTINE I don't remember. I don't think so. Your father and I had very little together. And so we had little to regret.

LILY I don't mean my father.

ALBERTINE (*After a long silence*) I came here because you were in trouble, or so you said. Not because I am. When I come to you for that reason, feel free to say what you wish. Until then, please do not.

LILY Julian couldn't have me last night, and when I cried he said please not to, that— And so I went out and walked and walked. I had never seen that street before. I heard noise way up, and I went in. There were people and a woman stood before them on a box. The people talked about themselves right out loud. One woman had lost a leg but she said it was growing back and she proved it.

(*There is a long pause*)

ALBERTINE My. Are you dozing off?

LILY And a man stood up and said how he used to drink and use a gun. And the lady on the box kept saying, "Truth, truth is the way to life, and the one way, the only way. Open your hearts with this knife and throw them here." (*Throws up her arm*) She had a knife in her hand—

ALBERTINE Do sit down, Lily.

LILY And she kissed the knife—

(*She kisses her hand in imitation*)

ALBERTINE Strange tastes people have. Don't kiss your own hand again, please.

LILY (*Sits down, speaks quietly*) Everybody left and there I was. The woman said, "You want me, child?" And I said, "Could I buy your knife?" "No," she said. "The knife is not for sale." But I wanted it more than I ever wanted anything and, well— (*Smiles, slyly*) —finally, we swapped something— And when it was in my hand, for the first time in my life, I just said everything, and asked. The lady said the knife of truth would dress me as in a jacket of iron flowers and though I would do battle, I would march from the battle cleansed. Then I fell asleep—

ALBERTINE Your many religious experiences have always made me uneasy, Lily—

LILY When I woke up I knew that I must begin my struggle up the mountain path of truth by asking you—

ALBERTINE You telephoned at two this morning to speak with me about a journey up a mountain path of truth?

LILY And Henry came instead, and made me get in the car, and brought me *here*. He stood in the way— But he

251

can't. Because I must ask truth, and speak truth, and act with truth, now and forever.

ALBERTINE   Do you think this is the proper climate? So hot and damp. Puts mildew on the truth.

LILY   Did you sell me to Julian, Mama?

(ALBERTINE *rises, comes to* LILY, *stares at her, and takes her by the shoulders*)

ALBERTINE (*Softly*)   Lily, take hold of yourself. Take hold.

LILY   Answer me.

ALBERTINE   You are my child, but I will not take much more of this.

LILY (*In a cry*)   Mama, Mama, I didn't mean to hurt you. (*Puts her hand on* ALBERTINE'S *chest*)   But it's so bad for me. Julian may leave me now, and he's all I ever had, or will, or want— Mama, did he marry me for money?

ALBERTINE   He married you because he loved you. Shame on you, Lily. You are looking for pain, and that makes me sad and always has.

LILY   I told you there is another woman. I saw them. I followed them and they went places where people wouldn't see them and they talked. And she has something to do with his getting rich.

ALBERTINE   Do you intend him never to speak to another woman? I don't know what you are talking about, getting rich, but it's good for people to have money of their own. The day comes when they don't like taking it from others. I know people thought of Julian as a charming man who didn't care about such things. But I never thought so.

LILY   Last night when I lay waiting for him, and he knew it, he said he'd had too much champagne and he wanted to sleep alone. It's been like that since the lady came to Chicago.

ALBERTINE   You've learned women's chitchat very fast.

I'm not good at this, but since we've started I can tell you everybody wants to sleep alone sometimes— (*Laughs*) —maybe most of the time.

LILY He liked to come to bed with me. You didn't know that, did you?

ALBERTINE I have not read it in the newspaper. But, as you know, I'm a large stockholder, and if you'd like it reported in detail— (*She breaks off, puts her hand over her eyes*) Forgive me.

LILY You'd never believed anybody could want me. I didn't believe it, either. I was so scared at first that I— But there I was, good for the man I loved. He said I was better than anybody, and that I must learn to cook because he'd always believed that a woman who was good in the bedroom was good in the kitchen— (*She laughs happily*) And I did learn. What do you think of that?

ALBERTINE I think well of it.

LILY (*Softly*) I was beloved, Mama, and I flourished. Now I'm frightened. Help me.

ALBERTINE (*Gently*) How can I help you when I don't understand what you're talking about? Are you really saying that if Julian stayed dependent on you, all would be safe, but if he has money for himself, and need not crawl to you—

LILY That's an ugly way to speak, Mama.

ALBERTINE On your struggle up the mountain path, you will find that truth is often ugly. It burns. (*After a second*) I don't believe there is any other woman, but in any case, be wise enough to wait and find out.

LILY I don't want to be wise, ever, Mama, ever. I'm in love.

ALBERTINE Then be happy that Julian has finally had a little luck. Lily, he would have come to hate your money. *That* was the danger I feared for you.

LILY I never wanted us to have money. I hate money. You know that, Mama.

ALBERTINE   Then be very careful. Same thing as loving it. (*The phone rings and* LILY *wheels and makes a dash for the house. At the same minute,* ANNA, *who has been moving in and out of the room, packing the valise, now turns from the valise and crosses to the phone.* LILY *falls over the porch steps and rolls to the ground.* HENRY *runs toward her*)

LILY   Anna! Anna!

ALBERTINE   Lily.

ANNA   (*Into the phone*)   I will wake him. Just a minute. (*She moves out.* ALBERTINE *moves to help* LILY *rise*)

LILY   (*Calling to* ANNA)   That's the woman. I want to speak to her. I want to ask her— (*She makes a sudden, violent movement up the porch steps*)

ALBERTINE , No. (*Very sharply*)   No.
    (HENRY *touches* LILY'S *arm as if to keep her from moving*)

LILY   (*To* HENRY)   Leave me alone. I told you that last night. I told it to you years ago when I rolled down the hill. I meant to roll down the hill and kill myself, but you didn't know it.

HENRY   I knew it.
    (JULIAN *appears in the living room, dressed in a robe, the envelope of money in his pocket. He moves to the phone*)

JULIAN   Hello. Sorry about the call last night. I was dying to tell you the good news, but of course I couldn't call you back. Did the cough medicine work? Did you have a good night's sleep? This is the great day, so stop worrying. Everything went fine. Got it right here in my pocket, nice clean bills. Eleven o'clock, waving a fortune at you. Where we agreed. (*He listens, smiling*)   I did everything the way you told me, only better. Don't worry about me. He just beats women. (*Gently, affectionately*) I'll be there. Good-bye, my dear. (ANNA *enters the living room carrying a glass of juice and a dress.* JULIAN *takes the juice from* ANNA, *kisses her*) What's good for breakfast?

ANNA   Pancakes?

JULIAN   (*Looks around at the old dress she is packing*) Why are you taking all that old stuff? Throw out everything old. (*Stares at* ANNA) What's the matter with you. You look terrible.

ALBERTINE   (*Through the window*)   Morning, Julian.
   (ANNA *exits toward the kitchen*)

JULIAN   Well, look who's here. Hello. (*He starts out for the porch, stops, kicks aside a few packages, grabs a small one and runs out*)   A present for you.

ALBERTINE   Thank you.
   (*He turns to* LILY)

JULIAN   Hello, darling. (*Stares at her*)   What's the matter with you? (LILY *shakes her head. He kisses her, and moves toward* ALBERTINE, *with whom he shakes hands. He sees* HENRY *and they shake hands*)   How's the fishing? Been up the bayou?

HENRY   Been up. But nobody got anything. Except crayfish.

JULIAN   Anybody asked what I missed most in Chicago, I'd have said a bayou, a bowl of crayfish, a good gun for a flight of wild ducks coming over— Going to buy a little place up there, first thing. You're welcome all the time. (*Sees that* LILY *has not moved and is staring at the ground*)   What's the matter, Lily? (*When she doesn't answer, he speaks to* ALBERTINE)   I sure manage to depress my ladies. Never used to be that way. Do I depress you?

ALBERTINE   (*Laughs*)   I'm very glad to see you.
   (*She has now unwrapped the package and taken out a flame-red lace mantilla supported by a giant comb. She arranges it on her head*)

JULIAN   What's it meant for?

ALBERTINE   I don't know.

JULIAN   When do you wear it?

ALBERTINE   I'll wear it for reading in bed. How very nice of you to bring it to me.

JULIAN (*As if the tone of thanks puzzles him*)   How nice of *you*. You put it on. Nobody else— (*Turns to* LILY) Lily, did you show your mama your new ring? (LILY *shakes her head*)   Oh. Go and get your ring and show your mama. (LILY *hesitates and then moves inside. He smiles ruefully at* ALBERTINE, *points to the mantilla*) Silly present, isn't it? It cost a lot.

ALBERTINE (*Laughs*)   Nice to buy, nice to get, silly presents. Who wants a roast of beef?

(*She removes the mantilla and carefully folds it*)

JULIAN (*Smiles with pleasure*)   That's what I thought— (*Confidentially, points inside*)   I think I bought, got, brought— Well, they're sort of upset and they don't think I know it. I should have had sense enough to know that when you've been poor and wanted things you couldn't have, your stomach gets small and you can't eat much right away. I brought too much, and everything too grand, and, well. Guess they got a little sick. They're so happy that it comes out unhappy. You know how it is?

ALBERTINE   I don't think so.

JULIAN   It's a crazy old world. For years, they— (*Points inside*)   —tell me about what's going to be, what I'm going to do, you know, get rich and big time. The more I fail, the louder they cheer me with what we're all going to have, want. And so all my life I dream about coming up those steps carrying everything, and I make up what they will say, and what I will say— (*Smiles*)   Well, when it came, I guess it was hard to believe, maybe even frightened them, I never thought of that, and I just bought anything if it cost a lot, and made Carrie sick on caviar, and everybody acted scared, and like they were going to cry. Lily did cry— Natural enough. You know?

256

ALBERTINE (*Carefully*) No, I don't know. You've had good fortune and brought it home. There's something sad in not liking what you want when you get it. And something strange, maybe even mean. (*Sharply, as if in warning*) Nobody should have cried about your good fortune, nobody should have been anything but happy.

JULIAN No, no. You don't understand. They're happy. They just haven't had time— I scared them, Europe and a house and fancy things all in a day. Who wouldn't be scared? They thought I'd come home broke— God knows I always had— You don't know about that, but *they* do, and they got ready to give me all they had, and tell all the same nice lies about how the next time. And then there I come, strutting like a kid— (*Laughs with great pleasure*) Rich. Rich. Rich. (*As a child would say it*) I'm as good as you now. Isn't that true?

ALBERTINE (*Laughs*) I'm not sure.

JULIAN We'll have to have long talks and consultations.

ALBERTINE About money? I don't think so. I like it very much. But it makes dull talk.

JULIAN Oh, I just bet you don't really think that. (*He pokes her with his finger; she stares at him and sits very straight*) That's just the way *you* people want *us* to think. Not dull at all. Why, I had more fun this week— Know what I did?

(*He pokes her again. She reacts sharply and* HENRY *laughs. She turns to look at* HENRY *and then turns back to* JULIAN, *smiling*)

ALBERTINE Henry doesn't like people to poke me, do you, Henry?

HENRY I never saw anybody do it before.

JULIAN I went to see a man I hated the two times I ever saw him and the many times I heard about him. Once when he teased me as a boy, and once when he made fun of me as a man. (*He stops, remembers, sighs*) I guess he's the only man I ever hated. Well, I went right

257

in his office and said I got something you want, and I'll take a hundred and fifty thousand dollars for it. After he said all about being crazy, and to get the hell out, he said, "Get your money from women—your sisters or your wife. You married her for it"— (JULIAN *rises, speaks softly to* ALBERTINE) Did people think that? Did they?

ALBERTINE   I don't see people. I never thought it.

JULIAN (*Leans down, kisses her hand*)   Maybe I'll knock you down later, I said to him, but right now let's keep our minds on a hundred and fifty thousand dollars delivered a week from today. (*To* ALBERTINE) Want to see?

(*He takes the envelope from his pocket and holds it open for her*)

ALBERTINE (*Laughs*)   It does look nice. I don't think I ever saw anything larger than a hundred-dollar bill.

JULIAN   I tell you, the rich don't have any fun with money.

ALBERTINE   Smells rather nice, too.

JULIAN   I put a little cologne water on it. (*As he puts the envelope back in his pocket*)   One hundred and fifty thousand dollars. Do people like you think it's a lot of money?

ALBERTINE   It's money. (*Very deliberately pokes him*) People like me think it's a good beginning. It's not a great fortune, but if you want one it will start you off.

JULIAN   You know, I think so, too. (*Smiles at her*)   Isn't it funny? I liked you, but I never talked easy with you before. Now you just seem to me like anybody else.

ALBERTINE   I'm sorry.

JULIAN (*Leans over and kisses her cheek*)   I didn't mean it quite like that. I just mean that you always scared me, and now you don't. I guess most people like you scared me. (*Smiles*)   I was kind of, well, kind of broken. I knew it, but I showed off to keep— (*He points inside*)

—them from— (*He turns to* HENRY) It's bad for a man to feel gone. (*Then, very gaily*) Like a miracle. I go in to see this bastard shaking, and I come out knowing I did fine, knowing I'm going to be all right forever. You understand it wasn't just the money?

ALBERTINE (*Laughs*) I don't understand very much. Why don't you wait and tell me when you can?

JULIAN All I mean, you do something right. *Just right.* You know a man's got to have what you've got—very different from trying to get a job or selling something he don't want. I just sat there calm and smiling until he got through trying to find out how I, *I*, bought two acres of swamp land before he did, and how I could know how much he needed it. I thought to myself, so this is the way the big boys do it, you poor fool for being so scared all your life. So I said, "Get through, will you, I got a board of directors meeting and have no more time for you." (*Laughs with pleasure*) I don't know where I got that from. Maybe the movies. You and my lawyer can attend to the rest, so agree or don't agree, I don't want to be in the room with you too long. He got white but he didn't say anything, so I got up and started out and he said, "All right. Give us two weeks to draw the papers"— My lawyer said, "Fair enough, sir," and I guess it was the "sir" that made me angry because I said, "No. I'll take it next Tuesday at two o'clock. Have it ready." And I walked out the happiest man in town. I paid back my life some way or other— (GUS *appears carrying ice*) You can lose for just so long— When you win, everything on you grows bigger, know what I mean? (*He laughs and pokes* ALBERTINE)

ALBERTINE And I grow black and blue.

GUS Hi. Home to stay?

JULIAN Gus, just look at that new icebox. (GUS *turns, stares in through the porch door*) Bought it more for you than for them.

GUS   In Chicago they keep it in the parlor?

JULIAN   Gus, my old friend Gus. You're going to have that farm, kid. Go find it and start with this.

(*He hands* GUS *several large bills.* GUS *looks at them, but doesn't take them*)

GUS   You at that again?

JULIAN   This time I made it. Throw the ice away—

(*He shoves the money into* GUS' *hand*)

GUS   Julian, I don't want that kind of trouble again.

JULIAN   Nobody'll come for it this time. I'm telling you the truth. And there's as much more as you want. Now get going and find the farm.

GUS   Who the hell wants a farm? Got enough trouble. Where'd you make up the farm from?

(*He goes around the garden and disappears*)

JULIAN   He said since we were kids about a farm— People talk about what they want, and then— How's that?

ALBERTINE   I guess most of us make up things we want, don't get them, and get too old, or too lazy, to make up new ones. Best not to disturb that, Julian. People don't want other people to guess they never knew what they wanted in the first place.

JULIAN   That's real sad. I know what I want and *I'm* going to be happy getting it.

ALBERTINE   Well, I like nice, rich, happy relatives, although I never had any. But I have bad news for you, Julian—it's not simple being happy, and money doesn't seem to have much to do with it, although it has to do with other things more serious.

(CARRIE *comes in, moving slowly. She stops when she sees the group*)

JULIAN   Morning. Where you been?

CARRIE   I—I've been downtown.

JULIAN   Buying things, I hope. (*To* ALBERTINE) My sisters are going to Europe tomorrow. Isn't that fine, after years of—

CARRIE Your sisters are not— (*Then, softly*) come inside, please.

JULIAN What's the matter?

CARRIE (*Starts toward the steps, sharply*) Come inside.

JULIAN (*Playfully, but with meaning*) Carrie, stop talking like that. You got a new man on your hands. You got to talk to me different now, like I'm a tycoon. (*To* ALBERTINE) What's a tycoon? How much, I mean?

ALBERTINE Miss Carrie can tell you. She works for one.

JULIAN Barrett? Is he? I don't want to be like Barrett—

CARRIE He knows what you think of him. He'd already read your letter when I got there. I can't tell you what I felt. All I could think to say was that it was a joke and you'd be down later to apologize.

JULIAN (*After a second*) Did you? Did you really say that? Don't ever say that again, Carrie. That's one of things I don't ever have to do any more. That's one of things money's going to buy us all.

CARRIE I want to see you alone, Julian.

JULIAN I don't think you should have gone to see him at all. We'll talk about it another time. I'm busy today. (*She wheels around, angry.* JULIAN *is grinning at* ALBERTINE) How you like me? See? Got no time for small matters.

CARRIE Small matters? After nineteen years. He said he didn't believe you wrote the letter. He said I wrote it, that it was like me, that he always had known about— (*She gasps*) —things in me. After nineteen years of loyalty— I want you to get dressed and go tell him that if you owe him an apology, he owes me an apology for the awful words he said—

JULIAN (*To* ALBERTINE) That's how tycoons act toward loyal ladies?

ALBERTINE I don't know how they act toward loyal ladies.

CARRIE Julian—

ALBERTINE I do know tycoons are not romantic about money and the happiness it buys.

JULIAN Ah, can't I be romantic for a month?

(CARRIE *moves into the living room and stands waiting*)

ALBERTINE All right. We'll give you a month. After a month I suggest venality. You'll find more people understand it and are less suspicious of it. Right now it's my impression that everyone around here thinks you held up a bank.

JULIAN No, a poker game. Or a jewel robbery. Hey, Lily. Lily! Come and show your mama your ring. Lily! (*To* ALBERTINE) *You* don't think I stole the money, do you? (*He looks at his watch, then moves quickly toward the porch as* LILY *appears*)

ALBERTINE (*Because* JULIAN *is going up the steps of the porch, and because she speaks very softly, he does not hear her*) No. I think I know where you got it.

JULIAN (*As he passes* LILY, *he picks up her left hand*) Go show your mama— Where's your ring?

LILY Somewhere.

JULIAN Where is somewhere?

LILY Don't be angry, please—

JULIAN Why not? (*He moves into the room, sees* CARRIE, *smiles*) Seen a large diamond ring?

CARRIE Up to yesterday we never had such problems. How does one look for a diamond ring? Julian, he said bad things to me. Julian. (*He doesn't answer, and starts to leave the room*) Julian. Please answer me.

JULIAN Answer you what?

CARRIE Once, and not long ago, you'd have known by my face, and you'd have kissed me and said, "What is it, my Carrie?"

(*Behind* CARRIE, ANNA *appears carrying a breakfast tray. She stops*)

JULIAN (*Gently*) What is it, my Carrie?

CARRIE I want to talk to you— Let's go by ourselves, the way we used to—

JULIAN I'm due downtown—

CARRIE You have no time for me. We're coming apart, you and I—

JULIAN What are you talking about?

CARRIE You've come home in all this mystery, and not said a word with me alone—

JULIAN When I take you to the boat tomorrow, I'll tell you all about "this mystery"—

CARRIE I want to speak to you now. Now.

JULIAN (*Softly*) Did you always use that tone with me? Did you? (*To* ANNA) Did you? (*When she doesn't answer*) Say something, so I can tell the way you talk to me.

ANNA Breakfast.

JULIAN (*Takes the tray from her*) Will you press a shirt for me?

(*She nods and moves off with him*)

CARRIE You're saying no to me, when I need you?

JULIAN I'm not saying no to you. I'm saying that I'm busy.

(*He sings as he exits*)

ALBERTINE (*To* LILY, *who is on the porch*) What did you do with the ring?

LILY I don't want it.

ALBERTINE He will be hurt. I suggest that you pretend that you do want it.

LILY I don't want it.

(CARRIE, *nervously moving about, comes to stand at the window and to listen to the voices in the garden*)

ALBERTINE There are many ways of loving. I'm sure yours must be among them. Put white flowers in your hair, walk up your mountain path of truth with a white banner in your hand and as you drop it on his head, speak of love.

263

LILY I gave her the ring and she gave me the knife.

ALBERTINE I beg your pardon?

HENRY (*Quickly*) I know what she means.

LILY I gave the lady the ring and she gave me the knife.
I didn't want the ring, and I didn't know Julian would
care. But I will go and tell him the truth now and—
(*She starts into the room*)

ALBERTINE You asked my advice and here it is: You do
too much. Go and do nothing for a while. Nothing. I
have seen you like this before. (*With force*) I tell you
now, do nothing. (*To* HENRY) You know the address
of the upstairs knife lady?

LILY Mama, don't make fun of her—

ALBERTINE No, indeed. We will try to find your ring. Decide whether your costume is meant for day or night,
and rest yourself. (*Softly*) Lily, don't tell Julian about
the ring. (LILY *nods and enters the house. She sees*
CARRIE, *smiles at her, and exits toward the kitchen.*
ANNA *appears carrying a shirt and crosses the room toward the kitchen*) Well, there it is.

HENRY You are not wise with Lily.

ALBERTINE No. I never was. Well, it's been a good year,
hasn't it? The best I ever had.

HENRY Nothing has happened.

ALBERTINE I know Lily. You do, too.

HENRY She is jealous and scared—

ALBERTINE And nothing I say will stop her from being
foolish. And of course there is another woman. But
Julian isn't sleeping with her. (*Laughs*) They raised
him to be a very, very moral man.

HENRY Very, very moral men sometimes sleep with
women. I think.

ALBERTINE But it shows on them. Do you think he's
sleeping with another woman?

HENRY He's not sleeping with her, and he won't. But he
used to.

ALBERTINE Yes? (*When there is no answer*) Cy Warkins is the man he's talking about, Cy Warkins who bought what he calls his two acres of swamp land. I'm not sure why Cy wanted it so much, but if it's down by the river I can make a good guess. Warkins owns fifty percent of the stock of the interstate agreement to take the railroad route along the docks. (*Laughs*) If my guess is right, he must have been surprised that Julian knew about the best kept secret in years. I regret not being there when Julian told him. But who told Julian? Mrs. Warkins? (HENRY *does not answer*) She never liked Warkins and that was the only thing I ever knew about her. But she must be forty now. (*When there is no answer*) But of course she wasn't always forty. (*She points inside*) They knew each other? And she told him about the railroad? I'm not gossiping, you know that.

HENRY I think that's what happened. She was in love with Julian once. She hates Warkins and has wanted to leave for years. Maybe this is the money to leave with.

ALBERTINE (*Softly, in a new tone, as if it is forced out of her, and she is ashamed*) How do you know about Mrs. Warkins? Please.

HENRY I don't know about her any more, but I used to. She's a cousin to me.

ALBERTINE (*Stares at him, and then laughs*) She's part colored? Isn't that wonderful! Did Warkins know when he married her?

HENRY He doesn't know now. But Julian did, and didn't care. She's a foolish woman and grateful for such things.

ALBERTINE That's understandable, God knows.

HENRY Not to me. I am not grateful, nor ungrateful, nor any word like that.

ALBERTINE Nor should you be. You are in a bad humor with me this morning. You are disapproving. What have I done or said?

HENRY (*Softly*) You look tired.

ALBERTINE (*Rises, goes to him*) The world has many people who make things too hard for too little reason, or none at all, or the pleasure, or stupidity. We've never done that, you and I.

HENRY Yes, we've done it. But we've tried not to.

(ALBERTINE *touches his hand.* HENRY *smiles and puts her hand to his face.* ALBERTINE *turns and, as she does, she sees* CARRIE *in the window.* ALBERTINE *pauses, turns slightly to where* CARRIE *has been sitting as if to ask herself what* CARRIE *could have heard*)

ALBERTINE Are you writing a book, Miss Carrie?

CARRIE (*Softly*) This is our house, Mrs. Prine.

ALBERTINE (*Sighs*) Indeed.

(HENRY *takes her arm and they move off.* LILY *comes running into the room, holding her right hand in her left hand. She is followed by* ANNA, *who carries a bottle and gauze bandage.* LILY *runs toward the hall, calling out*)

LILY Julian, I—I cut my hand.

ANNA Lily.

LILY Julian. I cut my hand. (*Then she turns and calls out loudly toward the garden*) Mama. Mama. I cut my hand.

CARRIE Your mama has left with her friend.

(JULIAN *appears, rubbing his wet hair with a bath towel*)

JULIAN What's the matter?

LILY I cut my hand.

JULIAN (*He picks up* LILY's *hand, holds it for* ANNA *to bandage*) It's a deep one. You ought not to have rusty knives in the kitchen.

(ANNA *looks up as if she is about to speak, but changes her mind*)

LILY Ouch. (*She turns her hand toward* JULIAN. *He kisses it and she gently touches his face. She rubs her thigh*) And last night I fell in here and hit my leg. You could cure that, too. Please. Make me cured, Julian. Let's go to bed and maybe you'll be pleased with me— Maybe. (*She puts his hand on her breast.* ANNA *turns away;* CARRIE *stands staring at them*)   And if you're pleased with me, then all the bad will go away, and I will pray for it to be that way. But if you're not, I'll understand, and won't ask why— (*She laughs gaily, slyly, and presses his hand on her breast*)   But *if* you are pleased with me, darling— (JULIAN *leans down to kiss her*)   I have missed you.

(*He picks her up in his arms and begins to move out of the room*)

CARRIE (*Sucks in her breath; loudly*)   I read in a French book that there was nothing so abandoned as a respectable young girl.

JULIAN (*Laughs*)   That's true, thank God. (*He leans down to kiss* LILY's *hair*)   Otherwise nobody could stand them.

(LILY *laughs merrily*)

CARRIE (*Comes toward them*)   You didn't fall in here last night. When I turned on the light—

LILY   Yes, ma'am. I fell. I didn't see the spinet—

(JULIAN, *carrying* LILY, *exits*)

CARRIE   You did not fall against the spinet. You were on this side of the room, hitting—

ANNA   Carrie.

CARRIE   She was hitting herself against that table. Just doing it. I saw her. I tell you, I saw her.

ANNA   I believe you.

CARRIE   He doesn't know she went out last night. He doesn't know she gave her ring away—to some woman— She's told him lies. She lies to him, she tricks him. I think she's a crazy girl— (*Points to the garden*)   And that woman knows it. I think there's a crazy girl in there—

ANNA (*Softly, as if to herself*) She cut her hand, quite deliberately and calmly, with a knife she took from a valise. She said a kind of prayer over the knife—

CARRIE (*Moves swiftly toward* ANNA) You saw her do that? You saw her cut herself? I tell you she's crazy. (*She moves toward the door, right*)

ANNA No.

CARRIE How can you stand what's happening here? He comes home with all this money nonsense. He's married to a crazy girl. I think he's in bed with a girl—

ANNA —he wanted. It's not our business.

CARRIE It is our business that our brother sells something to Mr. Cyrus Warkins for a fortune Mr. Cyrus Warkins doesn't want to pay. Warkins is a powerful and dangerous man in this town, and Julian would be a baby in the hands of such a man—

ANNA What are you talking about?

CARRIE I don't know all it means. (*Points out to the garden*) But I heard them say this money, or whatever, has to do with Warkins' wife.

ANNA He slept with Charlotte Warkins ten years ago. It's been over that long.

CARRIE How do you know such a thing? How do *you* know?

ANNA Because he told me.

CARRIE I don't believe you. You're a liar.

ANNA Be quiet, Carrie.

CARRIE You've made it up, you always made up things like that. It didn't happen. He was an innocent boy— (ANNA *laughs.* CARRIE *unbuttons the neck of her dress as if she were choking*) He would never have told *you.* He would have told me. He was closer to me— There he is, another man, not our brother, lost to us after all the years of work and care, married to a crazy little whore who cuts her hand to try to get him into bed— (*Points to the garden*) The daughter of a woman who keeps a nigger fancy man. I'll bet she paid Julian to take that crazy girl away from her—

ANNA   Stop that talk. You know that's not true. Stop talking about Julian that way.

CARRIE   Let's go and ask him. Let's go and ask your darling child. Your favorite child, the child you made me work for, the child I lost my youth for— You used to tell us that when you love, truly love, you take your chances on being hated by speaking out the truth. (*Points inside*)   Go in and do it.

ANNA   All right. I'll take that chance now and tell you that you want to sleep with him and always have. Years ago I used to be frightened that you would try and I would watch you and suffer for you.

CARRIE   (*After a second, in a whisper*)   You never said those words. Tell me I never heard those words. Tell me, Anna. (*When there is no answer*)   You were all I ever had. I don't love you any more.

ANNA   That was the chance I took.

CURTAIN

ACT THREE

CARRIE *is as she was.* ANNA'S *suitcases are on the porch. She enters, puts another suitcase below the piano, and exits. Offstage, there is a loud whistling, from* JULIAN. CARRIE *crosses to the spinet and begins to pick out the melody he is whistling. He enters, dressed except for his shirt, and carrying his coat. He is singing and he smiles pleasantly at* CARRIE.

JULIAN (*Singing*)
   This is the big day, this is the great day
   This is the Berniers day.
   Never been one, no, never never,
   Never been such a Berniers day.
   Never been such a day before.
   Going to be more and plenty more.
   Oh, it's money day, the end of trouble day,
   And going to be more and plenty more.
   Never been such a day before.
   Not for Mama, not for Papa,
   Not for Sister, not for Brother—
   Going to be more and plenty more.
   (*Shouts off*)   Anna! Where's my shirt?
CARRIE (*Softly*)   Do you know that all I want in this
   world is what will be good for you?
JULIAN   And I for you (ANNA *appears carrying his shirt. He crosses to take it from her, puts it on, and sings to* ANNA)
   Now every day she going to be
   She going to be a Berniers day.

270

Say every day she going to be
She going to be a Berniers day,
And for Mama and for Papa
And for Sister and for Brother
Going to be just a Berniers day.

(*To* ANNA) It's the best day of my life since I won the bag of marbles from old Gus. You made me give them back. You said he was a poor colored boy. But I was a poor white boy so I didn't know what you were getting so fancy about. Well, I'm on my way to the best day. (*To* CARRIE, *pointing to valise*) Getting packed? Getting excited?

CARRIE (*Pats the spinet*) I'll practice today and tonight I'll give a little concert for you and we'll sing all the pieces you used to like.

(ANNA *begins to move out of the room*)

JULIAN Er. We'll be leaving today. (ANNA *stops, turns.* CARRIE *rises*) We'll be going. (*Nervously*) And *you'll* be leaving tomorrow, so just one day. 'Course I'll wait until tomorrow if you need me—

CARRIE Where are you going?

JULIAN Maybe a camping trip, maybe New York—

CARRIE A few weeks?

JULIAN I don't know. No. A year or so. And then back here, of course. This is where I belong. Where I want to be, where I was meant to be. (*Overcheerful*) And by that time you world travelers will be back and—

CARRIE *You* want to go? Or *Lily* wants to go?

JULIAN Never seen New York, either of us.

CARRIE Lily wants to go.

JULIAN I don't know. I just decided. We'll come back, don't worry, and—

(*He crosses to the chest and takes out savings bankbook*)

CARRIE Why did you suddenly decide to go? Why?

JULIAN (*Holds up the bankbook*) Some people got a family Bible. We got a savings bankbook. (*Softly, to*

271

CARRIE) Don't look like that. (*Points inside*) She's young and— I don't think she wanted to come back. I didn't think about it before but— And maybe we should be alone for a while. That's all. (*Points to the bankbook*) Twenty thousand going in here this morning. Twenty thousand dollars. That going to be enough? (*Laughs with pleasure*) For six months maybe? Enough?

ANNA   I don't know anything about twenty thousand dollars.

JULIAN   You got to learn fast. Fast, I say. What was the word Mama used to use?

CARRIE (*In a cry*)   Julian, don't go—

ANNA (*Very fast*)   Faner. Elle commence a se faner. The leaf came in the spring, stayed nice on the branch in the autumn until the winter winds would blow it in the snow. Mama said that in that little time of holding on, a woman had to make ready for the winter ground where she would lie the rest of her life. A leaf cannot rise from the ground and go back to the tree, remember that. I remember it. But when it came there was nothing I could do.

JULIAN (*Gently, touches her*)   Mama was mean.

CARRIE (*Shrilly*)   Anna always says something about Mama when things are wrong. Always. Mama wasn't mean to you. Just to us.

JULIAN   Did you think I liked it that way? Did you? Mama had a tough time, I guess. That often makes people mean. (*Softly, to* ANNA)   You're still on the tree, still so nice and pretty, and when the wind does come, a long time from now, I'll be there to catch you with a blanket made of warm roses, and a parasol of dollar bills to keep off the snow. Dollar bills make a mighty nice parasol, I just bet you. (*Smiles*)   For another good lady, too. (*As if to himself*)   Well, I'm off to give them to her. I'll walk right down Sailor's Lane and she'll be waiting for me. I'll take her arm, we'll have a cup of coffee, and I'll try to say thank you. No, I won't. People are always saying thank you so they can forget what they said it for. (*Holds up one envelope*) I'll just hand this to her and say, "Have a good life, baby," and then I'll walk her down to the depot and put her on the train. A happy day. (*Holds up other envelope*) Then I'll go around and bank our share. That'll make me respectable, won't it?

ANNA (*After a second*) Is she *fanée*?

JULIAN Yes. A long time ago.

ANNA Then wish her well from me.

JULIAN I will.

CARRIE Is the lady going to New York?

JULIAN I don't know where she's going. I guess so. Doesn't everybody go to New York? (LILY, *on the last of* CARRIE'S *speech, comes into the room.* JULIAN *turns and grins at her*) Want to go to New York, or a fishing trip to Canada, or the Grand Canyon, or— Today?

LILY With you?

JULIAN (*Crosses to her, holds her face with his hand*) How would you like that? Time we found a place. Wherever.

LILY You and me?

JULIAN You and me.

LILY In a room?

JULIAN (*Laughs*) In a room, or a boat, or a tent—

LILY Just you and me. And will the not happening, happen to us again?

JULIAN (*Sharply*) Lily, stop that. I was tired and I had too much to drink last night. And I was nervous the last few days and am now. Any man will tell you that happens. (*Then, smiling*) Only you must never talk such things with any man, hear me?

273

LILY (*Giggles*) I won't.
(*She drops the knife from her right hand. She looks down at it as if surprised*)

JULIAN (*Leans down, picks up the knife, stares at it*)
What in the name of God is this?

LILY The knife of truth. Will you swear on it? Swear that you will keep me with you whatever—

JULIAN For Christ's sake, Lily. What the hell's the matter with you? (*He drops the knife on the table*) Stop talking foolish and stop playing with knives. Maybe kiddies should marry kiddies. But I'm thirty-four. Stop talking about last night and what didn't happen, because it's the kind of thing you don't talk about. Can't you understand that? (*Gently*) Now go pack your bags and go tell your mama we're going away.

LILY (*Laughing with pleasure*) Can I say we're going away forever? Just us.

JULIAN Forever. Just us. (*Turns, sees* CARRIE *and* ANNA, *and stops*) I mean we'll come back here, or the folks will come to us— (*Very fast*) You'll see. You'll come to visit us, we'll come to visit you— Buy us a little house up the bayou. Sometimes I wish I had gone on up the bayou years ago—

ANNA You did.

JULIAN Maybe I should have stayed. They said I was better with a muskrat boat than any Cajun, better with a gun. A nice little shack and a muskrat boat, all the bob-white you could ever want— (*After a second*) Fine morning to be talking like this.

ANNA (*Sharply*) Go on.

LILY (*She runs toward* JULIAN, *holds him; he puts his arms around her*) Will you be coming back for me?

JULIAN What? What are you talking about? Lily, for Christ's sake. (*He kisses her, moves away; stops, looks pleadingly at all of them*) What's the matter? Please.

It's the best day of my life. Please somebody look happy.

ANNA   Go on. (*He smiles, moves out at a run.* LILY *follows him to the porch. He turns and kisses her and runs off. After a second,* LILY *sits down on the porch, as though she is very tired.* ANNA *speaks to* CARRIE) I wanted to be around the children he will have. I wanted something nice to grow old for. I held on to that and prayed for it. (*Very softly*)   This time he will go forever.

CARRIE   I don't believe it. You must have your headaches again. He will not go forever, or even for long—

ANNA   This time I say he will go forever. You lusted and it showed. He doesn't know he saw it, but he did see it, and some day he'll know what he saw. (*With great violence*)   You know the way that happens? You understand something, and don't know that you do, and forget about it. But one night years ago I woke up and knew what I had seen in you, and always seen. It will happen that way with him. It has already begun.

CARRIE   I told you I didn't love you any more. Now I tell you that I hate you. We will have to find a way to live with that.

ANNA   I don't think so.

(*She moves out to the porch on her way to the garden*)

LILY   Will he come back for me, Miss Anna?

ANNA   What's the matter with you, child? You must go and dress and pack your things. Julian won't be long and he'll want you to be ready. Shall I call your mother?

LILY   She talked cóld to me. (*She imitates her mother*) "Try not to excite yourself, Lily. Try to make yourself clear, Lily." But when she talks to Henry— (*In another voice; soft and gentle*)   "Lily has gone to bed. Sit down. What shall we read tonight?" (*In her own voice*)   And one night she said to him, "Oh, God, make the time when we can be alone; make it come before we are both too

275

old to have pleasure from peace." (*Softly*) She would have paid anything for that time. Did she? Did she pay Julian? Is that why he took me?

ANNA (*Very sharply*) How dare you speak that way of Julian? What a bitter thought about a man who loves you.

LILY No. Who would want me for any other reason?

ANNA (*As she moves away*) Your modesty does not excuse you.

LILY I love him, Miss Anna. If he said he loved somebody else— Well, I'd just go away and he'd be rid of me. But this way—I know you understand.

ANNA A woman who marries a man she loves should have a little more happiness from it and talk a little more sense. That's all I understand.

LILY I've upset you, Miss Anna.

ANNA Yes. You're rather an expert.

(*She disappears around the garden.* CARRIE *has been sweeping the living room. She now moves to sweep the porch*)

LILY Cleaning day? (CARRIE *does not answer*) Do you like to sweep? I like to mop.

CARRIE Have you done much? Twice, say?

LILY I'm sorry you don't like me. I wanted you to.

CARRIE (*Gestures inside*) I would like to sweep the porch. Would you—

LILY Last night, in bed, Julian was thinking, I watched him. And thinking isn't the way to make love.

CARRIE I don't know much about gentlemen in bed and I don't want to learn from you.

LILY Haven't you ever slept with a man?

(CARRIE *turns and stares at* LILY)

CARRIE Shall we have a pillow fight or make fudge? I don't like these girlish confidences.

LILY I only thought you might like to know he was thinking of you, although, of course, I can't be sure. And maybe of Miss Anna, but most probably not.

CARRIE You'll be leaving here in an hour. Be satisfied with that victory and don't trust me with your dreams.

LILY Oh, Miss Carrie. I wanted you to like me.

CARRIE There is no need to worry about me any more.

LILY Oh, I do. And I will. I'm frightened of you.

CARRIE (*Angrily*) Your favorite word. Did it ever occur to you that other people are frightened, too?

LILY You? No. No, indeed. Of what, Miss Carrie?

CARRIE Of my hair which isn't nice any more, of my job which isn't there any more, of praying for small things and knowing just how small they are, of walking by a mirror when I didn't know it would be there— (*She gasps*) People say "Those Berniers girls, so devoted. That Carrie was pretty, and then one day she wasn't; just an old maid, working for her brother." They are right. An old maid with candied oranges as a right proper treat each Saturday night. We didn't see people any more, I guess, because we were frightened of saying or hearing more than we could stand. (*Very angrily*) There are lives that are shut and should stay shut, you hear me, and people who should not talk about themselves, and that was us.

LILY Why don't you come away with us, Miss Carrie?

CARRIE Stop sticking your baby pins into me. Go inside and pray that another woman won't do it to you. I want to clean the porch.

LILY There is another woman. I've seen her. Nobody believes me.

CARRIE I believe you.

LILY I don't know who she is. Do you?

CARRIE Your mother knows. Ask her.

LILY (*Giggles*) I just bet that's true. But Mama won't tell me because she doesn't like me and doesn't tell me things.

(*Runs to* CARRIE) You know what does the harm? I keep thinking that Mama paid Julian to marry me. And then sometimes I think that's not true; he does love me. God made him love me because God knew how much I needed him. (*Smiles; ingratiating*) He just worships you, Miss Carrie, and I know he confides in you. Did he ever tell you Mama paid him? (*Grabs* CARRIE'S *arm and, in the force of the movement, throws* CARRIE *off balance*) Tell me. Be good to me. Tell me.

CARRIE (*Pulls away*) I tell you what I think: You're going to drive him crazy.

(*She starts to move off.* LILY *grabs her*)

LILY Did my Mama—

CARRIE (*Angry*) I don't know what she did. All he told us was that he had fallen in love and was going to be married.

LILY (*In a transport of pleasure*) Oh. (*Laughing with happiness*) Miss Carrie; Miss Carrie! (*She pirouettes*) He told you he was in love! Isn't that nice?

CARRIE I remember wondering why he had picked that Sunday to tell us. Anna was going to the hospital the next morning for her eye operation. None of us had ever been in a hospital before, and we didn't know about the costs, and being in a ward, and all of that. So Julian came home and told about you, and then he said that Anna was going to have the best room in the hospital and he had called the great Dr. Kranz in Philadelphia, and the great Dr. Kranz was already on the train. He wouldn't let Anna say a word, said he won the money in a poker game. I don't know— Anna was more worried about that than about her eyes. And she fussed and fussed and never liked the fancy room and the uppity private nurses. But Dr. Kanz did a wonderful operation and when she came out of it, the first thing she said to Julian was, "My eyes were not made to make all this trouble for you." And he said a beautiful thing to her, he said, "Look, I'd give my both arms and one leg for you, but not two legs, so maybe I don't love you as much as I think," and how we all laughed. (*She smiles at* LILY) A few days later he brought you to see Anna. Do you remember?

LILY (*Who has been staring at* CARRIE) Yes.

CARRIE I was happy that Julian was to be married.

LILY You said so. (*Very loudly, as if out of control*) I didn't believe you.

CARRIE Oh, I could have stopped the marriage, even you must have guessed that.

LILY Even I. But you didn't stop it because you knew my mother had paid Julian—I'm glad I helped Miss Anna, I really am—would go on paying him, and you didn't have to worry about a little girl who didn't mean anything more to anybody than a bank check.

CARRIE I have said none of that: You have been looking for it, and you would have found it in anything I, or anybody else, could say.

LILY I don't mind, not much. It's better to know. I will take Julian any way I can have him. *If* I can have him. I feel most bad and sad, Miss Carrie, because what he married me for, he doesn't need any more. Isn't that true?

CARRIE I don't know. Take your questions to Mrs. Cyrus Warkins. She'll be in New York. You can have many a cozy evening.

LILY She's coming with us?

CARRIE No. She's going on the morning train.

LILY I see. Is she a tall, dark lady?

CARRIE I've never seen her. But Henry is tall and dark and she's his cousin, so perhaps. Your mother was very amused that the great lawyer Warkins had married a part nigger and didn't know it.

LILY Does Julian love her?

CARRIE I used to think I knew about Julian. I didn't. Ask your mother and her fancy man. They said Julian and

the woman were together years ago. And my sister confirms the alliance.

LILY (*Giggles too loudly*) Together? Alliance? Together
in bed? Alliance in bed? What a funny way to say it.
Julian told me that you talked like an old maid when
you were twelve years old, and that Gus used to say you
kept your vagina in the icebox, that he'd seen it there
and shut the door fast.

CARRIE (*Very loudly*) Stop that filthy talk. Julian never
said a thing like that—

LILY Oh, please, I didn't mean to offend you. Julian said
it in fun. Afterwards in bed, we always talked fun. That's
almost the best time, when you laugh and say things
you'd never say anyplace else, and it's all in honor bright.
It's then that you ask about other girls, everybody does
Julian told me, and every man thinks it's a big bore he's
got to get through for the next time, if you know what
I mean. Julian said there was only one woman that ever
mattered, long ago, and I wasn't to worry— (*She laughs*)
—and that she was married to a bastard who beat her,
and if he ever made money he'd give it to her to get
away. (*She smiles*) So now she's coming with us.
What will they do with me? (*She screams*) It pains
me. I can't tell you. I'll ask her not to come. (*She turns
and runs up the porch and into the room, toward the
phone*) I'll tell her I don't blame her, of course, and
I'll swear on my knife of truth that if I have just one
more year— (*Grabs the phone book, drops it, holds it
out to* CARRIE) Please find it for me.

CARRIE Mrs. Warkins isn't home. She's waiting for Julian.

LILY (*Runs toward the porch*) I'll run.

CARRIE Put your clothes on first. You've got a long way
to go in your underwear.

LILY (*Stares down at her nightgown*) Please you go, Miss
Carrie.

CARRIE Oh, I don't think so.

LILY Say I'm not angry, not anything like that. Say I know what it is to love and if at the end of a year, she wants and Julian wants— Well, then. Then.

CARRIE I don't think I could say those things.

LILY You don't talk the way you did. You talk real mean.

CARRIE In the last day I lost my brother, my sister, my job. That's all I had to lose. Perhaps it's the fear of losing people that makes us talk nice or better. (*Very loudly, sharply*) Don't you think? Don't you think maybe?

LILY Do I talk different?

CARRIE You are still the baby-rich girl, teething on other people. In a few years I think you'll have to start doing something for yourself.

LILY A few years? A few days will be too late, a few minutes— What time is it? What time is Julian going to take her away?

CARRIE (*Carefully*) I did not say he was going to take her away. He has gone to meet Mrs. Warkins, evidently to give her a share.

LILY What time is it? I know Mr. Cyrus Warkins, he's Mama's lawyer. Mrs. Warkins is a sad lady, if she's the one who was on the train.

CARRIE She's ailing, I've always heard, and doesn't go into society. But I suppose the real reason is that she's part nigger and thought somebody would find out. Julian didn't mind. Imagine that. He didn't mind.

LILY Why should he? I don't mind Henry's being colored. I like negro people, and Jewish, and once I met two Irish ladies. I just hate Henry because he's Henry.

(*There is a long pause; as if* LILY *has dozed*)

CARRIE (*Watching* LILY, *sighs*) Your mind wanders, doesn't it? Go pack your bags now.

LILY You're a fine lady. He'd listen to you. Miss Carrie, please call Mr. Cyrus Warkins.

CARRIE I will not call Mr. Cyrus Warkins. His wife is not going to New York with me.

281

LILY Mama should call him. Where's Mama? She went for my ring. Will Mr. Warkins listen to me. Nobody does. (*She runs to pick up the phone book, opens it, and drops the book*) Don't you want to help me? It's hot.

CARRIE Wait for your Mama.

LILY It will be too late.

CARRIE I think so.

LILY You're teasing me. It's not nice to tease me and to pretend that you're not (*As* CARRIE *moves away*) Miss Carrie, please.

CARRIE (*Sharply*) What do you want of me? What is that you want?

LILY I don't want to be in the room alone. (*Points down to the telephone*) It's for the best, the best for everybody, isn't it?

CARRIE What's the sense of answering you? You just go on talking and talking.

LILY No, please. Please. Isn't it best for everybody?

CARRIE I don't know about everybody. I'm not used to thinking that way. I just think about what's best for us, for Julian.

LILY That's what I want, too. What's best for Julian. Please tell me.

CARRIE (*Carefully, as if anxious to impress the words*) I don't know that I can. The people in the bank always talk of Mr. Warkins as a low-high-born man, tough and tricky, with plenty of riffraff friends to do his dirty work. Julian isn't fit to deal with such a man and God knows what could happen. Warkins is not a man to joke with.

LILY (*After the words "what could happen,"* LILY *has picked up the phone and given the operator the number "LaFitte 1707." Her voice is firm*) Tell Mr. Warkins that Lily Berniers, Lily Prine, must speak to him immediately and does not wish to be kept waiting. (*Waiting, she smiles at* CARRIE) I think that's the way Mama would say it. Oh, hello, Mr. Cyrus, this is Lily. (*She puts the phone down, wipes her hand on her nightgown, picks up the phone, waits*) Mr. Cyrus, you mustn't blame anybody if I tell you something. Will you promise a sacred promise on the life of your child?

CARRIE He hasn't got a child.

LILY But you haven't got a child. (*Pause*) Then why did you make a sacred promise on a child you haven't got? You mustn't joke with me, Mr. Cyrus, you must not. Oh. I see. Well, please tell your wife I'm not mad a bit. That's first. Just ask her to give me one more year with Julian and then I'll promise— Well, that's all. Just ask her that. (*She listens*) I wouldn't like to say because I don't understand much myself. Why does it matter? I don't see why it should. Oh. Well, Miss Carrie heard— (CARRIE *wheels about*) A lady heard Henry say it. Henry? Why, the Henry of my mother—you know. Just that once, a long time ago, Julian had been kind to your wife, and that maybe she was helping him now. I don't know how Henry knew. (*After a second*) Oh, yes. I do. Henry is cousin to Mrs. Warkins. Yes, cousin. (*She waits, looks puzzled*) Mr. Cyrus? Mr. Cyrus? No, I don't think your wife's coming here. If she were, I could have asked her myself. I thought you could go right away, before she gets on the train— (*To* CARRIE) He wants to know where he can find her to give her my message. (*Into phone*) I don't know.

CARRIE Something about Sailor's Lane near the depot.

LILY Something about Sailor's Lane near the depot. Yes. Nobody's done anything bad, you understand, Mr. Cyrus, and tell her I know that, but I'd just like to ask to have Julian for one more— Mr. Cyrus? Well, thank you. (*She puts the phone down, sits, smiles*) He says he sure will go talk to her.

(CARRIE *sighs, waits, and then turns away.* ANNA *comes*

into the room, dressed in a suit. She looks at LILY, *who
does not notice her. She crosses to the table and picks up
the envelope with the boat tickets*)

ANNA We can't go together now. What would you like to
do about these boat tickets?

CARRIE We can't go together *now*? I don't know what you
mean. Were we ever going?

ANNA I thought so. When Julian brought these home to
us, he thought so.

CARRIE How strange you are. Did Julian think that? I
suppose so; one piece of nonsense makes for ten. We
never in our lives had any intention of going, you know
that as well as I do.

(ANNA *picks up the valise, takes it to the porch and exits*)

LILY I did right, just exactly. Didn't I? And I'll take the
knife of truth and swear to keep my word—

CARRIE Yes. But would you do it someplace else? It would
be nice to see you in a dress. Why don't you try it?

LILY Oh. All right.

(*She exits.* CARRIE *sits down, as if exhausted. She looks
at her watch.* ANNA *comes back into the room, wearing
a hat now, and carrying a coat*)

ANNA You never wanted to go to Europe? Never meant
to go?

CARRIE How do you know such things? You go on talking
the way you always talked, saying you like or want what
you always said. (ANNA *doesn't answer.* CARRIE *begins
to recite in a make-fun singsong*)

"On the fairest time of June

You may go, with sun or moon

Or the seven stars to light you

Or the polar ray to right you,"—

Do you still like it, all the nights you read it to us?

ANNA Yes. (*Slowly*) I don't know. I suppose it doesn't
mean much to me any more.

CARRIE   I can hear you, all your cultured evenings. (*Recites*)

"To see the laurel wreath on high suspended,
That is to crown our name when life is ended."

ANNA (*Standing near the piano, she plays*)   And you this? So deeply felt, your favorite.

CARRIE   Was it?

ANNA (*Smiles*)   And the candied oranges I brought each week?

CARRIE   I was sick of them ten years ago.

ANNA (*Softly*)   Well, people change and forget to tell each other. Too bad—causes so many mistakes. (*She crosses to the table, takes a ship's ticket from the envelope, puts the envelope back on the table*)   I've taken my ticket, left yours in the envelope. You'll explain about that to Julian.

CARRIE   What are you talking about?

ANNA   I'll spend the night at the hotel. I'm going to Europe tomorrow.

CARRIE (*Moves toward her, stares at her, starts to laugh*)   You will be lonely.

ANNA   That's all right. I always have been.

CARRIE   You will look very silly, a middle-aged, scared-to-death woman, all by herself, trying to have a good time.

ANNA   You will stay here until you sell the house?

CARRIE   I don't believe you mean to go anywhere. It's just too crazy. You've never been anyplace in your life.

ANNA (*Moves toward the door*)   We have said good-bye.

CARRIE   You're showing off. You're just plain showing off. You're not going anywhere— (*As* ANNA *reaches the door*)   You can't go before Julian. It would kill him to know that anything was wrong between us.

ANNA   You don't love me, but you want me to stay with you.

CARRIE   We will find a way to live.

ANNA No.

CARRIE You need me. You always have. Julian, everybody, always thought you the strong and sturdy—

ANNA And you the frail, the flutterer, the small. That's the way you wanted them to think. I knew better. Our patched-together supper, a little talk, sometimes a book, long ago on the piano, a game of casino, your bath, then mine, your room and my room, two doors closed.

CARRIE All those years of nights, all the things you knew and never said. Does everybody live like that, or just two old maids?

ANNA I loved you and so whatever I knew didn't matter. You wanted to see yourself a way you never were. Maybe that's a game you let people play when you love them. Well, we had made something together, and the words would have stayed where they belonged as we waited for our brother to need us again. But our brother doesn't need us any more, and so the poor house came down.

CARRIE I think our brother will need us. Now or someday. And we must stay together for it (*Softly*) You're the kind of woman with no place to go, no place to go. (*Smiles*) You see? Some of those nights I thought about you, too. We must find a way to live.

ANNA I don't wish to find a way to live with you. I am a woman who has no place to go, but I am going, and after a while I will ask myself why I took my mother's two children to be my own.

CARRIE Go unpack your bags.

ANNA (*With great force*) Pretend it's last week. You've just told the girls in the bank that you can't have coffee, you have to hurry home, that Anna will be mad at you for being late, that Anna gives the orders to the soft and tender you. Go back and pretend it's still last week. (*She moves out to the porch, picks up a camellia plant and carries it down the steps.* MRS. PRINE *appears.* HENRY *is with her, he waits beyond the garden fence)* Will I look very foolish carrying a camellia plant to Europe?

ALBERTINE I don't think so. It's most becoming. Soft around the face.

(LILY *appears. She is dressed, has on her hat, and is neat and cheerful*)

LILY (*To* ANNA) Are you coming to New York with us? I would like that, Miss Anna.

ANNA You shouldn't like it, and I'm not coming with you. (*She moves around the side of the house*) I guess two plants ain't more foolish than one.

LILY Good-bye, Mama. We're going away. Good-bye. (*Smiles*) I know that will make you happy.

ALBERTINE Here's your ring, Lily.

LILY Oh. Thank you. I had forgotten— Oh. Madame Celeste gave it to you?

ALBERTINE Madame Celeste sold it to me.

LILY That's not fair, is it? Now I must give her back the knife of truth. (*She turns as if to leave*) I'd like to keep it, but she'd never sell it.

ALBERTINE (*Very sharply*) Sit down. (LILY *sits down;* ALBERTINE *sits opposite her, and speaks very quietly, but as if the words had been rehearsed*) I've had enough of whatever you're doing. However innocent is your innocence, I've had enough. More important, it is leading you into dangerous alleys. Not even for you will I again spend time in what you call an upstairs room with a morphine addict who holds séances to cover up what she sells.

LILY (*In a fury*) I don't believe you, I don't believe you, I don't believe you. You want to take my friend from me—

ALBERTINE I am tired. I am sad. It is not good to know that my child swore fidelity to such a woman, and gave her wedding ring as proof.

LILY My friend is a sweet friend. I gave her my ring because she loved me and gave me courage—

ALBERTINE   You are a pure girl and I believe you. Now listen: I am going to give you a good-bye present. Try to make use of it: the pure and the innocent sometimes bring harm to themselves and those they love and, when they do, for some reason that I do not know, the injury is very great.

LILY (*Who hasn't heard a word*)   You have talked this way about my friend because you want to bring me pain. Henry makes plans to pain me— (*Outside the fence,* HENRY *turns*)   As you lie in bed with him, Henry makes the plans and tells you what to do.

ALBERTINE (*Pleasantly, turns toward* HENRY)   Is that what we do in bed? (*To* LILY)   You think that's what we do in bed? You're wrong. It's where I forget the mistakes I made with you.

HENRY   Stop it.

ALBERTINE (*Ignores him; as if she is out of his control*)   If something is the matter with you, come home and I will care for you, as I should, as I should. But if nothing is the matter with you, have pity and leave me alone. I tried with you all your life, but I did not do well, and for that I ask your pardon. But don't punish me forever, Lily.

LILY (*Softly*)   Is something the matter with me, Mama? (HENRY *moves toward* ALBERTINE *and holds up his hand.* ALBERTINE *stares at him, then nods*)

ALBERTINE (*Very gently*)   No, darling. Certainly not.

LILY   If Julian leaves me—

ALBERTINE   Julian loves you, Lily.

LILY   I have sent a message and will keep my word. If Mrs. Warkins will give me one year—

ALBERTINE (*After a second*)   You sent a message to Mrs. Warkins? Why?

LILY   Oh, because. I spoke to Mr. Warkins and told him to ask her to wait for Julian for one more year. (ALBERTINE *moves forward.* HENRY *moves toward her.* ALBERTINE *turns and stares at* HENRY)   After that, if Julian doesn't want me— Where would I ever go, who would ever want me? I'm trouble, we all know that. I wouldn't have anywhere to go.

ALBERTINE (*After a long pause*) You will come home to me. You are my child.

LILY (*Warmly, sweetly*) Thank you, Mama. Nice of you. But I couldn't go home to you any more, as long as—

HENRY If it ever happens, I won't be there. I won't be there.

LILY Oh, thank you, Henry. That will be fine.

(*On the first part of* LILY's *speech,* HENRY *sees* JULIAN *in the street.* HENRY *makes a sudden move toward him, stops.* JULIAN *appears, stumbling toward the house. His face and hands are cut and bruised. He has been beaten, and one leg is injured. He moves toward the garden in great pain; his face is so stern that the people who see him know that to assist him would be to undignify him.* ANNA, *who has seen him from the back of the house, starts toward him, then moves swiftly back as if on an errand.* LILY *does not move, but makes a loud sound.* JULIAN *tries to go up the steps of the porch, slips, and then clings to pillar of the porch.* CARRIE *moves toward him, and then backs into the room.* HENRY *goes toward* JULIAN, *but* JULIAN *puts up a hand, and* HENRY *halts*)

JULIAN I took Charlotte to her brother's house. She'll be all right, but not her face. She's safe there, I think— Do you know what Charlotte I'm talking about?

HENRY Yes.

JULIAN She'd better not stay where she is. Just in case. Not in this town.

HENRY All right.

(*Painfully, slowly,* JULIAN *moves into the room.* CARRIE, *standing near the phone, points toward it*)

CARRIE (*Softly*) Doctor?

JULIAN No. (ANNA *comes in carrying a basin and bandages*) My friend. My poor friend. All she wanted,

saved for, thought about— (*He gasps as if he is sick*)
—to get away forever. Standing there, standing in the
alley, they slashed us up.

ALBERTINE (*Who is standing on the porch; softly*) Who?

JULIAN I don't know who. I saw two men and then I
didn't see anything else. Two thugs he sent—

ALBERTINE Who sent?

JULIAN (*In a shout*) Mr. Cyrus Warkins sent his men to
meet us. (*He takes the money envelope from his coat
pocket where it has been arranged as if it were a handkerchief, crumbles it, and throws it to the ground*) Nobody knew she came to Chicago to tell me, nobody knew
she put up the money for the land, nobody knew her
name. Tell her I swear it, I swear it. (*To* ANNA, *who
comes toward him with bandages*) Go away. (*To*
HENRY) I told *nobody*. Tell her I swear it on my life—

HENRY No need to tell her that.

JULIAN *But somebody did know. Somebody told him.* My
friend—wanted to help me, took a dangerous chance
and did— (*Softly*) You should see her. You should
see her. Make her know I never spoke her name.

ALBERTINE She will not think you did. I am certain she
will not think you did.

JULIAN (*Points to the envelope*) That's what's left of the
money.

ALBERTINE Shall I go to the police for you, Julian?

JULIAN I went. High up, to Drummond.

ALBERTINE Then perhaps—

JULIAN No. I don't know what the thugs looked like—
No matter what I said I could see Drummond saying to
himself that I made it up, never could have had fifty
dollars in my pocket, not less a hundred fifty thousand—

ALBERTINE Shall I go to Warkins?

JULIAN What for? Is he going to tell you who told him,
who he hired to beat us up— What for?

ALBERTINE I don't know.

JULIAN   Christ, what a mess-ass I am. She handed me the
whole deal, told me every move to make, a baby could
have done it.

(*His leg collapses and he falls to the floor. Slowly, pain-
fully he lifts himself, moves toward the chair and table.
ALBERTINE turns away, as if the sight is painful. As
JULIAN falls to the floor, LILY makes a dash to the porch.
ALBERTINE moves toward her; puts out a hand to hold
her*)

LILY   Mama, I did it.

ALBERTINE   Are you very sure you love him?

LILY   Mama, I did it. God forgive me.

ALBERTINE   Go in and sit by him. Just sit by him and shut
up. Can you do that? Can you have enough pity for him
not to kill him with the truth? Can you love him enough
to go by him, sit down— (*Very softly, with great violence*)   —*and be still?* (LILY *nods*)   Then go and do it.
(LILY *moves into the house and timidly approaches*
JULIAN)

JULIAN   I don't look nice. Take off your hat, baby. We
ain't going nowhere. There ain't nothing to go with.

LILY   May I wash your face?

JULIAN   Don't look like that. I'm all right. Nobody ever
beat me up before, or slashed a friend.

CARRIE   Things can happen.

JULIAN   What did you say?

CARRIE   I said bad things happen to people. Doesn't mean
anything.

JULIAN   I mean the way you said it. Say it that way again.

CARRIE   I don't know what you mean. Why don't you go
rest yourself, darling. Good hot bath—

JULIAN (*Turns to stare at her*)   Why you start to purr at
me? As if I'd done something good— (*Moves toward
her*)   You're smiling. What the hell's there to smile at?
You *like* me this way? (*After a second, turns to stare at
the room*)   Pretty, all this. And the mortgage, and the

tickets to Europe, and all the fun to come. Pretty, wasn't it?

CARRIE We didn't want them. (*To* ANNA) Did we?

ANNA No, we didn't want them.

JULIAN Don't talk that way. Won't do me any good. Assing it up all my God damned life, all my life it's been the same. (*With violence*) Nobody ever beat me up before. Nobody's ever going to beat me up again.

(*There is a pause.* LILY, *who has been washing* JULIAN'S *face, turns away.* CARRIE *sighs and moves to the porch door. Then, as if a decision has been made, she moves out to the porch and leans down to pick up* ANNA'S *luggage*)

ALBERTINE (*Very sharply, to* CARRIE) Mean to see a man stoke his pride. The meanest sight in the world. Don't you think?

CARRIE Let's be glad nothing worse happened. We're together, the three of us, that's all that matters.

ALBERTINE I counted four.

CARRIE I mean the four of us.

ALBERTINE Someday you will tell him about Lily? Then there will be three of you. Before you tell him, let me know. I will want to come for her.

CARRIE (*Points inside*) All that stuff has to go back, and the debts, got to find ourselves jobs. So much to do.

(CARRIE *picks up the valise and moves into the room*)

JULIAN Old saying, money is a real pure lady and when the world began she swore herself an oath never to belong to a man who didn't love her. I never loved her and she guessed it. Couldn't fool her, she got good sense. (*Softly, desperately*) Nobody ever beat me up before. Maybe once it starts—

CARRIE There's bad luck and there's good luck. That's all.

JULIAN I guess so. Well, I've had the bad. Maybe I got a little good luck coming to me. Other men make it easy.

Plenty of room in this world for everybody. Just got to fight for it. Got to start again, start again.

(*He rises.* LILY *moves to help him*)

CARRIE   I'm going to get something nice to make soup with. You always liked a good soup when you didn't feel well. Meat and marrow, the way you like it. (*As she gets to the porch door*)   Tomorrow's another day. (JULIAN, *leaning on* LILY, *moves out.* CARRIE, *leaving the house, passes* HENRY *and* ALBERTINE *in the garden*)   Good-bye, Mrs. Prine.

(*She exits. After a second* HENRY *puts his hand on* ALBERTINE'S *shoulder*)

HENRY   Good-bye.

(HENRY *exits.* ANNA *crosses to pick up her large valise, and at the same time* ALBERTINE *rises to exit*)

CURTAIN

Saul Levitt

The Andersonville
Trial

/

FOR DENA

The basic source material for this play is the official record of the actual trial of Henry Wirz, which took place in Washington, D.C., in the summer of 1865. The play may be considered "documentary" to the following extent: that it is set in the time and place circumstance of the historical trial; that the formal roles and names of its characters repeat those of the historical participants; and that some of the dialogue derives from the trial record. It might be added that the theme expressed in the play inheres in the trial record. Essentially, however, the play expresses the author's own conception of the personalities and the occasion—and is to be read as "drama" and not as "documentary."

The Andersonville Trial was first presented by William Darrid, Eleanore Saidenberg, and Daniel Hollywood at Henry Miller's Theatre, New York City, on December 29, 1959, with the following cast:

(*In order of speaking*)

GENERAL LEW WALLACE, *President of the Court*
Russell Hardie
LIEUTENANT   Robert Burr
COURT CLERK   Heywood Hale Broun
LT. COL. N. P. CHIPMAN, *the Judge Advocate*
George C. Scott
OTIS H. BAKER, *the Defense Counsel*   Albert Dekker
CAPTAIN WILLIAMS   Al Henderson
HENRY WIRZ, *the Defendant*   Herbert Berghof
LIEUTENANT COLONEL CHANDLER   Robert Carroll
LOUIS SCHADE, *Assistant Defense Counsel*   James Arenton
DR. JOHN C. BATES   Ian Keith
AMBROSE SPENCER   Moultrie Patten
DR. C. M. FORD, *Prison Surgeon*   Douglas Herrick
JAMES H. DAVIDSON   James Greene
MAJOR D. HOSMER, *Assistant Judge Advocate*
Howard Wierum
JASPER CULVER   Robert Gerringer
GEORGE W. GRAY   Frank Sutton
UNION SOLDIERS   Robert Downey, Martin West, Lou Frizzell
COURT REPORTER   Vincent Donahue

NEWSPAPERMEN		Robert Mayer, Richard Poston, William Scharf
GENERAL MOTT		Clifford Carpenter
GENERAL THOMAS		Taylor Graves
GENERAL GEARY		John Leslie
GENERAL FESSENDEN	*Assisting Judges*	Owen Pavitt
GENERAL BALLIER		William Hussung
COLONEL ALLCOCK		Archie Smith
COLONEL STIBBS		Freeman Meskimen

DIRECTED BY José Ferrer

PRODUCTION DESIGNED AND LIGHTED BY

Will Steven Armstrong

ACT ONE

Scene One

The Court of Claims, Washington, D.C. A morning in August, 1865. The atmosphere is sweltering.

The set reflects the musty courtroom of the historical trial—a room framed by heavy columns rising to form high arches which support a vaulted ceiling. A chandelier is suspended above the JUDGES' table. A number of conference-type tables are arranged to form a courtroom area: defense and prosecution tables, right and left, are on opposite sides; the JUDGES' table is center and to the rear, so that the JUDGES will sit facing the audience; the witness chair is placed near the JUDGES' table. Next to the defense table we note the bizarre element of a chaise longue. It is for the prisoner, who is ill and who will recline through most of the trial. Two tall French windows take up a large part of one wall. Set in the opposite wall are the double doors which form the only entrance into the room. A bench has been placed near the windows, with a railing in front of it which separates it from the courtroom area. It will serve as the "press gallery." Set close to the railing is a small table for the use of both the COURT CLERK and the COURT REPORTER. An American flag is mounted on the wall behind the JUDGES' table. On a stand, behind the JUDGES' table, is a huge schematic drawing of the Andersonville stockade— a rectangle with a simple sketching in of elements such as a stream, walls, entrance gate, "deadline," "hospital," burial ground, etc.

At rise: all parties to the trial, with the exception of the JUDGES and the defendant, are present. Only the three

301

newspapermen and the two defense lawyers wear civilian clothes. The others wear the blue uniforms of the Union Army. The military trial will begin in a moment, but in the meanwhile people stand and sit and converse in small groups. The two soldiers standing guard at the open doors slouch negligently. The atmosphere as the play opens is casual.

The JUDGE ADVOCATE *and* ASSISTANT JUDGE ADVOCATE *are* LIEUTENANT COLONEL N. P. CHIPMAN *and* MAJOR D. HOSMER. *Opposite them are* OTIS H. BAKER *and* LOUIS SCHADE, *representing the defendant.*

Now CAPTAIN WILLIAMS *enters, moving to the* LIEUTENANT *in charge of the courtroom guard detail, to whom he whispers with an air of suppressed excitement. (As we will learn in a moment, the exchange refers to the absence of the defendant.) The* LIEUTENANT *imparts his information to* CHIPMAN *and starts in the direction of* BAKER, *then at a signal from one of the soldiers he goes swiftly toward the doors. He halts near them to stand stiffly, shouting, "Attention!" All parties come to attention as the* JUDGES, *eight Union officers of rank, take their places. They sit, flanking* GENERAL LEW WALLACE, *President of the Court. There is a quality of cold, overriding power and purpose in control as proceedings start.*

As WALLACE *speaks, he reveals a chill and remote authority. He is a major general, thirty-seven years of age.*

WALLACE (*Banging gavel down once*) This military court convened by order of the War Department is now in session. The Lieutenant in charge is advised to post additional guards in the corridor. A lane must be kept clear at all times to the courtroom doors.

LIEUTENANT Yes, sir.

(*He goes out*)

WALLACE Have all witnesses listed to appear in these proceedings reported to the Clerk of the Court?

CLERK   All have reported to the Clerk, sir, and are on hand.

WALLACE   I take it all concerned with these proceedings have signed the necessary oath of allegiance to the government of the United States.

CLERK   Yes, sir.

(*The* LIEUTENANT *re-enters and takes up his post at the closed doors*)

WALLACE   (*As he refers to counsel by name, they acknowledge their names by a nod*)   Lieutenant Colonel N. P. Chipman, for the War Department. Mr. Otis Baker for the defense. The defendant, Henry Wirz, is to be tried by this military commission consisting of— (*Glancing down the line of the* JUDGES)   General Mott . . . General Thomas . . . General Geary . . . General Fessenden . . . General Ballier . . . Colonel Allcock . . . Colonel Stibbs . . . and myself, General Wallace. Has the defense any objection to any of its members?

BAKER   No objection.

WALLACE   I do not see the defendant.

CHIPMAN   If the Court please, Captain Williams is here and will explain his absence.

(CAPTAIN WILLIAMS *comes forward*)

WILLIAMS   Sir, regarding the defendant. He will be brought here shortly.

WALLACE   Is he ill?

WILLIAMS   (*Blurting it*)   Sir, he is temporarily indisposed, following his attempt on his life early this morning which was foiled by the alertness of the guards—

WALLACE   Mr. Wirz attempted to take his life?

WILLIAMS   Unsuccessfully, sir.

WALLACE   Captain, you will explain to the Court how such an attempt could have possibly occurred.

WILLIAMS   Sir, Mr. Wirz tried to slash his wrist after breaking a bottle.

WALLACE   A bottle?

WILLIAMS   A brandy bottle which he receives daily as a
stimulant by order of Dr. Ford—

WALLACE   The incident should not have occurred— You
are charged with custody of the prisoner. You will take
the necessary steps so it will not occur again. You say the
prisoner is in condition to appear shortly?

WILLIAMS   Within a few minutes, and I will personally—

WALLACE   (*Cutting him off*)   That is all.

WILLIAMS   Yes, sir.

(*He exits, to re-enter later with* CAPTAIN WIRZ)

WALLACE   I will ask defense counsel to plead to the indictment in the absence of the defendant.

BAKER   We would prefer, if the Court will permit, that
Captain Wirz hear the charges against him directly—

WALLACE   This trial has been postponed several times and
the Court intends to proceed this morning without further delay. (*More a command than a question*)   Will
counsel plead to the charge?

BAKER   Counsel will plead.

WALLACE   If the Judge Advocate is ready.

CHIPMAN   Ready, sir.

WALLACE   The indictment will be read.

(CHIPMAN'S *movement reflects something of the man at
once. He is thirty-one, a battle veteran whose youthful
idealism has been hardened by war to a fierce unyielding
partisanship. We must sense humane impulses held un-
derneath a compulsion of bitterness toward the South—
warring feelings creating a quality of controlled tension*)

CHIPMAN   Charge— Criminal conspiracy to destroy the
lives of soldiers of the United States in violation of the
laws and customs of war.

Specification— That Henry Wirz, who was in charge
of the Confederate Prison at Andersonville, Georgia, did
keep in barbarously close confinement federal soldiers,
up to the number of forty thousand, without adequate

shelter against the burning heat of summer or the cold of winter and—

Specification— That the said Henry Wirz in carrying out this conspiracy did not provide the prisoners of war with sufficient food, clothing or medical care, causing them to languish and die to the number of more than fourteen thousand.

Specification— That he established a line known as the "deadline" and that he instructed the prison guards stationed on the walls of the prison stockade to fire upon and kill any prisoner who might pass beyond that deadline.

Specification— That he used bloodhounds to hunt down, seize and mangle escaping prisoners of war, through these various causes bringing about the deaths of about fifty federal soldiers, their names unknown.

Specification— That through direct order and/or by his own hand he brought about the murder of thirteen prisoners, their names unknown.

WALLACE Mr. Baker, pleading for the prisoner—how do you plead to the charge?

BAKER (*He is in his forties; a lawyer of polish, experience, and daring; of an ironic, worldly intelligence. Method must be sensed in his every move—even when he appears most angry. We hear the edge of irony in his voice as he makes his objections; aware that they are all going to be rejected*) We interpose a motion—that this military Court discharge itself as being without proper jurisdiction now that the war is over.

CHIPMAN This Court has jurisdiction under the war powers of the President, which are still in force. It is well known that diehard Rebel officers still refuse to lay down their arms. Officially and in fact the war continues. Move to deny.

WALLACE The motion is denied.

BAKER Motion to postpone . . . on the ground that potential witnesses who in more normal times might speak for the defendant refuse to do so now, for fear their motives will be misunderstood as signifying support of the late Confederacy.

CHIPMAN (*With open sarcasm*) If Mr. Baker's witnesses can in good conscience take the oath of loyalty to the government of the United States, they have nothing to fear.

BAKER The Court is aware of the temper of the times. It is only four short months since Mr. Lincoln was assassinated.

WALLACE (*A clap of thunder*) We will leave that name out of this trial!

BAKER Nevertheless, Mr. Lincoln's presence is in this room—his murder is felt in this room—and it swells the charge of murder against the defendant to gigantic size—

CHIPMAN For which the Southern cause is responsible. And counsel will not turn Mr. Lincoln's tragic death to his advantage here.

BAKER It is my general concern, sir, that the indictment leaves out Captain Wirz's military superiors, making him the single target of the national mood of vengeance against the South—

WALLACE (*Gavel*) That will be all, Mr. Baker. Motion denied. If you have no further motions—

BAKER I do. As to the specifications alleging the crime of murder and abetting murder against certain persons, move to strike them since no persons are named.

CHIPMAN Counsel cannot with his motions dispose of the horror of fourteen thousand unknown dead dumped into unmarked graves at Andersonville. Better records were kept of bales of cotton. Move to deny.

BAKER Will the Judge Advocate tell us where accurate prison records were kept during the war? (CHIPMAN *reacts with obvious annoyance*) The Judge Advocate owes me common courtesy here. He forgets that a person accused of crimes punishable by death is entitled to a proper defense.

CHIPMAN We know what is defended here. Counsel's political motives are well understood.

WALLACE (*Raps gavel*) The exchange will stop.

BAKER I only remind the Judge Advocate that he is in a court of law and no longer on the battlefield. He behaves as if the horror of war was not universal. The North had its Andersonvilles.

WALLACE The government of the United States is not on trial here, Mr. Baker.

BAKER That remains to be seen.

WALLACE (*Rising*) Mr. Baker—!

BAKER Meaning no offense to the Court— The remark stated in full would have been . . . "That remains to be seen through the testimony that will be offered here." I was referring to what the record will show, sir . . .

WALLACE The Court is not misled— (*The courtroom door is opened from the outside by* CAPTAIN WILLIAMS, *who indicates to the* LIEUTENANT *in charge that the prisoner is ready to appear*) In the future you will exercise care in your remarks to this court, Mr. Baker. Motion denied.

LIEUTENANT Prisoner to the Court!

(WIRZ *enters, followed by* DR. FORD, *who carries his medical bag and who is followed by* CAPTAIN WILLIAMS. FORD *and* WILLIAMS *go above witness chair to sit in reporters' area, in front of the windows. Dressed in shabby black clothes and a white shirt open at the throat, obviously not well,* WIRZ *still manages to suggest the bearing of a soldier. He looks about him as he moves toward the defense table—arrogant, defiant, fatalistic, contemptuous—a mixture of all these attitudes. He is in his forties*)

WALLACE (*To* BAKER) If you have no further motions, I will order the defendant to plead to the charge.

BAKER No further motion, but if the Court please, we have made a special request of the Judge Advocate on behalf of the defendant—which he has apparently forgotten.

CHIPMAN (*Cold*) It has been requested that the prisoner be permitted to recline on a sofa during the proceedings on his claim of great pain and weakness owing to a so-called war wound—

WIRZ (*He speaks with a slight Germanic accent*) Not so-called, Colonel. I was a soldier in the line. I was honorably wounded at the Battle of Seven Pines, and—

CHIPMAN The defendant is not the only man in this room who bears the scars of war.

WIRZ I will not be slandered.

WALLACE Permission is granted for the prisoner to recline during the proceedings, and he will now plead—

WIRZ (*Breaking in swiftly; speaking with heavy irony; he is still standing*) I thank you, General. I wish to make a statement, sir, as to my—

WALLACE You will have an opportunity to do so—

WIRZ (*Finishing*) —as to my attempt on my own life this morning, if the Court is interested—

WALLACE Make your statement.

WIRZ It was not guilt of conscience that drove me to that act. I have no guilt of conscience. None whatsoever—

WALLACE If that is all you have to say—

WIRZ Only a few words more, sir. I calmly sized up the situation, as a soldier. As I see it I have simply no chance whatsoever and I decided not to give the government the satisfaction—

WALLACE (*Overlapping*) That will be all, Mr. Wirz.

WIRZ One other matter, sir—

WALLACE That will be all.

WIRZ Then the Court will not permit me to mention a personal matter that should be the concern of the Court?

WALLACE You will speak to the point—what is it?

WIRZ I write letters to my family and do not know if they are received.

WALLACE The Court has nothing to do with mails. Possibly your letters are delayed. Conditions are still unsettled.

WIRZ General, I was taken from the midst of my family without warning and under the eyes of my children arrested. I do not care what the newspapers call me—let them call me the butcher of Andersonville. But what my children think of their father—that is important to me. I have a right to present myself as I wish to my children. *I have that right.* It is a cruelty that I do not know if my letters are received.

(*The* JUDGES *confer briefly*)

WALLACE If you wish, we will see to it that your letters go by military packet to your home—

WIRZ (*Appearing to fawn; but with irony*) I thank the Court most kindly. They have been most considerate to me. The medical care, the spiritual comfort of the priest who is permitted to visit me daily in my cell. The Court has been most kind. (*With sudden venom*) All that is wanted of me is my life. I am not fooled!

BAKER (*Crosses to* WIRZ *and escorts him to the couch as he addresses the Court*) Will the Court make due allowance for the strain the defendant is under—?

CHIPMAN (*Overlapping*) Defense counsel must share guilt with the prisoner for that outburst—

(*As* CHIPMAN *and* BAKER *now quarrel,* WALLACE *remains stonily silent*)

BAKER (*Overlapping*) Everything is conspiracy in the eyes of the Judge Advocate— I'm not here to help you make your case—much as you would like—

CHIPMAN I would like you to be still now—

BAKER (*Overlapping*) And I remind you—that normal courtroom behavior—

CHIPMAN Nothing is normal here, sir—

BAKER —that normal courtroom behavior calls for the outward appearance—I don't care what you *think*—that one's opponent is acting in good faith—

CHIPMAN Which I cannot assume, sir, since I know where you stand—

BAKER And where is that, Colonel?

CHIPMAN On the side of those who secretly opposed this government when it was fighting for its life. Who pays you here?

BAKER Not the government.

CHIPMAN No, not this government but the remnants of that other—still active.

BAKER Make a political accusation against a man and nothing he says will be considered for its own sake. The Judge Advocate is suspicious of my politics and wants to know who pays me. (*Glancing toward* WALLACE) If the Court please, I'll oblige the Judge Advocate. (WALLACE *says nothing and* BAKER *moves to confront* CHIPMAN *at close range*) I am paid by a committee formed to defend Captain Wirz. I am not involved in this case in the way the Judge Advocate would wish. I take my cases where I find them, subject to one condition—I must feel there's a shade—the smallest shade of doubt—as to a man's guilt. (*As he strides back to the defense table*) Regarding my politics, in my home city of Baltimore, a city of divided loyalties, some held that I was an enemy to the Confederate side because I felt that slavery was not worth dying for since it was an unworkable institution that was doomed to extinction anyway. And there were the others who suspected me because I was lukewarm on the glorious future that would follow a Northern victory. The Colonel might make his own position clearer.

CHIPMAN I will try to do that, Mr. Baker. I was brought up to believe that slavery was evil. I answered Mr. Lincoln's second call for volunteers because it was natural for me to go to war against a cause which wished to perpetuate human bondage. And I am here in the service of the Union to secure justice for men barbarously murdered by that Southern cause. I am personally involved here, Mr. Baker, if you are not—

BAKER   As a lawyer or as a clerk under orders to process Wirz through to the hangman? (CHIPMAN *comes to his feet, is restrained by* HOSMER, *sits.* BAKER *gestures toward* CHIPMAN *as he speaks to* SCHADE, *his voice cool*)   As I thought. We can make the bull charge.

(WALLACE'S *glance moves from* CHIPMAN *to* BAKER *in a long, silent chastising, after which he speaks in a flatly powerful tone*)

WALLACE   I take it the gentlemen are through . . . Under military law we could of course dispense with defense counsel; the defendant would not have to be present. And this case could be heard in a small room. But the government has seen fit to set it here in the Court of Claims and before an audience. Conceding the temper of the times and the emotions of all parties, we intend to hold this trial within bounds. I do not advise further testing the power of the Court to maintain order . . . (*Briskly*) Defense counsel has stated he has no further motions and I will now order the defendant to plead to the charge. Prisoner, how do you plead?

BAKER   The prisoner enters a plea of not guilty to the charge and all specifications.

WALLACE   The Judge Advocate will summon his first witness.

(*As* CHIPMAN *begins,* WIRZ *beckons to* BAKER)

CHIPMAN   On the general charge of criminal conspiracy, we summon Mr. D. T. Chandler.

(*In the time it takes for* CHANDLER'S *name to be bawled out by the* LIEUTENANT, *for* CHANDLER *to appear, walk to the witness chair, and be sworn, we hear the exchange at the defense table.* BAKER *tries to confer with* SCHADE, *but is interrupted by* WIRZ. *We must sense* BAKER'S *quiet distaste for* WIRZ *as a person*)

WIRZ   Baker, you have all the necessary documents—

LIEUTENANT (*Calls off*)   Mr. D. T. Chandler!

BAKER   Yes.

WIRZ   And the evidence that I released the youngest Northern prisoners on parole—you remember how I let them out to pick blackberries—

(CHANDLER *enters and crosses to the* CLERK)

BAKER   I know.

(CHANDLER *is sworn in by the* CLERK)

WIRZ (*Pause*)   But it will do no good. (*The tone is cryptic*)   I must die . . . Yes . . . I must die . . . (*Pause*)   The real crime I have committed, Baker—you understand what it is of course.

BAKER   Well?

WIRZ   That I chose the losing side.

CHIPMAN   Before we begin we will state briefly the rule of evidence applying in cases of criminal conspiracy. The evidence of a common design to commit a criminal act is sufficient to convict—and we shall prove that such a common design existed at Andersonville—to which the defendant willingly lent himself. (GENERAL WALLACE *indicates that* CHIPMAN *may start interrogation. We should see* CHANDLER *as a man of breeding and courage, caught through the questioning between loyalty to his defeated cause and his essential humanity*)   Mr. Chandler, please state how you were employed during the year 1864.

CHANDLER   I served in the Army of the Confederacy, with the rank of lieutenant colonel.

CHIPMAN   What was your official duty?

CHANDLER   I was assigned by the War Office to inspect and report on the military prisons maintained by the Confederacy.

CHIPMAN   Did you, in the course of an official assignment, go to the Andersonville military prison situated in Sumter County, Georgia?

CHANDLER   Yes, sir. There had been civilian complaints forwarded to Richmond.

CHIPMAN   How long did you remain at Andersonville?

CHANDLER   Two weeks.

CHIPMAN (*Moves to the map, indicating with a pointer*) I ask you if that is a fair map of the Andersonville stockade?

CHANDLER   Yes, it is.

CHIPMAN   Will you state the dimensions of the stockade—its area?

CHANDLER   A thousand feet on the longer side, from north to south. Eight hundred feet from east to west, covering about sixteen acres of ground.

CHIPMAN (*Crosses to the prosecution table*) What was the nature of the terrain?

CHANDLER   Simply earth—bare ground.

CHIPMAN   Was that the condition of the terrain in advance of its being selected as a site for the camp?

CHANDLER   No, sir. The tract was originally part of a section of pine woods.

CHIPMAN   And what can you tell us of the climate in that part of Georgia? I refer now to extremes of temperature. Of summer heat and winter cold.

CHANDLER   In July and August it would be quite high, at times over a hundred degrees. Winters, it could be near freezing and rainy.

CHIPMAN   Was that camp laid out with provision for shelter of any kind?

CHANDLER   No, sir.

CHIPMAN (*Moving to the map again, using the pointer*) This outer stockade wall—describe it, sir.

CHANDLER   A wall some fifteen to twenty feet high, consisting of rough-hewn timbers. A platform ran along the

313

top of the wall and at regular intervals there were sentry boxes.

CHIPMAN   This line inside the wall—

CHANDLER   That was a line of posts running parallel to the outer wall—about twenty-five feet inside it.

CHIPMAN   It had a name, did it not?

CHANDLER   The deadline—so called because a prisoner going beyond it could be shot by the guards.

CHIPMAN   This meandering line?

CHANDLER   That would be the stream that ran through the camp, entering under the wall on the west . . . and emerging under the east wall of the stockade.

CHIPMAN   Its width and depth?

CHANDLER   No more than a yard wide and perhaps a foot in depth . . . (*As* CHIPMAN *indicates with the pointer*) The marshy area around the stream.

CHIPMAN   That marshy area could better be called swamp, could it not?

CHANDLER   Yes, sir; swamp.

CHIPMAN   Of what size?

CHANDLER   Extending about a hundred and fifty feet on either side of the stream.

CHIPMAN   And having a considerable oozy depth, did it not?

CHANDLER   Anyone venturing across it would probably sink to his waist . . . (*Following the pointer*) That would be the cookhouse . . . The burial trenches . . . The deadhouse . . . The main-entrance gate—

CHIPMAN (*Crosses to his table*)   Now, sir, as to the history of the camp. Will you state the circumstances under which it was established?

CHANDLER   By the latter part of '63 our prisoner-of-war camps were overcrowded. The War Office then decided to create a new camp.

CHIPMAN   Who was responsible for the establishment of this new camp?

CHANDLER   General John H. Winder.

CHIPMAN   Now deceased?

CHANDLER   Yes.

CHIPMAN   And what was his official function?

CHANDLER   He was in charge of all military prisons for the Confederacy, east of the Mississippi.

CHIPMAN   You have said the tract of land on which the camp was located was originally part of a section of pine woods. The cutting down of every tree that might have provided shade—was Winder responsible for that?

CHANDLER   Yes, sir.

CHIPMAN   And this site—and the arrangements made for the care of the prisoners was known to and approved by the War Office?

CHANDLER   (*Tightly*)   I cannot say how much knowledge or approval. The Colonel knows how a line of command operates.

CHIPMAN   (*Moves to the witness*)   Wasn't it their responsibility—? Withdrawn for the time being. Will you now describe conditions in the prison at Andersonville as you observed them?

CHANDLER   The area was tightly crowded with men when I inspected it.

CHIPMAN   Giving each prisoner—how much room, would you say?

CHANDLER   Thirty-five-and-a-half square feet per prisoner.

CHIPMAN   A space equivalent to a cell only six feet on each side. What else did you find at Andersonville?

CHANDLER   (*Tightly*)   There was a general insufficiency— of water, shelter, and food. I think that would cover it.

CHIPMAN   (*Over the witness; his intensity is palpable*)   I think not. When you say an insufficiency of water you mean that the available water supply for all purposes— for drinking, washing, cooking—all came from that narrow brook, is that correct?

CHANDLER   Yes, sir.

315

CHIPMAN And that stream was at the same time the repository for all the waste matter at the camp, was it not?

CHANDLER Yes, sir.

CHIPMAN All waste was emptied into that stream; the waste from the cookhouse and the bodily waste of the prisoners?

CHANDLER Yes, sir.

CHIPMAN Making that stream into a foul, sluggish sink, isn't that so?

CHANDLER Yes—

CHIPMAN (*Circling*) And that foul, stinking stream a few feet wide was the water supply for forty thousand men, and that is what you meant by an insufficiency of water, isn't it?

CHANDLER Yes.

CHIPMAN And as to the insufficiency of shelter, there was in fact *no* shelter and the men lived on bare ground winter and summer or dug themselves into the ground, into burrows—is *that* correct?

CHANDLER Yes, sir.

CHIPMAN And as to the sort of clothing they had. You will please be specific, sir.

CHANDLER (*More and more uneasy*) *Some* wore shirts and trousers—

CHIPMAN *Some.* You mean the newly arrived prisoners *still* had their shirts and trousers, don't you?

CHANDLER Yes.

CHIPMAN You mean the rest, the vast number of them, were in rags, don't you?

CHANDLER Yes.

CHIPMAN You mean those men were simply in a state of nakedness and near nakedness under the terrible weather conditions you described a moment ago—isn't that so?

CHANDLER Yes.

CHIPMAN And the food?

CHANDLER Mostly corn meal.

CHIPMAN   Ground fine or coarse?

CHANDLER   Unbolted meal.

CHIPMAN   Unbolted meal. Meaning meal ground so coarse it was as good as swallowing a knife for what it did to a man's insides considering the weakened condition those men were in. Isn't that so, Mr. Chandler?

CHANDLER   Yes, sir.

CHIPMAN   Did the men ever get anything else to eat outside of this meal?

CHANDLER   A bit of meat now and then.

CHIPMAN   What sort of meat?

CHANDLER   Not very good.

CHIPMAN (*Moves to* CHANDLER) Not very good. The prisoners had a joke about that meat, didn't they? A grim kind of a soldier joke to describe that meat from sick, dying mules and horses. They told you that the animal that meat came from—it had to be held up on its legs to be slaughtered—didn't they?

CHANDLER   Jokes of that sort—yes.

CHIPMAN   And you saw with your own eyes it was rotten, maggot-ridden meat, and that is what you meant when you said it wasn't very good, didn't you?

CHANDLER   Yes—

CHIPMAN (*Moving*) And the conditions they were living under drove them to extreme measures in the effort to survive, isn't that so?

CHANDLER   Extreme—yes, sir.

CHIPMAN   To the point where they regarded rats as a delicacy, isn't that so?

CHANDLER   Yes, sir.

CHIPMAN   To the point that when one of them died, the others, in the desperation they had been driven to, stripped his body clean of whatever was on it in five minutes—of boots or trousers if he had any, or bread, or greenbacks to bribe the guards—anything that might help them stay alive—isn't that correct?

CHANDLER   Yes, sir.

CHIPMAN   Driven in their desperation to the point of cannibalism, isn't that so?

CHANDLER   Yes—

CHIPMAN   You were able to establish that in your mind for a fact?

CHANDLER   Yes.

CHIPMAN (*Close to the witness*)   How? (*As* CHANDLER *hesitates*)   As delicately as you wish, Mr. Chandler.

CHANDLER (*After a moment; with difficulty*)   Well—by the condition of some bodies—very rough surgery had been performed.

CHIPMAN   And so, in that place, men had been driven to the disposition of beasts—

CHANDLER   Yes.

CHIPMAN (*Crosses to the map, his voice flaring*)   And if I were now to sum up Andersonville as a pit—an animal pit in which men wallowed—the sick, the dying, the insane wallowing among the dead—would I exaggerate the picture of that place?

CHANDLER   No.

CHIPMAN   Concerning what you saw there . . . you submitted a report with recommendations to General Winder and your War Office, did you not?

CHANDLER   I did.

CHIPMAN (*Handing over a document to* CHANDLER)   This is a copy of that report?

CHANDLER (*Glancing at it and handing it back*)   That is the report.

CHIPMAN   Offered in evidence. (*He hands the report to* WALLACE, *who scans it and returns it to* CHIPMAN)   You say in this report that Andersonville is a blot on the Confederacy. You recommend that all prisoners be transferred to other prisons without delay and that Andersonville be immediately closed down.

CHANDLER   I did; yes.

318

(CHIPMAN *hands the report to the* CLERK)

CLERK   Exhibit one for the government.

CHIPMAN   And that report was ignored, was it not? Ignored, disregarded, the condition allowed to continue—?

CHANDLER   Colonel, I am not here to indict the leaders of the cause for which I fought, as plotting the murder of defenseless men.

CHIPMAN (*Boring in*)   The report revealing how Winder and Wirz were operating that camp was ignored—

CHANDLER   I have told you I could not endure Andersonville. You people act as though you were better human beings than we were!

CHIPMAN   No, but our cause was. Your report was ignored?

CHANDLER   Due to the crisis—the bitterness—the disorder —with General Sherman marching through Georgia burning his way—

CHIPMAN   It was ignored—?

CHANDLER   As your officers would have ignored it, sir, if it had been General Lee marching through Pennsylvania into New York!

WALLACE   Mr. Chandler—

CHANDLER   This situation is difficult for me.

WALLACE (*Stern, but not hard; he respects* CHANDLER) Nevertheless, you must answer the question. The Judge Advocate will repeat the question and you *will* answer it.

CHIPMAN   Your report on Andersonville was ignored, was it not?

CHANDLER   Yes, sir.

CHIPMAN   Did General Winder ever express to you his disposition toward those prisoners?

CHANDLER   When I spoke to General Winder he had hard and bitter feelings toward them.

CHIPMAN   And how did he express those feelings?

CHANDLER   He finally said that if half of the prisoners died, there would then be twice as much room for the rest—

319

CHIPMAN And the half slated for the grave were well on their way at Andersonville, weren't they? Mr. Wirz set up certain rules for that camp, rules relative to punishing prisoners attempting to escape—?

CHANDLER Yes, sir.

CHIPMAN His command of that camp conforming to Winder's inhuman disposition toward those men?

BAKER I must ask the Judge Advocate what he means by that suggestive, ambiguous phrase, *conforming to*.

CHIPMAN Withdrawn. Those rules Mr. Wirz set up at Andersonville—were they rules violating the customs of war?

CHANDLER Well—yes.

CHIPMAN Were they, in addition, cruel and inhuman rules?

CHANDLER Yes.

CHIPMAN Was Wirz the personal choice of Winder for superintendent of that camp?

CHANDLER Yes.

CHIPMAN That will be all.

(*He crosses to his table*)

BAKER Colonel Chandler, you made a second report on Andersonville to the Confederate War Office, did you not?

CHANDLER I did, yes, sir.

BAKER That is a copy of that report?

(*He hands the report to* SCHADE, *who shows it to* CHANDLER)

CHANDLER (*Scrutinizing it briefly and handing it back to* SCHADE) It is.

(SCHADE *hands it to* WALLACE, *who examines it quickly and indicates that it is acceptable*)

SCHADE Submitted for the defense— (*Handing the report to the* CLERK) Entered in evidence.

CLERK Exhibit one for the defense.

BAKER   In this report—to which the Judge Advocate has failed to call attention—you recommend the dismissal of General Winder.

CHANDLER   Yes.

BAKER   But *not* of Captain Wirz.

CHANDLER   No.

BAKER   Why not?

CHANDLER   At the time I inspected Andersonville, I saw nothing in Captain Wirz's conduct of a malignant disposition toward those men, that would have justified asking for his dismissal.

BAKER   I note in the same report that you took various prisoners aside, urging them to speak freely as to any instance of ill treatment by Captain Wirz—and they had no complaints on that score?

CHANDLER   No, sir.

BAKER   In other words, neither you nor the prisoners, who were presumably being subjected to Captain Wirz's cruel and inhuman treatment, blamed him for it, did you?

CHANDLER   No, sir.

BAKER   No more questions. Thank you, sir.

CHIPMAN   Mr. Chandler, very often, as you know, commanders are forewarned of inspection and dress up their commands in advance. Couldn't that have occurred in your case?

CHANDLER   Possibly.

CHIPMAN   And isn't it possible that the prisoners would fear the consequences of complaints against Wirz? Those men did not know you, and Wirz would still be in command after you were gone. And under those circumstances, isn't it very possible that they would not answer you truthfully?

CHANDLER   Perhaps. I did the best I could with that Andersonville situation—

CHIPMAN   (*Inwardly raging; silent for a moment*)   Did

Wirz do the best he could? (*Rises and crosses to the witness*) In spite of Winder's orders, couldn't he have chosen to . . . (*Frustrated*) . . . there are ways!

BAKER Ways of doing what? Evading the orders of his superior? What is the Judge Advocate suggesting?

CHIPMAN (*Crosses to his table, sits*) Withdrawn. That will be all, thank you, Mr. Chandler.

WALLACE If there are no other questions the witness may step down. The Court thanks the witness.

(CHANDLER *goes.* CHIPMAN'S *tone is becoming more peremptory*)

CHIPMAN We call Dr. John C. Bates to the stand.

LIEUTENANT Dr. John C. Bates.

(BATES *comes in and is sworn. He is a type of country doctor; an honest man with small vanities*)

CHIPMAN Dr. Bates, were you in the service of the Confederate Army during the year 1864?

BATES Yes, sir.

CHIPMAN Were you at any time inside the Andersonville stockade?

BATES Yes, sir. For about eight months during '64.

CHIPMAN In what capacity were you there?

BATES As a medical officer—assigned to the camp by the Surgeon General. I can't say I asked for it.

CHIPMAN I suppose not. Describe your activity there as a physician.

BATES Writing prescriptions for drugs that were not available, amputations of limbs due to gangrene—quite a lot of that—and certifying the dead in my section each morning—quite a lot of that too.

CHIPMAN Did you in the course of your stay there make any estimate of the rate of death at that place?

BATES I did; yes, sir. I had always kept a ledger book covering the ailments and treatment of my patients in civil life—farmers—their families—their horses too. And I decided to keep some sort of a record in that camp

The Andersonville Trial

. . . because I was deeply shocked by that place when I came there.

CHIPMAN Please tell the Court what your estimate of the death rate was.

BATES In the spring months it averaged fifty, sixty, seventy men a day . . . in spells of extreme heat during the summer reaching a hundred men a day. More in May than in April, more in June than in May, and in July, August, September, three thousand men a month were dying.

CHIPMAN What were the principal causes for that high rate of death?

BATES The lack of sanitary facilities—the lack of exercise —the anemia of the men from lack of food rendering them subject to fatal illness from the slightest abrasion or infection—the lack of medical supplies.

CHIPMAN And, Dr. Bates, in your professional opinion, how many of the thousands who died there would have lived if conditions had at least been sanitary?

BATES I would estimate—seventy-five to eighty per cent.

CHIPMAN Ten to eleven thousand of those fourteen thousand men—

BATES Yes, sir.

CHIPMAN Can you think of sanitary measures which, if taken at Andersonville, would have saved lives—?

BATES A number; yes.

CHIPMAN Were such measures suggested to Wirz?

BATES Yes, sir. By myself—perhaps others.

CHIPMAN And what did he say?

BATES He said I was a doctor and didn't understand his difficulties running a huge camp like that. He was downright incoherent—damned me for a Yankee sympathizer —and cursed me out in English, German and some other foreign dialect—

WIRZ French. That was French, Dr. Bates—

BATES French, eh?

WALLACE (*Brings down the gavel*) For your own good, Mr. Wirz, keep in mind that your situation here is not amusing.

WIRZ No, sir—and I can't explain it to myself or to the Court, why I have this feeling to laugh, hearing how I killed all those men. Perhaps the Court can explain it.

WALLACE Do not play the clown here . . . Continue, Colonel.

CHIPMAN Only one more question—on that not so humorous occasion when you spoke to Wirz and he complained to you that his job was difficult . . . did you understand him to mean his job was difficult administratively or difficult— (*Searching for his thought*) —humanly?

BATES Mr. Wirz dwelt on *his* difficulties—not the men's.

CHIPMAN That will be all, Doctor. Thank you.

(*He sits*)

BAKER Dr. Bates, you regard yourself as a fair-minded man, don't you?

BATES I do.

BAKER The fact that you dislike Captain Wirz has not influenced your testimony here in any way, has it?

BATES No, it has not—

BAKER But you *did* dislike him, didn't you?

BATES Not so as to influence my professional objective judgment—

BAKER I now address myself to that professional *objective* judgment, Doctor—strictly to that. So far as you know, by whose authority was the amount of food per prisoner decided on?

BATES By the Commissary General at Richmond, I believe.

BAKER And not by Captain Wirz. And by whose authority was the amount and type of medical supply to the camp decided on?

BATES The Surgeon General.

BAKER And not by Captain Wirz. He was responsible

324

neither for the lack of food nor the inadequate medical supplies.

BATES   I would have to agree.

BAKER   You would have to agree. You don't want to agree but you would have to agree, is that what you mean, Dr. Bates? You seem to have found Captain Wirz rather calloused toward the condition of the prisoners.

BATES   That was my honest impression.

BAKER   Well, we are all entitled to our honest impressions. I recall you saying a few minutes ago that you were shocked at the high rate of death in the Andersonville prison when you came there.

BATES   Deeply shocked.

BAKER (*With a show of sympathy*)   One can understand how unnerving it must have been. That was in what month by the way?

BATES   In February.

BAKER   And you had to face that unnerving scene day after day and month after month—it's difficult to understand how you could do that.

BATES   Well, sir, I had to steel myself and gradually the shock of it became endurable.

BAKER   I'm curious, Doctor—how gradually did your feeling of shock lessen? For example, how did you react to the dying—by June, let us say?

BATES   Not as much.

BAKER   And by September?

BATES   Far less—

BAKER   So that by September, when, as you said, three thousand men a month were dying, you hardly reacted at all—?

BATES   I meant—I had grown accustomed—

BAKER (*Gesturing in the direction of* WIRZ)   Of course you had. Any human being to save his sanity would have had to do that. So Captain Wirz's "callousness" in that place wasn't so strange after all, was it?

BATES (*Rattled*)   Well—my impression of Mr. Wirz remains the same, despite that.

BAKER   Thank you, that will be all.

(BAKER *returns to the defense table;* CHIPMAN *comes forward*)

CHIPMAN (*Sharp*)   Dr. Bates, do you remember one single instance, in conversing with Wirz, when he expressed any criticism of the orders or disposition of his superior?

BAKER   Objection. I find that a strange question to be asked by a counsel for the War Department, himself a soldier. Is it being held against Captain Wirz that he did not make a public judgment of the motives of his military superior?

WALLACE (*Considering. The question has implications and there is a noticeable stir among the* JUDGES. *They confer briefly*)   The Court must agree Wirz was not bound to comment on the order of his military superior.

CHIPMAN (*Facing* JUDGES, *driving*)   If the Court please, we are concerned here with the frame of mind of a man carrying out his superior's inhuman design. We are bound to explore his thinking when he obeyed those orders—

BAKER (*Rising*)   His thinking when he obeyed those orders? And if he did not like those orders what was he supposed to do? Disobey them? If conscience is the measure by which soldiers obey or disobey orders, one can hardly condemn the Army officers who went over to the Confederacy, since they did so on the ground of conscience— (*The gavel comes down*)   And on that ground Robert E. Lee deserves a monument—

WALLACE (*Obviously perturbed*)   That will be all, Mr. Baker . . . (*To* CHIPMAN)   I am certain it was not in the mind of the Judge Advocate to raise the issue of disobedience to a superior officer—

CHIPMAN (*Crosses slowly to table, sits, inwardly resisting*

326

the Court)   Under certain circumstances that issue may require consideration—

WALLACE (*With great deliberation—cueing, ordering and warning* CHIPMAN *at the same time*)   The Court is not, of course, suggesting the line of inquiry the Judge Advocate is to take here. But the Court will say that it is disposed to draw its own inference as to a criminal design from evidence of the defendant's words and acts—and not from an examination of moral factors which can drop us into a bottomless pool of philosophic debate . . . I am certain the Judge Advocate will agree and that he will withdraw that question as to whether or not Wirz criticized his superior officer.

CHIPMAN (*His glance travels slowly and sullenly down the line of* JUDGES, *fighting them, and then—*)   The question is withdrawn. (*Moves to the witness; in a temper*) Dr. Bates, you never grew so accustomed to that place as to forget your human obligation to those men, did you? You made it your daily business to bring in food from the outside for those starving men, didn't you?

BATES   Of course.

CHIPMAN   And there was plenty of food in the region of Andersonville to draw from, if Wirz had wished to bring it in—the yield of grain and vegetables in the region was considerable, wasn't it?

BAKER   Is Dr. Bates put forward as qualified to testify on the agricultural situation?

CHIPMAN   Withdrawn! If the Court please, we wish to change the order of appearance of witnesses. We would like at this time to call a witness qualified to speak with accuracy on the available food supply in the vicinity of Andersonville.

WALLACE   Does defense counsel offer objection to a change in the order of the government witnesses?

BAKER   Not at all.

CHIPMAN   Ambrose Spencer to the stand!

WALLACE   The Court thanks you, Dr. Bates. You may step down.

LIEUTENANT   Ambrose Spencer!

BAKER (*Cool and amused; pointing up* CHIPMAN'S *failure to thank the witness*)   *We* thank the witness.

CHIPMAN   Thank you, Dr. Bates! (BATES *exits.* SPENCER *enters, is sworn in and takes the stand. A somewhat glib, unctuous, coarse country squire type.* CHIPMAN'S *questioning is now more impatient; he treads on the tail of* SPENCER'S *answers*)   Mr. Spencer, tell us where you reside.

SPENCER   I reside in the town of Americus, in Sumter County, Georgia—

CHIPMAN   Your occupation?

SPENCER   I operate a plantation in that county—corn, cotton, tobacco and—

CHIPMAN   Is that plantation in proximity to the site of Andersonville?

SPENCER   Practically bordering it.

CHIPMAN (*Pacing*)   You are therefore in a position to know as well as any man the yield of grain and vegetables in the region of Andersonville.

SPENCER   I would say so.

CHIPMAN How would you estimate yields for the years 1863 and 1864?

SPENCER (*With obvious satisfaction*)   Both good years. Sumter and the adjoining county, Macon, I may point out, are part of a very productive area—sometimes termed the garden of the Confederacy, and—

CHIPMAN   Yes, yes. We will have some details as to the yield.

SPENCER   Corn averaged about eight bushels to the acre, wheat six. That is the general average but we have land in Sumter County producing thirty-five—

CHIPMAN   And as to vegetables?

SPENCER   We had an uncommon amount during the war since there was so little cotton planted and all the ground was pretty well planted in provisions.

CHIPMAN   And, if Mr. Wirz had solicited food for the prisoners from the farms and plantations in the area— what in your judgment would have happened?

SPENCER   He would have gotten it.

(*As* SPENCER *goes on,* WIRZ *sits up.* BAKER *restrains him*)

CHIPMAN   What makes you so certain of that?

SPENCER   The proof, sir, is that without it being solicited, there were people in the vicinity who came forward and made an effort to get food into that camp. In one case a group of women in Americus, including my wife, made that attempt.

CHIPMAN   Tell the Court what happened on that occasion.

SPENCER   Well, sir, the ladies thought it would be the Christian thing to do, having heard that the prisoners were doing so poorly. They obtained enough food through contributions to fill four wagons and had them driven—

CHIPMAN,   How large were those wagons?

SPENCER   The largest farm wagons they could find—each requiring four to six horses to pull it.

CHIPMAN   Making a load of how much food for those men?

SPENCER   Oh, maybe twenty tons.

CHIPMAN   Continue, sir.

SPENCER   They had those wagons driven up to the gate of the stockade. Mr. Wirz was at the gate when those ladies arrived. He would not permit the food to be brought in— He cursed those women. He told them they were giving aid and comfort to the enemy—that Yankee soldiers were unlawfully invading—looting the South—that those women were traitors—and worse. He used the violentest and profanest language I have ever heard in a man's mouth. He said if he had his way he would have a certain kind of a house built for those women and he would put them all in there where the Confederate soldiers would teach them loyalty in a hurry and teach it to them in a way they wouldn't forget—

CHIPMAN We understand the remark, sir. And those ladies were turned away by Mr. Wirz from giving food to those starving men—

SPENCER They were turned away and they wept.

CHIPMAN And if Mr. Wirz had solicited food—on Christian grounds and on behalf of the good name of the Confederacy—you think that would have brought in large amounts of food—?

SPENCER I am certain the people of Georgia would have responded—

CHIPMAN You were acquainted with the defendant, were you not?

SPENCER Knew him quite well.

CHIPMAN And you knew General Winder—

SPENCER Knew him too.

CHIPMAN And from your knowledge, what can you tell us about the disposition of General Winder toward those prisoners?

SPENCER When he came there once, Winder said that the Yankees had come South to take possession of the land and that he was endeavoring to satisfy them by giving them each a small plot—pointing to the grave site.

CHIPMAN And did you ever hear Wirz speak along the same lines?

SPENCER I can tell you that he stated that he wished all those men in hell—that he boasted he was killing more Yankees at Andersonville than Lee was at Richmond—

CHIPMAN You heard those remarks—?

SPENCER Yes—to wipe out those men. That was the scheme.

CHIPMAN Thank you.

(*He goes to his table*)

WIRZ (*As* CHIPMAN *finishes*) That was my scheme, you

The Andersonville Trial

say? To wipe out those men? On my head all those men?
(*He rises,* BAKER *and* SCHADE *come to him*)

WALLACE (*Overlapping*)   Mr. Wirz . . . !

WIRZ   I was a man like other men—

WALLACE (*Overlapping*)   Counsel, you will restrain—

WIRZ (*Breaking away from* BAKER *and* SCHADE *and crossing to* JUDGES' *table*)   Who will understand? An ordinary man like me—assigned—!

WALLACE (*Overlapping*)   Guards!
(*The two* GUARDS, *the* LIEUTENANT, CAPTAIN WILLIAMS *and* DR. FORD *move in on* WIRZ)

WIRZ   The drummer boys I saved—and now— (*In a drawn-out cry*)   —I am surrounded!
(*As the* GUARDS *reach for him, he slumps down in a faint. He is carried to the sofa*)

FORD (*To* SCHADE)   A bottle of brandy, in the bag.

BAKER   I ask for a postponement.

WALLACE   Dr. Ford?

FORD   A fainting spell from which he recovers. He lacks strength and suffers from strain but should be well enough to continue—I suppose.
(WIRZ *comes to consciousness, raising himself to lean on an elbow, watching*)

WALLACE   This trial must go on—

BAKER   If the Court please—

WALLACE   It is no use, Mr. Baker—

BAKER   The open bias of the witness is a case in point. I need not remind the Court of the bitterness in our time—

WALLACE   It is no use, Mr. Baker—

BAKER   Even the sight of a tattered Confederate blouse is a cause for riot in the streets. The very air is charged.

WALLACE (*The case is beginning to coil about him*)   We are not empowered to move this trial into the next century— This trial will continue. You will make clear to the defendant that should there be another demonstration here he will be tried *in absentia*—

331

WIRZ   *In absentia.* Latin for absence. I understand all languages but the language of this trial—

BAKER   The Court has suffered sufficient provocation to send Captain Wirz from this courtroom but I suggest it does not—

WALLACE   (*In a cold, deadly tone*)   You suggest we do not—

BAKER   Since it is not he alone in this room who is stripped down to naked hatred and anger—

WALLACE   Counsel will cross-examine or stand down.

BAKER   Counsel will cross-examine! Mr. Spencer, you don't regard yourself as prejudiced against Captain Wirz, do you?

SPENCER   I don't.

BAKER   Then why have you chosen to leave out of that touching tale about those women bringing food to that camp the fact that General Winder was there at the time and that it was he who ordered that food kept out?

SPENCER   Why?

BAKER   Yes, why. You were at the main gate of the camp together with other civilians and you heard General Winder say loudly and emphatically that that food was not to be brought in—

SPENCER   Wirz wouldn't have tried in any case. I know that man.

BAKER   Answer the question— Why didn't you say so?

SPENCER   I wasn't asked.

BAKER   You weren't asked. Motion to dismiss Mr. Spencer's testimony as irrelevant in that it offers nothing other than that Captain Wirz was carrying out a direct order.

CHIPMAN   Move to deny.

BAKER   Will the Judge Advocate offer a ground for denial? Is he saying that Captain Wirz should have defied that direct order of General Winder's?

CHIPMAN   Will you deny that was an inhuman order?

BAKER   Which he should have disobeyed?

The Andersonville Trial

WALLACE   Defense motion is denied.

BAKER (*With restrained, deliberate fury*)   Of course denied. It is now plain enough why the government has chosen to try Captain Wirz on a conspiracy charge. On that charge the accused may be convicted without any direct evidence against him—

WALLACE (*Rising*)   Mr. Baker!

(WALLACE, *half-risen, remains in that position as* BAKER *continues, his eyes fixed on* BAKER, *head cocked as if to make sure he will not miss one word*)

BAKER (*Going on*)   —and if there is a conspiracy, it is one directed against Captain Wirz. I say now that the motives which bring Wirz to trial here dishonor the government of the United States; and that contradicting its own military code—the Army will have this man though he was only doing his proper duty.

WALLACE   Are you through, Mr. Baker?

BAKER   I am through, sir.

WALLACE   You have been in contempt since the beginning of that outburst. The Court will consider a formal charge against you. You are dismissed from this proceeding forthwith, and will immediately leave this room.

BAKER   Let Captain Wirz be without counsel—so this trial may be judged for what it is—

WALLACE (*Not waiting for* BAKER *to finish*)   Guards—escort Mr. Baker from the room.

(BAKER *starts for the door. His manner is cool. The* JUDGES *look at one another and then toward* CHIPMAN. *The dilemma is theirs*)

WIRZ (*Crying out*)   I appeal to the Court! I will have no counsel— (*And then, almost with satisfaction*)   No counsel then. It makes no difference.

CHIPMAN (*Swiftly*)   I respectfully request the Court . . .

(BAKER *halts on hearing* CHIPMAN *begin to speak*)   The Court has borne the provocative behavior of defense counsel with the utmost patience—I request that Mr.

Baker be allowed to purge himself of contempt if he so wishes. (*Making his meaning clear despite the elaborate phrasing*) I pray that the magnanimity of the Court extend itself so that not even in the wildest misrepresentation of this trial may it be said this defendant was denied counsel of his choice.

WALLACE (*After a pause*) Mr. Baker. For the single reason that Mr. Wirz may have counsel of his choice, you may now purge yourself of contempt if you so wish. You may do so by recanting those remarks impugning the integrity of the government and Army of the United States, by apologizing to the Court and by giving us your oath such outbursts will not occur again.

BAKER (*With great deliberateness, aware of the face-saving involved*) I do so recant and apologize and give my oath that I will not hereafter impugn the fairness of the Court or the motives of the government and Army of the United States.

(*He crosses to the table and sits*)

WALLACE The Judge Advocate will— (*Notices the witness*) Are we through with this witness? (*Both lawyers indicate that they are*) The Court thanks the witness and he may step down. (SPENCER *exits*) Call your next witness, Colonel.

(*During the following speech, as the lights begin to dim out,* CHIPMAN'S *voice is heard, dying away*)

CHIPMAN On the specification that the defendant did keep in barbarously close confinement soldiers numbering at times forty thousand men without adequate shelter from the rain and heat of summer and the cold of winter, we call . . .

THE LIGHTS FADE OUT

Scene Two

A week later. The weather continues hot.

As the lights come up to full, the witness, JAMES DAVID-
SON, *is in the chair, and we hear* CHIPMAN'S *voice coming
back as he examines* DAVIDSON. CHIPMAN *is examining him,
with a driving, desperate quality, his tunic unbuttoned, collar open.*

DAVIDSON *is young. War and prison experience haunt his
face. He is feeble and ill at ease and his postwar motley costume of Army tunic and civilian trousers hangs loosely on
his gaunt frame. One may imagine how deeply he longs for
a quiet, restful place.*

CHIPMAN (*Close to the witness; his voice rasping*)   Now,
   Mr. Davidson, Captain Wirz *knew* the dogs tore and
   killed prisoners of war?
DAVIDSON   It was commonly known, yes, sir.
CHIPMAN   Knew it, and permitted it, and as far as you
   know, never took steps to put an end to that practice—
   (BAKER *starts to object*) Withdrawn! Mr. Davidson,
   during the time you were a prisoner at Andersonville, did
   you ever see a man torn by dogs—I mean on an occasion
   when Wirz was present?
DAVIDSON   Yes, sir.
CHIPMAN   Tell us about it.
DAVIDSON (*Slowly; too slowly for* CHIPMAN)   Saw that
   after tunneling out of the stockade with another prisoner.
   We got maybe fifteen miles from the camp when the dogs
   treed us. The guards ordered us down. And I saw those
   dogs tear my companion.
CHIPMAN   And Captain Wirz was there, wasn't he?
DAVIDSON   Captain Wirz rode up a minute after that pack

335

of dogs had treed us, yelling, "Get those Yankee bastards"—beggin' your pardon.

CHIPMAN   And he was present while those dogs were tearing your companion?

DAVIDSON   While they were tearing him, yes, sir.

CHIPMAN   And what was Wirz doing while they tore him—?

DAVIDSON   Damning that man to hell—beg—his eyes starting out of his head—like a fit was on him.

CHIPMAN   Can you recall another instance—an instance where—

WALLACE (*His irritation is obvious*)   Before we hear the answer we will ask the Judge Advocate if he expects, as he stated yesterday, to conclude his case today—

CHIPMAN   We shall make every effort to conclude—
(*They are fighting now*)

WALLACE   The Court does not wish to exclude pertinent testimony but we have heard a great number of the former Andersonville prisoners testify—

CHIPMAN   I am now trying to establish Mr. Wirz's attitude when he was present on occasions where extreme cruelty was practiced— The Court will understand that we call only those witnesses we think necessary . . .

WALLACE   Of course—

CHIPMAN   —and we cannot altogether control the time required for thorough examination of witnesses—

WALLACE   Naturally. However, the Court does not consider it necessary to hear further evidence corroborating facts alleged many times over. Will the government conclude this afternoon?

CHIPMAN   We will conclude this afternoon, sir.

WALLACE   Continue, Colonel.

CHIPMAN .   Mr. Davidson, the question is, did you know of any instance where an escaped prisoner was tracked down and actually *killed* by dogs? And again, I am referring to an instance when Wirz was present. (DAVIDSON *does not answer*) Did you hear my question, Mr. Davidson?

DAVIDSON   Yes, sir.

CHIPMAN   Well?

DAVIDSON   I—want to forget about that place, Colonel.

CHIPMAN   (*Curtly*)   State the circumstances.

DAVIDSON   Was this time a man from my prison squad escaped. Tunneling through to the outside one night. But then we heard the rumor he'd been captured by the dogs.

CHIPMAN   You actually saw that man being brought back to the stockade—

DAVIDSON   Yes, sir. First through the gate is Captain Wirz on that big gray he rode and then come two guards and this man between them . . . And they was holding him . . . and letting him go once he was inside that gate . . . He fell down . . . his legs was torn and his throat laid open. His flesh torn about the legs and his neck bloody.

CHIPMAN   And did he get up or did he lie there?

DAVIDSON   Made as if to get up and then lay back. Didn't move after that.

CHIPMAN   And where was Wirz during all this time?

DAVIDSON   Right there.

CHIPMAN   Right *where?*

DAVIDSON   Like I said, sir—

CHIPMAN   We will hear it again, *please*, Mr. Davidson.

DAVIDSON   Like I said, he rode in as this man fell down. Captain Wirz rode around him looking down at him, reining in his horse which was skittering and rearing— that was a horse with a temper—then rode back through the gate.

CHIPMAN   That will be all. Thank you.

BAKER   (*His manner is gentle, in conscious contrast to* CHIPMAN'S)   Mr. Davidson, we will not detain you long, sir. In that first instance you have described—when you made your escape attempt—you say Captain Wirz cursed, urging on those dogs, that were tearing your companion?

DAVIDSON   Yes, sir.

BAKER   Tell me, Mr. Davidson, at any time in your career as a soldier—did you ever yell—"Get those Rebel bastards"?

DAVIDSON   I guess so.

BAKER   And what was it that Captain Wirz yelled—?

DAVIDSON   "Get—those—Yankee—" But that was different.

BAKER   How different?

DAVIDSON   He meant for those dogs to tear that man, and I saw them do that.

BAKER   You were close enough to see that—

DAVIDSON   Yes—

BAKER   Well—*how* close, would you say?

DAVIDSON   Ten, fifteen feet away maybe. No more 'n from here to there.

BAKER   And how was it, Mr. Davidson, those dogs did not tear you? (DAVIDSON *stares at* BAKER *in shocked, puzzled silence*)   How do you account for that? (DAVIDSON *shakes his head inarticulately*)   Can you think of any reason, Mr. Davidson?
(*After a pause*)

DAVIDSON   I wouldn't know why, sir.

BAKER   Now, since you admit those ferocious dogs didn't attack *you,* shall I understand you were completely unhurt when you were brought back to the camp?

DAVIDSON   (*Slowly*)   No, sir.

BAKER   You were bruised some, as a result of rushing pell-mell through the swamps, weren't you?

DAVIDSON   Yes.

BAKER   Bloodied a bit, too?

DAVIDSON   Some. From all that running and stumbling against rocks—

BAKER   Yes. And from bramble bushes and whipping branches and dead cypress limbs, some of them as pointed as knives?

338

DAVIDSON Yes, sir.

BAKER It would bruise and bloody any man, trying to beat a pursuit through a Georgia swamp, wouldn't it?

DAVIDSON I guess so.

BAKER So in that second instance you spoke of, when you saw a man brought back to the stockade—couldn't those marks on him that you say were caused by the dogs— couldn't they have been caused by his rushing headlong through the swamps, as yours were?

DAVIDSON That man was torn by dogs—

BAKER Well, now you didn't *see* him being torn by dogs, did you, Mr. Davidson?

DAVIDSON It was commonly known that the dogs—

BAKER Many things are commonly known, sir. Could you identify the bruises on this man as being indisputably caused by dogs?

DAVIDSON (*Feebly stubborn*) He was bit by the dogs and he died—

BAKER (*Shrugging*) Possibly. How long did you remain at that spot after this man—you don't happen to know his name, do you?

DAVIDSON No, sir.

BAKER How long did you remain there after that man fell down?

DAVIDSON Three—five minutes.

BAKER And did you have occasion to look that way later?

DAVIDSON Some time later—yes.

BAKER And was he still lying there?

DAVIDSON No, sir—taken off to the deadhouse—

BAKER Or to the sick ward? (*Waiting*) Mr. Davidson, you can't say this man died as a result of being mutilated by dogs and you can't identify this man, is that correct?

DAVIDSON (*To* WALLACE) Sir, please. I got to go back home.

BAKER And Captain Wirz riding around that man . . . without a word—that sounds mighty unfeeling. You wouldn't know whether he notified the guard at the gate to have that man moved, would you?

DAVIDSON   I got to go home.

BAKER   Thank you, Mr. Davidson. That will be all.

CHIPMAN (*Crosses to the witness; his temper is barely under control*)   Mr. Davidson, didn't Wirz openly show his contempt and hatred for those men torn and killed by dogs?

(DAVIDSON *glances toward* WIRZ)

DAVIDSON (*Wretchedly*)   I don't know.

CHIPMAN   You don't know? With Wirz coldly sitting his horse—indifferent to that man brought back to die—

DAVIDSON   I can't say for sure now how he felt—

CHIPMAN (*Hardly waiting for the answer; starting to lose control*)   But those were the marks of teeth and claws that you identified on that man, weren't they?

DAVIDSON   I guess so—

CHIPMAN (*Shouting*)   You were quite sure of all that at one time. You also said that he died—that the flies set on his face and he didn't move to brush them off—

DAVIDSON   I don't remember—

CHIPMAN   And Captain Wirz looking on—looking on— that dying man.

DAVIDSON   I—I—

CHIPMAN   All I am asking you to repeat is what you already have sworn to under oath—that his attitude was monstrously cold and indifferent to those dying men!

DAVIDSON (*High*)   Let me be, Colonel!

CHIPMAN   Mr. Davidson, I must warn you—!

DAVIDSON (*At absolute pitch*)   I got to forget that place—!

CHIPMAN (*Shouting*)   Or has it been suggested to you that you forget that place—!

WALLACE   Colonel Chipman! (CHIPMAN *turns away, crosses to the table and sits, fighting for control*)   I think the witness is through. (*Gently—pointedly looking at* CHIPMAN)   Are you now ill, Mr. Davidson?

340

DAVIDSON (*Steps off the podium*) Yes, sir. I got pains—

WALLACE You have told us about that incident as well as you can now recall it, is that correct?

DAVIDSON Yes, sir.

WALLACE How old are you, Mr. Davidson?

DAVIDSON Nineteen, sir.

WALLACE I believe you said you fought with the Second Vermont Cavalry.

DAVIDSON (*He straightens*) The Second Vermont Cavalry, sir. We turned their flank many times.

WALLACE You may now go home and the Court wishes you Godspeed in recovering good health and in forgetting what you have endured in war and in prison.

DAVIDSON Yes, sir. Thank you, sir. (*Starts out and stops; looking uncertainly from* CHIPMAN *to* BAKER, *searching himself*) Could be those dogs didn't tear me for the same reason Daniel was not tore in the lion's den. There was many died in that place. Many died. I hear those dogs baying at night. I hear voices cry out "Help, help" and no one to help. Many died. Many, many died.

CHIPMAN (*After a silence; terribly strained*) I apologize to the witness.

DAVIDSON Yes, sir.

(*He exits*)

WALLACE (*With deliberateness*) The weather continues hot and we have been at this trial longer than anticipated. I will ascribe tempers to the heat. Call your next witness, Colonel.

CHIPMAN Joseph Achuff to the stand—

WALLACE Is Mr. Achuff called to testify on the specification that dogs attacked escaping prisoners?

CHIPMAN Yes, sir.

WALLACE The Court considers it unnecessary to hear further testimony on that specification; it has been amply testified to by previous witnesses.

CHIPMAN If the Court please—

341

WALLACE That is the judgment of the Court. Call your next witness, Colonel.

(CHIPMAN *strides to the prosecution table*)

CHIPMAN (*To* HOSMER) Who next?

HOSMER Hardy.

CHIPMAN Baker will roast him and toss him back to me well done.

HOSMER (*With meaning; they have talked of this before*) He won't roast Gray—

CHIPMAN So Gray is here . . . I won't put him on— (*To the Court*) As our final witness on the specification that the defendant caused the death of prisoners by direct order, we call Jasper Culver to the stand.

(WIRZ *reacts*)

LIEUTENANT Jasper Culver!

(CULVER *enters. There is a punch-drunk suggestion in his walk. He smiles uncertainly. He is sworn in. As* CULVER *gets into his story, he will begin to act it out*)

CHIPMAN Mr. Culver, what was your regiment and when were you captured and brought to Andersonville?

CULVER I was connected with the Sixty-seventh New York Infantry—and was captured and brought to Andersonville in March, 1864.

CHIPMAN Did you ever see a prisoner of war killed? Inside the stockade?

CULVER I did.

CHIPMAN Who killed him?

CULVER The guard.

CHIPMAN And did that guard do so on his own or because of a direct order?

CULVER He was given a direct order to kill him.

CHIPMAN By whom?

CULVER By Captain Wirz.

CHIPMAN And where did that killing take place?

CULVER At the deadline.

CHIPMAN Who was the man you saw killed?

CULVER   We called him Chickamauga. Because he had lost a leg in that battle and because he had lost his memory there. So we called him by that name—Chickamauga.

CHIPMAN   And why did Chickamauga want to cross that line?

CULVER   He wished to lie down under a pine tree, he said, because a long time ago—but not that he could remember where—he had laid down under a pine tree. "I can't remember nothing before Chickamauga" is what he said to the guard . . .

CHIPMAN   State the circumstances—when did this occur?

CULVER   It was in the early fall, I believe . . . I remember the smell of burning leaves.

CHIPMAN   Continue, sir.

CULVER   I watched Chickamauga go toward the deadline and called to him to stop, but he went on as if not hearing. At the line he shouted to the sentry to let him cross, but the sentry waved him back. Chickamauga then began to move up and down the line, hopping back and forth on his one leg, begging to be let out of the stockade for ten minutes. The guard let him stay on the line but he was nervous and telling Chickamauga to get— (*He laughs*) —back and Chickamauga laughed. And then Chickamauga, he said for the guard to tell Captain Wirz that he knew of a plot whereby all the men would escape and he would tell Captain Wirz about that plot in exchange for being let out a few minutes, and with that the guard called for the Captain to come. And Wirz came. And when Chickamauga saw Wirz he made the Captain promise to let him rest a few minutes under that pine tree if he tells him that plot and the Captain says he will do that, and then Chickamauga he says to the Captain, "I will tell you that plot to escape. Here it is in a nutshell. Why, you know Uncle Billy Sherman in his white socks is marching through Georgia and what he is going to do is blast Andersonville open from the outside and that is how the men will get free." And Wirz began to rave and he said to Chickamauga, "I am going to give you a pass to hell," and Chickamauga said, "You can't give me no pass to hell on account I'm in hell now." And Captain Wirz turned to the guard and said, "Get that man back across the line or shoot him." The guard said, "I can't shoot no cripple." And Captain Wirz said, "If you don't obey I will have you court-martialed." And the next thing the guard shot Chickamauga and he fell over the deadline. Done for.

CHIPMAN   That will be all.

BAKER   Mr. Culver, I am thinking of how accurately you told that story. You remember the details down to the exact words said back and forth. That sense of detail makes you a most excellent witness.

CULVER   Thank you, sir.

BAKER   And one might add—it is also the characteristic of a good soldier—which I am sure you were before Andersonville—

CULVER   (*Echoing in mingled emotions of pain and pride*) Before Andersonville!

BAKER   When you were in the line.

CULVER   (*Beginning to chant*) In the line! Antietam Bridge, Chancellorsville and Stafford Court House—

BAKER   And you must remember the nighttime bivouacs, around the fires, listening to the sentries—

CULVER   Around the fires! Hearing them calling through the dark, "All is well"—post one to post two, "All is well"—

BAKER   And that outpost line—that of course was a line which a man dare not cross on pain of being shot by the sentries—

CULVER   On pain of being shot by the sentries!— And "Who goes there?" is the cry, "Who goes there?" "Who goes—"

BAKER   And of course you can tell us why such lines are

set up by commanding officers, Mr. Culver. As you remember it, sir, by the book.

CULVER (*Very correct; sounding out*) By the book, sir—
And that is for the order and safety of the camp.

BAKER And inside the stockade at Andersonville—were
there signs posted warning men not to cross the line?

CULVER (*With an air of modesty*) I recall some—yes,
Counsel, there were.

BAKER That story you told about Chickamauga. With the
great interest people have in anecdotes about the war,
you have undoubtedly had occasion to tell it a number of
times already, Mr. Culver, haven't you?

CULVER I have been requested to tell it a number of times.

BAKER I'll wager you could tell it a hundred times and it
would come out exactly as you told it today—

CULVER A thousand times, Counsel, and it would come
out the same way.

BAKER And always told with great effect, I imagine.

CULVER With great effect, yes, sir.

BAKER It would hardly be as effective if Captain Wirz did
not come out the villain of the piece, would it?

CULVER Hardly— (*Starting; staring at* BAKER. *A grim,
sober expression coming into his face*) You wish to
make a fool of me, Counsel. I'm not lying—

BAKER (*In a sad anger*) No, Mr. Culver, you are not. A
man can't help it if fables grow in his head, can he?

CULVER No, he—*fables?*— I don't know what you're talking about—!

BAKER (*Moving to address the Court*) I'm looking for
facts and I'm hunting for them through fairy tales of
good and evil— Mr. Culver, you say you heard Captain
Wirz say, "Get that man back across the line or shoot
him." Didn't Wirz actually say, *"For God's sakes,* get
that man back across the line or you will have to shoot
him"?

CULVER It is frozen into my memory as I have said it—

345

BAKER   And when Chickamauga said, "I am in hell now," didn't Wirz say, "You and I both"—"You and I both are in hell"—as indeed they both were?

CULVER   I have said it as I remember it—!

BAKER   As you need to remember it. That will be all, Mr. Culver, thank you. Move to dismiss all counts under this specification since the deadline was a proper military line required for the order and safety of that camp.

CHIPMAN   (*Moving to the map*)   It was not a purely military line! Mr. Culver, look at the map. Where the stream entered the camp under the west wall. There! What was that water like?

CULVER   (*Dazed*)   Somewhat fast-flowing, yes, sir.

CHIPMAN   Was it drinkable?

CULVER   Somewhat drinkable, yes, sir. (*Pointing to* BAKER) That man there!—

CHIPMAN   And inside the deadline, what was the water like there?

CULVER   Not fittin' to drink, no, sir.

CHIPMAN   It was by that time filthy and clogged with waste matter—driving the men to do *what*—?

CULVER   To try for a drink near the west wall.

CHIPMAN   (*Circling the witness*)   And they had to wade waist-deep through that swamp to get that drink of water, didn't they?

CULVER   Waist-deep and further—

CHIPMAN   And when they succeeded in getting to that water, what did the guards do?

CULVER   Opened fire on us—yes—

CHIPMAN   Killing men?

CULVER   Killing and wounding—yes, yes!

CHIPMAN   Killing and wounding for a drink of water! And Wirz knew that and he let those men get shot down, didn't he?— And Counsel calls that a purely military line! Move to deny defense motion as to that deadline in

346

that it was clearly part of the cold, inhuman design of that camp.

BAKER   Inhuman?

CHIPMAN   Yes.

BAKER   Immoral?

CHIPMAN   Yes.

WIRZ   I can explain—

BAKER   (*Gesturing to quiet* WIRZ)   Will the Judge Advocate openly and finally admit his belief that Captain Wirz's duty was to make a moral, not a military choice?

CHIPMAN   The *human* choice.

WALLACE   This arguing over an irrelevant issue becomes intolerable—parties are warned. Defense motion denied. (BAKER *sits down;* WALLACE'S *tone is deadly*)   The Judge Advocate will now state the connection between the moral issue and the charge of conspiracy.

CHIPMAN   (*After a pause; tired*)   The Judge Advocate will not attempt to make that connection.

WALLACE   Thank you, Mr. Culver, you may stand down. (CULVER *exits*)   If you have concluded your case, Colonel, we will now adjourn until tomorrow morning, at which time the defense will be ready—

CHIPMAN   We may wish to call further witnesses—

WALLACE   If so they will be witnesses bringing in new criminal evidence. I say *new* criminal evidence in the precise legal meaning of the term, bearing *directly* on the charge of conspiracy. I hope that is understood.

CHIPMAN   Yes, sir.

WALLACE   The Court stands adjourned.

(*General exit. Opposing counsel remain in the room.* BAKER *takes his and* SCHADE'S *hats from the rack and gathers up his papers*)

BAKER   The choices in this world are bitter, Colonel, aren't they? On the one hand to follow your decent instincts and on the other— Tell me, if you can, Colonel, how does your role in this room differ from Wirz's at Andersonville—seeing that he too did nothing more nor less than carry out policy?

CHIPMAN   You compare me to him?

BAKER (*Starting for the door*)   You know in your heart that you condemn him only for carrying out the orders of his superior. (*Pausing near* CHIPMAN)   You have as much as said so. But this Court will have no part of that argument. And what then do you do but withdraw it? You obey, as Wirz obeyed.

CHIPMAN   You compare me to him?

BAKER   Oh, of course, you're governed by purer motives. After all, you're on the edge of a brilliant career. You'll walk out of this case the envy of every struggling young lawyer in the country; the successful prosecutor of the one war criminal to be hanged out of this war. Yes, your future's assured . . . if you don't jeopardize it. Shall the government's own counsel at this time preach disobedience to orders? How does it feel to be an instrument of policy, nothing more?

CHIPMAN   Goddamn you—

BAKER   Get as angry as you wish—that's the truth of it. Good afternoon, gentlemen.

(BAKER *and* SCHADE *exit*)

HOSMER   Don't you see what he's trying to do? Provoke you into playing the idealist here?

CHIPMAN (*Moving restlessly*)   I see—

HOSMER   It would suit him perfectly to lead you down that path—

CHIPMAN   I know—

HOSMER   —to turn things so it's you arguing with the government—

CHIPMAN   All right! (CHIPMAN *brings himself under control as he moves slowly to the doors and closes them before speaking*)   I shout at you—I shout at Davidson— only a boy—a sick boy . . . (*He is silent for a long*

348

moment) Where do we stand after days of those witnesses we've put on—those sick, broken survivors of that place? We haven't really proved conspiracy and we haven't proved criminal acts. And yet I know that behind Wirz's screams of innocence and persecution—behind that stance of the honorable wounded soldier who was only obeying orders, he hides something dark that must be smoked out— (*Breaking off, frustrated*) I ask you: What kind of case do we bring in here?

HOSMER   If you want a better one, close with Gray. (*As* CHIPMAN *looks knowingly at him*)   Eyewitness evidence that Wirz murdered—

CHIPMAN (*Withering*)   Eyewitness evidence—

HOSMER   Let the Court decide—

CHIPMAN   You've heard Gray—do you believe him?

HOSMER   Let the Court decide—! (HOSMER *watches* CHIPMAN *move restlessly*)   If you put him on you will finish strong. Gray furnishes the name of the murdered man; name and regiment. Good God, what difference does it make in the end, Chipman? Wirz is doomed anyway.

CHIPMAN   And the kind of case we bring in doesn't matter, does it?

HOSMER   Not—really.

CHIPMAN (*Flaring*)   But if there's a moral issue here—I mean if we feel that Wirz should have disobeyed—and if we evade that issue—if we're afraid to raise it—how are we actually any better than that creature was at Andersonville? Are we all Wirz under the skin? Feeding where we're kept alive? At a trough?

HOSMER   So Baker *has* reached you!

CHIPMAN (*With hard amusement*)   Do you think that? Or is it that he raises an issue which has been in this case from the beginning—and which we haven't wanted to face?

HOSMER   We don't *need* to face it. I'll say it again—Wirz is doomed no matter how our case looks. But you can make it hard for yourself if you turn it the wrong way. You're a soldier, you know how the Army has to function, if it is to function at all. It has ways of dealing with irregulars. Are you thinking of a Washington career or will you be satisfied with a law practice in some county seat in Iowa? (*Studying* CHIPMAN) Chipman, you seem to *want* to go a hard way.

CHIPMAN (*Sardonic; mimicking*) *I want to go a hard way.* This blood-spattered country—bleaching skulls in the woods—the dead of my own Iowa Second, names you wouldn't know—did any of us *want* to go a hard way? But we did—we did! As if we had any choice . . . as if I have any choice here. (*Pausing*) I asked for this case feeling *hard* against them—hating them enough to want to flog them through Wirz. (*At a pitch*) Do you think I *want* to shed that hatred? Understanding what Baker wants to do—to lock me in a quarrel with the government—I still can't go around that issue. I hate that damned Southern cause—and still I can't go around what Baker says. I'm partisan to my bones—and *still I can't go around it.* (*After a pause—in a lower voice*) I'd like to believe I'm more of a man than Wirz was; that, had I been in his place, I would have disobeyed if that was all that was left me to do to save those men . . . Yes, that's what sticks me . . . Am I more of a man than he was? (*Groping*) Either . . . either I press the Court to consider the issue of Wirz's moral responsibility to disobey or—I'm no better in my mind than he was! I can't go around *that.*

HOSMER And just how do you plan to go around raising the moral issue?

CHIPMAN I don't know— (*Reaching for something*) Let Baker put Wirz on the stand.

HOSMER Which he won't do . . .

CHIPMAN I know that. I know . . .

HOSMER Put on Gray. You don't have to like him . . .

Just put him on. Nail down your case with a clear statement of murder—and you will have your man . . . even if it's not in *your* way— The government has a point to make, too, you know: it struggles to pull together a divided country. Isn't that a worthy, an important thing? At least as important as the purity of your soul? (HOSMER *waits, but* CHIPMAN *turns away.* HOSMER *goes to the door*) You stay?

CHIPMAN   A moment . . . There are larger issues than a man's own convictions, aren't there?

HOSMER (*Tiredly*)   Sometimes. (*A pause; and then, almost fiercely*)   You make me feel old.

(*He exits.* CHIPMAN *paces slowly; and, finally, without seeming to realize it, sits down in the witness chair, turning his head to look back toward the Andersonville map. Then, as he grasps that he sits in the chair, he brings his hands down to grip the arms of the chair, as if to say, "Here I am, too!"*)

THE CURTAIN FALLS

ACT TWO

Scene One

Scene: the following morning.

At rise: the court personnel, lawyers and reporters stand about, chatting, waiting for the session to begin. The LIEUTENANT *enters.*

LIEUTENANT   Attention!

(*The* JUDGES *enter*)

WALLACE   At ease. (*The* JUDGES *and the others take their positions*)   This Court is now in session. What is the pleasure of the Judge Advocate?

CHIPMAN (*Standing*)   If it please the Court . . . on the specification that the defendant committed murder by his own hand, we call Sergeant James S. Gray.

LIEUTENANT (*Calling out into the corridor*)   Sergeant James S. Gray.

(*During the following exchange,* GRAY *waits at the door. He is a strong, tough-looking soldier—a type to bet on as the sole survivor of some desperate situation. He is dressed sharp, down to shiny cavalry boots*)

BAKER (*Seated*)   If the Court please, we do not see that name listed here.

CHIPMAN (*Moving to* WALLACE's *table, his voice noncommittal*)   Sergeant Gray was not listed since it was uncertain that his release from duty could be arranged in time. He is attached to General Thomas' headquarters at Nashville.

(WALLACE *glances inquiringly at* BAKER)

BAKER   No objection.

WALLACE   The witness may be sworn in.

(GRAY *enters, salutes smartly, is sworn and takes the stand*)

CHIPMAN (*The tone is flat*)   Sergeant Gray, what is your regiment?

GRAY   Seventh Illinois Cavalry, Company B, sir.

CHIPMAN   And how long have you been in the service?

GRAY   In my last term, two years and one month.

CHIPMAN   How long were you at Andersonville prison, Sergeant?

GRAY   I was taken to Andersonville on the tenth of June, 1864, and remained there until November.

CHIPMAN   Do you know anything about the defendant, Wirz, having shot a prisoner of war there at any time?

(WIRZ *tries to come to his feet;* BAKER *restrains him*)

GRAY (*His manner is calm and easy*)   He shot a young fellow named William Stewart, a private belonging to the Ninth Minnesota Infantry.

CHIPMAN   State the circumstances.

GRAY   Stewart and I went out of the stockade with a dead body—

CHIPMAN   Explain how you could get out.

GRAY   The regulations were that whenever a man died, prisoners could be detailed to take the body out past the gate to the deadhouse.

CHIPMAN   Continue, sir.

GRAY   Well, sir, I had begged for the chance to move that dead body and I was picked with Stewart to take it out. We went up to the gate with the dead man and they passed us out with a guard. It was my determination—I don't know whether it was Stewart's or not—to try to make an escape again. We went toward the deadhouse, not to put the body into the deadhouse because in that house they were piled like cordwood full up and the line of dead bodies extended out from it about fifty yards. Wirz then came riding up and dismounted and asked us what we were doing out there. Stewart replied that we had brought out a dead body to place in the deadhouse. Wirz said it was a lie, that we were trying to make our escape. Stewart said it was not so. We came for purpose stated. Wirz said if you say that again I'll blow your brains out. Stewart repeated what he said before. Wirz then struck him down and stamped him and then drew his revolver and shot him—

CHIPMAN (*Pointing to* WIRZ) Is that the man?

GRAY Yes.

(WIRZ, *in a spasm of energy, leans forward, facing* GRAY)

WIRZ Look close, Sergeant—make sure! I give you the chance to take back that lie before the great God judges you!

GRAY (*Cool and indifferent*) You knocked him down and shot him dead—

CHIPMAN That will be all.

BAKER I ask for a moment to confer with the defendant. We have no preparation for this witness. (WALLACE *signals affirmatively.* BAKER *crosses to* WIRZ) Quick, who is Gray?

WIRZ It's no use—

BAKER Who is Gray?

WIRZ I don't know.

BAKER What about Stewart?

WIRZ There was no William Stewart.

BAKER Are you sure?

WIRZ Yes—yes. I'm sure.

BAKER (*Turning toward* GRAY. *Restlessly searching*) Sergeant, will you describe once more this so-called Stewart's death?

GRAY Captain Wirz rode up and asked us by what authority we were out there. Stewart spoke up and said that we were out there by proper authority—

BAKER (*His manner sharper; openly skeptical*) So Captain

Wirz knocked him down and shot him simply because he said he was out there by proper authority?

GRAY Whether he shot Stewart because he said that to him or because he was a Yankee, I don't know. I don't know why Wirz shot him. I leave that to himself. But that was all Stewart said to him.

BAKER There were some guards about when this so-called murder occurred, were there not?

GRAY I recall some.

BAKER Did you speak to them after Stewart was killed?

GRAY I never spoke to Johnny Reb if I didn't have to.

BAKER How well did you know Stewart?

GRAY (*Shrugging*) We were in the same prison squad.

BAKER And under what circumstance did he oblige you with his name and regiment?

GRAY I don't recollect exactly.

BAKER Describe this William Stewart.

GRAY All looked alike there. Thinned out and not to be recognized by their own mothers—

BAKER (*Circling* GRAY) So you cannot describe him. You talked to him and you know his name and regiment but you cannot describe this man. Did he hide his face while he talked to you? (*As* GRAY *is about to speak*) I know —thinned out and not to be recognized by their own mothers. Can you refer to any third person who could identify this William Stewart?

GRAY No.

BAKER No! What does that answer mean? There were ninety men in that prison squad with you and Stewart. Then other men—at least one—must have known he was from the Ninth Minnesota—and could identify him.

GRAY Counsel, he happened to mention his name and regiment to me—

BAKER (*Through his teeth*) However, fortunately for the prosecution which until now has lacked for a clear crimi-

355

nal instance, it has dredged you up as the single witness to the murder of a man having at least a name— (*Very hard*) Sergeant, do you believe in an afterlife and that man's sins, including the sin of lying, will there be punished?

GRAY I believe there is such a thing as punishment after death—

BAKER Have you ever been arrested for a criminal offense?

GRAY No, sir.

BAKER I gather you like Army life, seeing that you have re-enlisted.

GRAY I would say that.

BAKER After all, the Army feeds you, keeps you comfortable, and judging by your sergeant's stripes, you are considered by your superiors to be a good soldier, one who knows what he is supposed to do without it being explained to him in so many words.

GRAY A man gets to know what is expected of him.

BAKER And if you felt—even if you weren't told—what was expected of you, you would carry it out, wouldn't you?

GRAY Certainly.

BAKER And if you felt—even if you weren't told—what the Army's real concern was in some situation and if you understood that to mean that you were supposed to lie—

WALLACE Finish your question along that line, Mr. Baker, and you will be in contempt—

BAKER Withdrawn. Sergeant, what did you do before entering the Army?

GRAY Farmed some; ran dogs.

BAKER Ran dogs—?

GRAY In hunting and so forth.

BAKER Where did you do that work?

GRAY In Illinois, Indiana, Virginia, and—

BAKER Virginia . . . (*In a sudden intuition*) For what

356

purpose did you run your dog pack in Virginia? Was it
by any chance to bring back runaway slaves?

GRAY   Yes, sir.

BAKER   I take it it was more profitable to track down runaway slaves in Virginia than to hunt deer in Indiana.

GRAY   Yes, sir. Being as the nigra was valuable property
that had to be brought back alive.

BAKER   Tell me, Sergeant. Did that valuable property ever
make human sounds when you caught it and beg you to
let it find freedom?

GRAY   I don't remember.

BAKER   Human feelings must be put aside sometimes,
mustn't they? (GRAY *doesn't answer*) And the truth
must be put aside sometimes, too. (GRAY *doesn't answer*)
And when you said you saw Wirz kill a man named Stewart at Andersonville, you were lying, weren't you?

GRAY   I saw that happen as I have described it.

BAKER   That will be all.

CHIPMAN   (*Coming forward; furious*) Sergeant Gray!
Were you lying when you said you saw Wirz kill a man
named Stewart?

GRAY   I saw that happen as I have described it.

CHIPMAN   Sergeant, I ask you again, did you see Wirz kill
a man named Stewart or did you hear about something
like that?

GRAY   I saw that happen as I have described it—*sir!*

CHIPMAN   . . . That will be all!

WALLACE   (*With distaste*) The witness will step down.
(GRAY *salutes and exits*) Has the Judge Advocate concluded his case?

CHIPMAN   (*Crosses to table, sits, and after a sullen silence*)
Yes, sir.

WALLACE   Is the defense ready?

BAKER   (*Rises; moves to face the Court*) Yes, sir. If the
Court please, since the defense regards the instance of

murder alleged against the defendant as the single charge
worth refuting—

WALLACE   The Court is not interested in your judgment of
the charges—

BAKER (*Finishing*)   —we shall waive our entire list of witnesses and will in their place put on the stand one witness.

WALLACE   One witness?

(WIRZ *stirs restlessly and turns to* BAKER *as if to speak*)

BAKER   Questioning will take no more than a few minutes
and will constitute the entire defense case.

WALLACE   Who is the witness?

BAKER   He is in the room—Dr. Ford, the physician in
charge at the Old Capitol jail, where the defendant has
been lodged since the trial began.

(WIRZ *mutters a protest to* BAKER, *who quiets him*)

WALLACE   Let Dr. Ford take the stand.

(FORD *steps forward and is sworn*)

BAKER   Dr. Ford, have you, during some time past, been in
the habit of seeing the defendant?

FORD   Since June, I believe, ever since his imprisonment he
has been under my care when sick.

BAKER   Have you during that time examined his right arm
and have you examined him today?

FORD   Yes, sir.

BAKER   What do you find to be the condition of his right
arm?

FORD   It is swollen and inflamed; ulcerated in three places;
and it has the appearance of having been broken.

BAKER   The fingers of his right hand?

FORD   Two fingers, the little finger and the next are slightly
contracted. The contraction is due to an injury to the
nerve leading down to the fingers.

BAKER   Have you examined the defendant's left shoulder?

FORD   Yes, sir. A portion of it is dead. There is a very large
scar on the left shoulder and a portion of the deltoid
muscle is entirely gone—I suppose from his war wound.

It has been carried away, only the front part of the muscle remaining.

BAKER   How does that influence the strength of the arm?

FORD (*Illustrating*)   He might be able to strike out with forearm from the elbow but he could not elevate the whole arm.

BAKER   And as to the right arm? Would he be capable with that arm of pushing or knocking a man down?

FORD   I should think him incapable of doing so with either arm, without doing himself great injury.

BAKER   Would he have been capable of using with force any heavy or light instrument—would he have been capable of pulling the trigger—let alone suffering the recoil of—a heavy revolver?

FORD   No—not likely.

BAKER   And as to his condition a year ago, in 1864?

FORD   I have spoken with Dr. Bates, who was at Andersonville and who examined Wirz there at the defendant's request, and he confirms my opinion that this condition was no better in 1864 than it is now.

BAKER   Then he could not have knocked down this so-called William Stewart—

FORD   I don't see how—

BAKER   He could not have pulled the trigger—

FORD   As I have said—

BAKER   He could not have killed him. The defense rests! Thank you!

WALLACE (*Harsh and strained*)   Will the Judge Advocate cross-examine?

(CHIPMAN *moves forward impetuously—stops*)

CHIPMAN (*Harsh*)   Dr. Ford has testified to Mr. Wirz's physical condition as he saw it and we are not here to dispute the medical findings . . . No cross-examination, but . . .

(CHIPMAN'S *voice dies away, but he remains standing, inwardly, silently fighting*)

WALLACE (*Waiting, and then—*)   Thank you, Dr. Ford.

WIRZ (*To* BAKER; *a loud whisper*)   What is it? Is it all finished? But I have not had the chance—

WALLACE   We will convene the day after tomorrow to hear government and defense summations.

CHIPMAN (*In a burst*)   If the Court please, we ask for a continuance—!

WALLACE   Continuance?

CHIPMAN   —until tomorrow morning. The Judge Advocate would like to determine if there is something pertinent to this trial—

WALLACE (*Sharp*)   Does the Judge Advocate wish to bring forward new evidence?

CHIPMAN   Possibly.

BAKER   The defense will welcome new evidence—particularly on the charge of violent murder attributed to a man who cannot raise his arms.

WALLACE (*Gavel; he waits for a moment*)   Unless the government contemplates other witnesses we must consider the presentation of evidence finished—

(WIRZ *reacts with a choked sound of protest*)

CHIPMAN (*Glancing rapidly at* WIRZ; *his manner terribly strained; speaking in bursts of thought*)   We do not feel that the situation at Andersonville has been thoroughly explored—that is why we ask the continuance—we feel there is more to be discovered—more to be said about what took place there—

WIRZ   I agree—yes! For once I agree with the Judge Advocate!

(WALLACE *raps*)

CHIPMAN (*Whirling to face* WIRZ)   Does the defendant desire to take the stand in his own behalf?

WIRZ   What?

BAKER   What is that? . . . No, the defendant will not take the stand.

CHIPMAN (*Looking straight at* WIRZ, *speaking with desper-*

ate speed) Of course he is not legally bound to do so, but it seems to the Judge Advocate that he might wish to make his position clearer than anyone else can possibly do for him—

BAKER (*Rising*) What is the Judge Advocate trying to do—?

WIRZ (*Leans toward* CHIPMAN) If I might wish *what? What*—?

BAKER (*Going on*) He addresses defendant over the head of counsel.

WIRZ (*Overlapping*) But what is it the Judge Advocate is saying—I would like to know what is meant—*that I might make my position clearer*—?

WALLACE (*The gavel rapping*) You cannot speak unless you take the stand, Mr. Wirz. The Judge Advocate is asking if you wish to take the stand. You have a right to do so, but cannot be compelled to do so. You have that right, though we suggest you listen to counsel.

(BAKER *and* SCHADE *stand over* WIRZ)

BAKER Are you out of your mind?

SCHADE I don't understand what's come over you!

WIRZ This legal game has been played back and forth and I am to die without a word to say for myself! I must explain—

BAKER *Listen.* The evidence they've offered is tainted from start to finish. And they know it! Let them bring in their verdict of guilty. But it must then go to the President, who may pardon as he values the reputation of the government. That's your single chance—

WIRZ And I say no chance. No chance—

SCHADE Wirz, listen to Baker—

BAKER You will not take the stand—

WIRZ (*Standing up*) I was a man like other men and I wish to show that!

BAKER You'll face Chipman alone. You will be alone—

SCHADE (*Overlaps*) Do you understand? Alone!!

WIRZ Yes, alone, as I have been alone—and neither you nor anyone here has been concerned for me as a *man*. And now— (*His manner is feverish. He crosses to face* CHIPMAN *and the Court*) I might wish to speak—since the Judge Advocate wishes me to take the stand—

WALLACE I don't understand you, Mr. Wirz. You may or may not take the stand as *you* wish. It has nothing to do with what the Judge Advocate wishes.

WIRZ And I am saying that I might do that. Since I have been slandered here I might do that. I don't understand what is the difficulty— (*Revealing a deep need, in spite of a tone of mockery. Moving to face the* JUDGES *at close range; glancing toward* CHIPMAN) So the Judge Advocate wants me to take the stand—

WALLACE The Judge Advocate cannot influence you to do that. He is not your counsel.

WIRZ No, no, of course he is not. He is my worst enemy. Oh, I know that. He wishes to destroy me. (*He looks steadily at* CHIPMAN *and* CHIPMAN *in turn looks back at him. There is something private between them now*) Take the stand, on my own behalf, eh, Colonel?

CHIPMAN On your own behalf.

BAKER (*Grimly*) Are you dispensing with counsel, Captain Wirz?

CHIPMAN (*Speaking with cool desperate calculation*) Mr. Wirz, if you take the stand, you will speak for yourself. And after that—let me warn you—I will try to search you out to the bottom of your soul.

WIRZ Hah! You think you can do that?

CHIPMAN I can try—

WALLACE (*Gavel*) Will the defendant say whether or not he wishes to take the stand!

WIRZ General! (*Moving to* BAKER) Hah—do you hear that? My worst enemy—what does he say? He will search me out, to the bottom of my soul!

BAKER   You think Chipman is here to save you?

WIRZ   I am to die—I must take the stand! I have been made a monster in the eyes of my children. I die with that mark on me if I do not speak up! And I will not have it that way—I will give them my words so they can say their father was a man like other men. Do you understand me? (BAKER *looks at* WIRZ *searchingly.* WIRZ'S *tone is strange*)   You will examine—and then I will fight him.

BAKER   And if you take the stand . . . how will I keep you from saying more than you should?

WIRZ   But you see, Baker, I must fight him . . . (BAKER *stares hard at* WIRZ)   I must . . . fight him.
(BAKER *shrugs finally, his expression tired and a little sad. He turns to face the Court*)

BAKER (*Slow*)   The defendant will take the stand in his own behalf.

WALLACE   He understands that he is not required to do so?

BAKER   The defendant understands and wishes to do so.

WALLACE   You may take the stand, Mr. Wirz.
(WIRZ *is sworn and takes the stand*)

BAKER (*His effort is plainly to be brief and to limit* WIRZ'S *answers*)   Captain Wirz, you are a naturalized citizen of the United States, is that correct?

WIRZ   Yes, sir.

BAKER   When and where were you born?

WIRZ   I was born in Zurich, Switzerland, in the year 1822.

BAKER   What year did you arrive in the United States?

WIRZ   In 1849.

BAKER   Describe briefly your activities prior to the outbreak of the war.

WIRZ   I worked at first in the mills in Lawrence, Massachusetts, and, not doing well there, moved with my family to various parts of the United States. I lived in Louisiana for a time and resided in Louisville, Kentucky, when the war broke out.

363

BAKER   State your war record prior to your appointment as superintendent of the Andersonville prison camp.

WIRZ   I enlisted in the service of the Confederacy as a private and was soon commissioned as a lieutenant, having had previous military training abroad. After being wounded at the battle of Seven Pines I was offered that assignment of superintendent, by General Winder.

BAKER   Over what period of time did you serve in that assignment?

WIRZ   From January, 1864, until February, 1865.

BAKER   Were you at any time given special or secret instructions as to how you were to run that camp?

WIRZ   No, sir!

BAKER   I refer specifically to instructions for the care of the prisoners.

WIRZ   No, sir—no special instructions beyond the prescribed regulations for the care of prisoners of war, and any statement to the contrary—

BAKER   Captain Wirz, were the food supplies at first furnished you sufficient for the prisoners?

WIRZ   Yes, sir, at first I was given ample supplies to furnish for each and every enemy prisoner a ration which was the same ration issued to Confederate soldiers as is the custom. It included bacon and fresh-baked bread daily. If not bacon, it was beef and those men did not starve, but later it became—

BAKER   Captain Wirz, state the circumstances under which that situation changed.

WIRZ   It began to change for the worse around March when we began to receive prisoners by the thousands but not sufficiently an increase in the ration. So I naturally had to cut down more and more that ration and I wrote to General Winder about that—

BAKER   When did you write that letter?

WIRZ   Sometime in May, 1864.

BAKER (*Holding up letter*)   I have here a letter written by Captain Wirz to General Winder, dated May 19, 1864.

(SCHADE *takes the letter to* WALLACE)

SCHADE   Presented to the Court.

WALLACE (*After glancing at it*)   It may be entered in the record.

SCHADE (*Giving the letter to the* CLERK)   Letter of May 19, 1864, offered for the defense.

CLERK   Exhibit nine, for the defense.

BAKER   Captain Wirz, tell us about that letter.

WIRZ   Yes, sir. I wrote to General Winder about the lack of food and requested additional supplies.

BAKER   Now, Captain, did General Winder reply to that letter?

WIRZ   He did so in person on one of his visits to the camp. He said we were taking care of the prisoners just as well as the enemy took care of *our* men in *their* hands. He said he had reports that our men were not well treated, particularly at a camp at Elmira, New York, where they were dying like flies. He was in a temper and he made it clear *that* closed the subject, and as an inferior officer I felt I could not pursue the matter further. However, I did what was in my power to do there—as about those drummer boys—

BAKER   We will get to that in a moment. Tell the Court now the origin of the deadline.

WIRZ   Yes, as to that deadline. Well—in that conversation I said to General Winder that the prisoners were getting desperate because of the lack of food and the guards consequently nervous, fearing a rush on the walls, and there was bound to be trouble. I asked for more guards there to quiet the prisoners down with a show of strength. But he said men could not be spared. But still—it was my responsibility they should not escape, don't you see, so I suggested that inner line, and General Winder approved that line. But that did not mean I did not consider those prisoners, as I started to say before about those drummer boys—

BAKER (*Curtly*) Very well. Tell the Court about those drummer boys.

WIRZ Yes, sir. There were sixty or seventy boys in that camp, drummer boys, little bits of boys and I felt bad that these boys, no more than children, should suffer there, having children of my own. So I asked them if they would take an oath not to try to escape and they did and they were put on parole outside the walls and lived outside the camp. I assigned them to pick blackberries to provide additional food for the camp, but that did not work. Being boys, they ate what they picked themselves— And that was not all I did there—

BAKER (*Trying to control* WIRZ) Captain Wirz. Tell us about Father Whelan—

WIRZ Yes. I gave permission for all priests and ministers to enter that camp and Father Whelan, of the Roman Catholic Church, came several times bringing fresh bread there. He was allowed to bring that in and he distributed it to all the prisoners, black and white. All religious people of any denomination were permitted to enter to give comfort to the prisoners—all. I believe that religion is— that religion—

BAKER Now, Captain, tell us about the women who tried to bring food into the camp.

WIRZ Yes, yes— General Winder at first graciously consented to let that food in, but when those women were about to do that he received some bad war news, some report that Sheridan was burning farmhouses and crops in the Shenandoah Valley and he then flew into a rage and said that food couldn't be brought in and being an inferior there I could hardly override his orders. That is how it was. In general that place was entirely on my head—

BAKER Did you try to get relieved—?

WIRZ (*Picking up in intensity as he goes on*) I have not finished! I was saying that place was entirely on my head and I had there the responsibility to keep order and keep those men from escaping and they kept trying and it was difficult to keep order there since the men kept trying. Naturally they had that right to try and I had my duty which was to prevent them.

BAKER But you did try to get relieved of that assignment, did you not?

WIRZ Yes, sir, I tried to do that. I wrote to General Winder, asking to be assigned to another post, but he informed me he could not relieve me. And, simply—I had there to stay and so it kept on being on my head.

BAKER I have here a letter written by defendant to General Winder, dated May 26, 1864, in which defendant requests that he be relieved of his post at Andersonville.

SCHADE (*Takes the letter to* WALLACE) Submitted for the defense.

WALLACE (*Glances at it*) It may be entered.

SCHADE (*Takes the letter to the* CLERK) Letter of May 26, 1864, offered for the defense.

CLERK Exhibit ten for the defense.

BAKER Captain Wirz, did you strike down and kill a man called William Stewart?

WIRZ (*Shouting*) There was no William Stewart and that is a lie— (WALLACE *raps the gavel.* WIRZ *repeats sullenly*) There was no William Stewart.

BAKER Did you, at any time, shoot down or kill a prisoner of war?

WIRZ No, sir; I never did that. I could not physically do that.

BAKER Captain Wirz, when you were arrested at the conclusion of hostilities, were you making any attempt to escape?

WIRZ No, sir; I saw no reason to do that. I was with my

family outside the stockade and, having heard of the general pardon, was on my way back to Louisville when a major of General Wilson's forces entered to tell me I was under arrest. I was taken away and held prisoner. I soon understood the awful charge against me—and that my fate was to hang—!

(BAKER *abruptly tries to close off the examination*)

BAKER   That will be all, thank you.

WIRZ   (*Shouting*)   Am I not to be asked my conception of my duty?

BAKER   Thank you, Captain Wirz.

WIRZ   I wish to explain how I understand the military rules!

BAKER   Very well. Explain your understanding of the military code.

WIRZ   (*With bite and growing bitterness*)   That one does as he is ordered. That he keeps his feelings to himself. That he does not play the heroic game which some people who are not in his position think he could play. That he obeys. That he does not concern himself with the policies of his superiors—but obeys. That he does his assigned job and obeys. That when the order to charge is given—he obeys. That when ordered to keep prisoners—he obeys. And if in so doing he must die, then he dies.

BAKER   Your witness, Colonel.

CHIPMAN   (*He is still for a moment*)   You have explained your sense of duty clearly, Mr. Wirz. When the officer is ordered to keep prisoners he obeys.

WIRZ   Yes, sir.

CHIPMAN   Meaning that he must keep the prisoners from escaping?

WIRZ   That is one of the things—yes.

CHIPMAN   Meaning that he must keep them alive—?

WIRZ   As much as it is within his power.

CHIPMAN   Which did you regard as more important? To keep them from escaping or to keep them alive?

WIRZ According to the customs of war, to keep them alive as it was within my power *and* to prevent them from escaping.

CHIPMAN One duty neither more nor less important in your mind?

WIRZ Both equal—

CHIPMAN You say you never at any time killed a prisoner of war?

WIRZ (*Raising his arms slightly*) It has been demonstrated that I could not—

CHIPMAN I ask *you*, sir, directly—did you or did you not—?

WIRZ I never did that. No, sir.

CHIPMAN In that letter of May 19, 1864, in which you tell General Winder of your increasing duties at Andersonville I note that you also ask him to consider a promotion in rank for you from captain to major. What were you concerned with when you wrote that letter? The overcrowding or your promotion?

WIRZ It was nothing wrong in the same letter to request that promotion—

CHIPMAN And in your letter requesting a transfer from Andersonville you make a point of your illness as the reason—

WIRZ To make it indirect, otherwise General Winder might not have liked that transfer request.

CHIPMAN But you were in fact seeking medical attention when you wrote that letter, weren't you?

WIRZ I had in mind at the same time to get away from that assignment.

CHIPMAN You say that what occurred at Andersonville was beyond your power to avert?

WIRZ Yes, sir.

CHIPMAN In the course of performing your duties you inspected the stockade—at times I imagine from the wall

where the sentries stood. You could look down into that
—how would you describe it, may I ask?

WIRZ   It has been described—

CHIPMAN   As a sort of hell—?

WIRZ   Oh, indescribable, sir. Indescribable. I suppose you
remember, Colonel, hearing me say that I could not bear
the sight of those young boy prisoners in there, sixty to
seventy of them, and sent them out to pick blackberries—

CHIPMAN   That is in your favor—

WIRZ   Thank you—

CHIPMAN   It is interesting that you keep referring to that
act—as if there is so much else you dare not remember—

WIRZ   You twist things, sir— I let Father Whelan bring
bread—

CHIPMAN   You went to your duties from your home every
morning?

WIRZ   Yes, sir.

CHIPMAN   And I take it you were a normal father and husband, concerned to raise your children properly and
teaching them the common virtues—?

WIRZ   Particularly in a religious way—yes.

CHIPMAN   And you saw nothing strange in leaving your
family and your grace at meals to go to your job of over-
seeing the dying of those men?

BAKER   Objection.

CHIPMAN   Withdrawn. You have said that keeping those
men alive was of equal importance in your mind with the
need to keep them from escaping?

WIRZ   Yes, sir.

CHIPMAN   The food was wormy and rotten. Did you think
of sending out foragers to commandeer supplies from
Georgia farmers?

WIRZ   It would have been illegal—

CHIPMAN   You could have signed vouchers—

WIRZ   I was not authorized—

CHIPMAN Payable by the Confederacy—

WIRZ Not authorized, sir—

CHIPMAN Sent out squads of prisoners to collect fire-wood—

WIRZ They would escape—

CHIPMAN Under guard—

WIRZ There were not enough guards—

CHIPMAN Enlarged the stockade—

WIRZ The size was prescribed—

CHIPMAN Let those prisoners among whom were carpenters, masons, and mechanics of all sorts, build the shelters which would have kept them alive—?

WIRZ As I have already said—not authorized—

CHIPMAN But those measures would have saved lives—

WIRZ I don't know how many!!—

CHIPMAN (*Flaring*) We will say only one!— Would you say that one, single human life is precious, Mr. Wirz?

WIRZ I do not follow—it would have been illegal for me to do the things you say—

CHIPMAN But morally right, Mr. Wirz?

BAKER Objection.

WALLACE We do not see how the Judge Advocate's questioning connects with the charge of conspiracy.

CHIPMAN (*Grimly*) Will the Court allow me to explore that issue one step further before deciding the connection cannot be made?

WALLACE (*With equal grimness*) You may explore it— one step further.

CHIPMAN Mr. Wirz, you are a religious man?

WIRZ As I have testified—I know how important religion is, and I allowed all ministers—

CHIPMAN Then, sir, professing religion as you do, would you agree that moral considerations, the promptings of conscience, are primary for all men?

WIRZ Of course I do! I observe that ideal like most men —when—I—can!

CHIPMAN When you can. Then you could not observe moral considerations at Andersonville?

WIRZ That situation was General Winder's responsibility —not mine.

CHIPMAN (*Rising, moving closer to* WIRZ) You regarded that situation as General Winder's responsibility because he was your military superior?

WIRZ Yes—

CHIPMAN And how far did you deem his authority over you to extend?

WIRZ To all circumstances, considering that was a military-war situation.

CHIPMAN To all circumstances. Are you certain of that?

WIRZ I am absolutely certain!

CHIPMAN And had he, in that military-war situation, given you a direct order to slaughter one of your own children without giving you an explanation, would you have done that?

WIRZ That is ridiculous—

CHIPMAN Would you have done that?

WIRZ It is ridiculous—I do not answer—!

CHIPMAN Would you have done that?

WIRZ No—!

CHIPMAN Why not?

WIRZ It would be an insane order—!

CHIPMAN Yes. Insane. Or inhuman. Or immoral. And a man therefore in his heart does indeed make some inner judgment as to the orders he obeys.

WALLACE (*Gavel*) The Judge Advocate will hold. The Court has stated more than once, it is not disposed to consider the moral issue relating to soldierly conduct. It has indicated to the Judge Advocate that we are on extremely delicate ground at any time that we enter into the circumstances under which officers may disobey their military superiors. However, the Judge Advocate apparently feels he must enter that area. He will now advance some legal basis for that line of questioning or withdraw it.

CHIPMAN   If it please the Court—we will endeavor to connect this line—

WALLACE   The Judge Advocate must in advance furnish a legal basis—

CHIPMAN   The Judge Advocate respectfully urges—

WALLACE (*Gavel*)   The Court must hear some basis for permitting this line of inquiry.

CHIPMAN (*Desperately; demanding*)   If it please the Court, military courts—judging war crimes—are governed by both the criminal code and by the broader, more general code of universal international law. In most cases that come before them, they will judge specific acts in which the nature and degree of offense is determinable without great difficulty. But, on rare occasions, cases occur demanding from a court a more searching inquiry. Should the Court allow such broad inquiry it becomes more than the court of record in a particular case; it becomes a supreme tribunal—willing to peer into the very heart of human conduct. The Judge Advocate urges that the Court does not in advance limit or narrowly define the basis for questioning. Should the Court insist on such a basis, then we are through with the witness.

WALLACE   Does the Judge Advocate offer the Court alternatives?

CHIPMAN   We did not mean to imply that—

WALLACE   The Court is flattered to think it may take on the mantle of a supreme tribunal— However, it is still a military court.

CHIPMAN   If it please the Court—

WALLACE   No, Colonel, I'm not through. The Court grants it may be philosophically true that men have the human right to judge the commands of their military superiors, but in practice one does so at his peril.

CHIPMAN (*Slowly*)   At his peril, yes, sir.

WALLACE (*His tone is deadly*)   We would want that the
peril of that line of questioning be understood most
clearly. We have a question for the Judge Advocate that
he may or may not answer—he is not, of course, on trial
here. The question is: What is it an honest man fights for
when he takes up arms for his country? Is it the state or
the moral principle inherent in that state? And if the state
and the principle are not one, is he bound not to fight for
that state and indeed to fight against it? The Judge Advocate need not answer, for we will make the question
more particular. If, at the outbreak of the war, the government of the so-called Confederacy had stood on the
moral principle of freedom for the black man, and the
government of the United States had stood for slavery,
would a man have been bound, on moral grounds, to
follow the dictates of conscience—even if it had led him
to the point of taking up arms against the government of
the United States?

CHIPMAN (*Anguished*)   It is inconceivable to me—

WALLACE   That is not the question—

CHIPMAN   That situation could not possibly occur—

WALLACE   That is not the question—

CHIPMAN (*Bursting*)   He would have been bound to follow the dictates of his conscience.

WALLACE   Even to the point of taking up arms against the
government of the United States?

CHIPMAN (*After a pause; slow*)   Yes.

WALLACE (*With deliberateness*)   The Colonel understands,
of course, that a man must be prepared to pay the penalties involved in violating the—let us say—the code of the
group to which he belongs. In other societies that has
meant death. In our society it can mean merely depriva-
tion of status—the contempt of his fellows—exile in the
midst of his countrymen. I take it the Colonel understands my meaning?

CHIPMAN   He understands what the Court is saying.

WALLACE   And he still feels that he must enter that dangerous area?

CHIPMAN (*Now he is pleading; no longer hard*)   General, I do not enter that area of my own free will. I enter because I have been forced to it by the nature of this case. (*Moving to the map*)   We have lately emerged from a terrible and bloody war and that war has spawned a most sinister and curious crime. Men in the thousands—fourteen thousand men—have been sent to their death—not by bullets on the battlefield, but in a subtle, furtive, hidden manner. We have in the course of this trial examined as it were the outward appearance of hell—its walls, deadline, swamp, dogs, its terrible heat and freezing cold. But we have not gotten to the heart of it. We are now faced with the necessity of exploring further into—let us say it again—hell. (*At last* CHIPMAN'S *underlying humanity comes through*)   I put it to this Court that we owe to those fourteen thousand who died there—to those who mourn them—something so true as to put us head and shoulders above politics, above sectionalism, above the bitterness in our own hearts. I admit to entering this room with that bitterness in myself—I admit to the mood of vengeance. I would now wish to go beyond that if I can. As we say—life is precious—as we cling to our humanity by our fingernails in this world—by our fingernails—let us have a human victory in this room.

WALLACE (*After a pause*)   The Court is not unmoved. (*The pause is long as the* JUDGES *confer,* WALLACE *sitting still in the midst of them, disturbed and considering*) The Judge Advocate considers as primary to the presentation of his case the moral issue of disobedience to a superior officer?

CHIPMAN (*Strained*)   Yes, sir.

(*Again* WALLACE'S *pause is long; and then, almost angrily—*)

WALLACE   The Judge Advocate may continue—

BAKER (*Losing control of himself for the first time; incredulous*) The Judge Advocate may continue? Defense counsel is amazed that the Court does not now recognize there is no legal case here. To attempt to connect normal obedience to orders with willful conspiracy is impossible and no fine-sounding statement about universal law or supreme tribunal can bridge the unbridgeable. The Court knows the Judge Advocate cannot possibly make that connection. The Court knows that! And yet the Court allows the Judge Advocate to proceed when it should forthwith dismiss the defendant—

WALLACE Is counsel ordering the Court to do that?

BAKER No, but he submits there is no legal case here.

WALLACE The Judge Advocate may continue— (*Sharply, as* CHIPMAN *takes a step toward* WIRZ) bearing in mind that the Court may conclude at any time that it feels there is nothing more to be gained from this line of questioning.

CHIPMAN (*Crosses slowly to* WIRZ; *tired*) Mr. Wirz, we have said that a man does make some inner judgment as to the orders he obeys. That implies that if those orders offend his humanity deeply enough he may disobey them. The authority of General Winder over you was not absolute. And so the question is, why did you obey?

WIRZ (*Looking about him rapidly*) Am I required to answer? . . . I did not think of my assignment at Andersonville in that way . . . I do not understand what happens here . . . I thought only in the normal way to obey him, since he was my military superior—

CHIPMAN But not your *moral* superior, Mr. Wirz. No man has authority over the soul of another. As we are men we own our own souls and as we own them we are equal as *men*—the general, the private, the professor, the hod carrier. *We are equal as men, sir*. And every man alive as he is a man knows that—as you in your heart knew that—

WIRZ But that is not—

CHIPMAN   And as that situation had become a grossly immoral situation, and as General Winder was not your moral superior, you did not have to obey him. So the question remains, *why did you obey?*

(WIRZ *glances toward* WALLACE)

WALLACE   The Court will hear the answer.

WIRZ (*Incredulously*)   I will say it clearly. I would have been most certainly court-martialed. And if my superiors wished, considering it was a time of war, and that the war had come to a desperate, bitter stage in which the word "traitor" could be sounded in a moment—I might have been executed—

CHIPMAN   It might at least have been for a reason. You might have saved fourteen thousand lives—were you afraid?

WIRZ   I? A soldier? Afraid?

CHIPMAN (*Standing over* WIRZ)   The question then still is—*Why did you obey?*

WIRZ   As I have explained. What heroic thing do you demand I should have done at Andersonville? I—an ordinary man like most men?

CHIPMAN   Mr. Wirz, we who are born into the human race are elected to an extraordinary role in the scheme of things. We are endowed with reason and therefore with personal responsibility for our acts. A man may give to officials over him many things. But not what is called his soul, sir—not his immortal soul. And the question therefore still is—*Why did you obey?*

WIRZ   Why? As I have said. As I say for the last time—it was to me a military situation.

CHIPMAN   But that was not a military situation, Mr. Wirz. Those helpless, unarmed men were no longer the enemy, whatever Winder said. Here was no longer a question of North and South; no longer a question of war; only a question of human beings. Chandler saw that. Those Southern women who brought food for those starving men—they saw that. Where was your conscience then?

WIRZ   Where!!??

CHIPMAN   In General Winder's pocket with his keys, his tobacco and his money. And worth no more than any of those things—

WIRZ   You speak high, Colonel—high! Ask them in this room if they can say in their hearts they would have done different if they had been in my place—ask them. (*In fury and contempt*)   You are all the victors here and you make up a morality for the losers!

CHIPMAN   Yes! The victor makes the morality since the loser cannot.

WIRZ   And I spit on that morality! I spit on it! And I say —ask them in this room if they would have done different—ask them—

CHIPMAN   And if they could not, then we must shudder for the world we live in—to think what may happen when one man owns the conscience of many men. For the prospect before us is then a world of Andersonvilles—of jailers concerned only to execute the commands of their masters. And freed of his conscience—fearing only the authority to which he had surrendered his soul—*might the jailer not commit murder then?*

WIRZ   I did not commit murder!

CHIPMAN   (*Circling*)   You did not kill William Stewart?

WIRZ   There was no William Stewart—

CHIPMAN   (*Fiercely*)   You were never in a fury with those men—a fury great enough to overcome the weakness of your arms?

WIRZ   It is as the doctors say—

CHIPMAN   (*Very close to* WIRZ)   To whom do you dare say that? You and I have both been on the battlefield. We've seen men holding their bowels in their hands and with their legs broken, still moving forward. You raised your arms—

WIRZ   No—!

CHIPMAN Yes! You were in a fury when you rode out to hunt down those men with that dog pack and when you caught them you raised those two dead arms—

WIRZ No—!

CHIPMAN (*Toward a crescendo*) Then how did you rein that hard-mouthed horse you rode to the left—and how to the right—and how bring his head down when he reared—if not with those two—dead—arms?

(*On the last phrase* CHIPMAN, *his face contorted, grabs* WIRZ *by the upper arms. As he does so,* BAKER *and* WALLACE *start, as if to speak, but* CHIPMAN *lets go as quickly as he had taken hold, horror in his face at his own act*)

WIRZ Possibly!— I raise my arms sometimes! Yes!—but I did not kill any William Stewart because there was no William Stewart, so help me God.

(CHIPMAN *stares at his hands. Both men are now near exhaustion*)

CHIPMAN We will leave Mr. Stewart aside—but you had to obey orders which you knew were killing men, didn't you?

WIRZ I had to obey—

CHIPMAN Even though you knew that to obey was to kill those men—and to disobey was to save them?

WIRZ (*Making a curiously helpless gesture*) Even though— Simply—*I could not disobey.* I did my duty as I saw it. I have made that clear. But you badger me. Which however way I explain it, it will not do for you—and you badger me—you badger me! I have made it clear that I had to keep order there. To keep the record monthly of the number of prisoners including those escaping—to report that to General Winder and the War Department—and you badger me. It has been made clear—and *you will not let go.* To prevent them from escaping—to report in writing the attempted escapes—that was my responsibility. Isn't that clear? Even though I had not enough men, that did not excuse me, though I found that

379

job overwhelming—isn't that clear? And you badger me!
It *was* overwhelming and I had to find ways and means
to block those escape attempts—that was my duty. It was
solely on my head. So it went, I preventing, they trying,
I preventing, they trying. And no move to stop them
completely successful. Nothing, nothing could stop them.
And that responsibility solely mine. The deadline—that
did not prevent them. Cannon mounted on the wall—that
did not prevent them. They kept trying. Tunneling under
the walls. Digging, burrowing, burrowing— In the night,
burrowing. Crushed from the weight of the wall timbers when they made the mistake to burrow directly under those logs. And the others continuing. Continuing.
Tracked down by the dogs and trying again . . . and
I having to anticipate . . . finding their tunnels . . .
learning their tricks. They trying, I preventing. They trying, I preventing. They bribing the guards with greenbacks . . . blacking their faces to pass as niggers to
bring the dead bodies out of the stockade . . . and I
charged to block those moves. But nothing prevents them
to try . . . that burrowing. At night. I'm awake. I don't
need to see them to know what they are doing. Burrowing. In the night. Digging, digging, in that hopeless effort
to escape—digging, crawling—like rats—

CHIPMAN   And rats may die and one may have no com-
punction about rats—

WIRZ   Yes— (*Catching himself*) I meant rats, so to
speak— You are playing a cheap lawyer's trick on me—

CHIPMAN   Very well, a cheap lawyer's trick—so they were
not rats to you—*but they were no longer men to you*. In
your mind you canceled them out as men and you made
them less than men, and then they might die and one
did not have to suffer over that, did he? (*Almost gently*)
Why did you try to commit suicide in your cell? (WIRZ
is silent)   Is it because you feel nothing? (*Silence*)   Is
it because you have no human feeling left and cannot

endure yourself feeling nothing? (*Silence. In sad contempt*) You speak too much of your children . . . ! Is it because you have already—in your mind—asked them— Should I have done my duty or should I have given a man a drink of water?—and you heard their answer? (WIRZ *starts;* CHIPMAN'S *tone is one of confirmation, very soft*) Yes . . . you wish to die. (*Silence.* WIRZ *stares off. And now* CHIPMAN'S *tone is one of pained, exhausted inquiry—no longer hunting*) I ask you for the last time, Mr. Wirz. Why—and it was not fear of court-martial or dismissal or any external thing— why—*inside* yourself—couldn't you disobey?

WIRZ (*In a low, relieved exhalation*) Simply—I—could not. I did not have that feeling in myself to be able to. I did not have that feeling of strength to do that. I—could —not—disobey.

CHIPMAN (*Moving with slow, dragging, exhausted steps to the government table*) The government rests.

THE LIGHTS DIM OUT QUICKLY

Scene Two

A week later.

As the lights come on, WIRZ *stands erect, and* WALLACE *is well into the reading of the verdict.*

WALLACE . . . and on the charge that the prisoner did with others conspire to destroy the lives of soldiers in the military service of the United States in violation of the laws and customs of war— Guilty. And on the various specifications that he aided and abetted murder and did commit murder— Guilty. And the Court do therefore sentence him, the said Henry Wirz, to be hanged by the neck till he be dead, at such time and place as the President of the United States may direct, two-thirds of the members of the Court concurring therein. The business of this military court being now terminated, we declare the Court dissolved.

(*The gavel raps once.* WIRZ *is led out. The* JUDGES *go out quickly. Then there is a general exit.* BAKER, *with* SCHADE *at his shoulder, crosses to* CHIPMAN)

BAKER I'll say this for you, Colonel. At least you fought on your own terms.

CHIPMAN I asked for Wirz's guilt—not his death.

BAKER But he dies anyway. His life for the Union dead. No matter that you so stubbornly fought to purify the occasion—it was a political verdict—whatever you said.

CHIPMAN I charged him for what he is. Perhaps, deep down, the Court did, too.

BAKER Perhaps. It was a worthy effort though it hasn't anything to do with the real world. Men will go on as they are, most of them, subject to fears—and so, subject to powers and authorities. And how are we to change *that* slavery? When it's of man's very nature?

CHIPMAN Is it?

BAKER Isn't it?

CHIPMAN I don't know. We try.

BAKER (*Ironically*) We redecorate the beast in all sorts of political coats, hoping that we change him, but is he to be changed?

CHIPMAN We try. We try.

(BAKER *goes out, followed by* SCHADE. HOSMER *looks at* CHIPMAN'S *grave face, pats him gently on the shoulder and goes out. For a moment longer* CHIPMAN *looks at the map—the hieroglyphic which bespeaks a more engulfing disaster than he grasped in the beginning. He goes out. The lights dim, leaving only a light on the Andersonville map, which fades slowly as*

THE CURTAIN FALLS

PADDY CHAYEFSKY

Paddy Chayefsky must be considered television's greatest gift to the legitimate theatre, because it was with such masterful TV scripts as *Marty, Bachelor Party, Middle of the Night,* and *The Catered Affair* that his name first became known to the playgoing public.

Chayefsky was born in the Bronx in New York City in 1923, and was educated at De Witt Clinton High School and C.C.N.Y. He enlisted in the Army during World War II and was sent to Germany, where he ran afoul of a booby trap; while convalescing in an Army hospital, he wrote the book and lyrics for a servicemen's musical that enlisted the interest of Producer Garson Kanin.

Chayefsky's *Marty* was the first TV play to be successfully transformed into a motion picture. It won the Academy Award. His first original screenplay, *The Goddess,* won the Critics' Prize at the 1958 Brussels Film Festival. His first play for Broadway, *Middle of the Night,* ran for almost two years, with Edward G. Robinson in the lead.

It remained for *The Tenth Man,* however, superbly directed by Tyrone Guthrie, to establish Paddy Chayefsky once and for all in the very top rank of contemporary American playwrights. The play was originally called *The Dybbuk from Woodhaven,* and was considered a dubious commercial prospect on its tryout tour. By the time it opened at the Booth Theatre in New York, on November 5, 1959, all the rough edges had been ironed out, and by ten the next morning the line before the box office was a block long. "All we need in the theatre," acclaimed Brooks Atkinson in the New York *Times,* "are writers, directors, and actors. In *The Tenth Man* they are happily met in a new play for the first time this season: a happy marriage of literary imagination and affection for people."

LORRAINE HANSBERRY

A Raisin in the Sun, winner of the New York Drama Critics' Circle Award as the best play of the 1958-1959 season, is Lorraine Hansberry's first play to achieve production, but she has been engrossed in the world of the theatre ever since, as a child, she was taken to see *Dark of the Moon* in her native Chicago.

Miss Hansberry was born in 1930, attended the University of Wisconsin and Roosevelt College in Chicago, and moved to New York in 1950. She lives now in Greenwich Village with her husband, Bob Nemiroff, a songwriter and music publisher.

In 1957 another music publisher named Philip Rose, a friend of the Nemiroffs, determined to produce *A Raisin in the Sun.* The necessary capital was raised with the aid of a veritable army of small but enthusiastic investors. For months no New York theatre could be found to house the play, but ecstatic notices from out-of-town tryouts had a magical effect, and *A Raisin in the Sun* opened triumphantly at the Ethel Barrymore Theatre on March 11, 1959. At the conclusion of the premiere, Sidney Poitier, best-known member of the cast, jumped down to the orchestra and carried Miss Hansberry onstage, where the audience cheered her for ten solid minutes.

John McClain, in the New York *Journal American,* hailed *A Raisin in the Sun* as "a wonderfully emotional evening." Walter Kerr in the New York *Herald Tribune,* called it "an honest, intelligible, and moving experience." John Chapman, in the New York *News,* was most enthusiastic of all. *"A Raisin in the Sun,"* he wrote, "is a beautiful, lovable play—a work of theatrical magic in which the usual barrier between audience and stage disappears."

LILLIAN HELLMAN

Lillian Hellman is one of a score of subsequently famous literary folk who cut their eyeteeth in the strange but exciting publishing house presided over by the late Horace Liveright. There she demonstrated for the first time the fierce dedication to her ideals, the limitless capacity for work, and the constant striving for perfection that has ever since characterized her career. Tough, unyielding, brilliant, she is also capable of an understanding and compassion that found expression in her tender care of the author Dashiell Hammett in the tragic twilight of his career.

Miss Hellman was born in New Orleans in 1905, and moved with her family to New York five years later. She returned frequently to New Orleans for long visits, and went to public schools both there and in Manhattan. She attended both New York University and Columbia, but did not graduate.

Herman Shumlin persuaded her to leave Liveright's to become his chief play reader (she "discovered" Vicki Baum's *Grand Hotel*), and it was he who produced her first smash hit in 1934—*The Children's Hour.* Close on its heels came *Days to Come* (1936), *The Little Foxes* (1939), *Watch on the Rhine* (1941), *The Searching Wind* (1944), *Another Part of the Forest* (1946), and *The Autumn Garden* (1951), not to mention several remunerative detours to Hollywood, mostly under the aegis of the persuasive Sam Goldwyn.

Toys in the Attic, which opened at the Hudson Theatre on February 25, 1960, is one of Miss Hellman's most substantial hits. "It brings the theatre back to life," exulted Richard Watts, Jr., in the New York *Post;* and John Chapman, in the *News,* proclaimed "Lillian Hellman has jolted the theatre out of its childishness with a smackingly vigorous drama!"

SAUL LEVITT

Saul Levitt was born in Hartford, Connecticut, but he has been a New Yorker since the age of three, and is a graduate of New York's City College. During World War II he was a radio operator on a B-17, and then Staff Representative for the Army magazine *Yank,* attached to the Third Army.

Mr. Levitt has written a novel, *The Sun Is Silent,* and short stories which have appeared in *Cosmopolitan, American Mercury* and *Harper's* magazine. He has written extensively for television and documentary films.

The Andersonville Trial is his first play. A shorter version was presented on television in 1957.

VINTAGE FICTION, POETRY, AND PLAYS

VINTAGE BIOGRAPHY AND AUTOBIOGRAPHY